I0759679

MORDECAI M. KAPLAN

Mordecai M. Kaplan

Restless Soul

JENNA WEISSMAN JOSELIT

Yale
UNIVERSITY
PRESS
New Haven and London

Yale University Press books may be purchased in quantity for educational, business, or promotional use. For information, please e-mail sales.press@yale.edu (U.S. office) or sales@yaleup.co.uk (U.K. office).

Frontispiece: A younger version of Mordecai M. Kaplan painted by Fred Bretten, n.d. (Courtesy of the Library of the Jewish Theological Seminary, New York)

Set in Janson Oldstyle type by IDS Infotech Ltd.
Printed in the United States of America.

Library of Congress Control Number: 2025945300
ISBN 978-0-300-26434-0 (hardcover)

A catalogue record for this book is available from the British Library.

Authorized Representative in the EU: Easy Access System Europe, Mustamäe tee 50, 10621 Tallinn, Estonia, gpsr.requests@easproject.com

10 9 8 7 6 5 4 3 2 1

ALSO BY JENNA WEISSMAN JOSELIT

Books

Our Gang: Jewish Crime and the New York Jewish Community, 1900–1940

New York's Jewish Jews: The Orthodox Community in the Interwar Years

The Wonders of America: Reinventing Jewish Culture, 1880–1950

Parade of Faiths: Immigration and American Religion

A Perfect Fit: Clothes, Character and the Promise of America

Set in Stone: America's Embrace of the Ten Commandments

Museum Catalogues

Getting Comfortable in New York: The American Jewish Home, 1880–1950 (with Susan L. Braunstein)

A Worthy Use of Summer: Jewish Summer Camping in America (with Karen S. Mittelman)

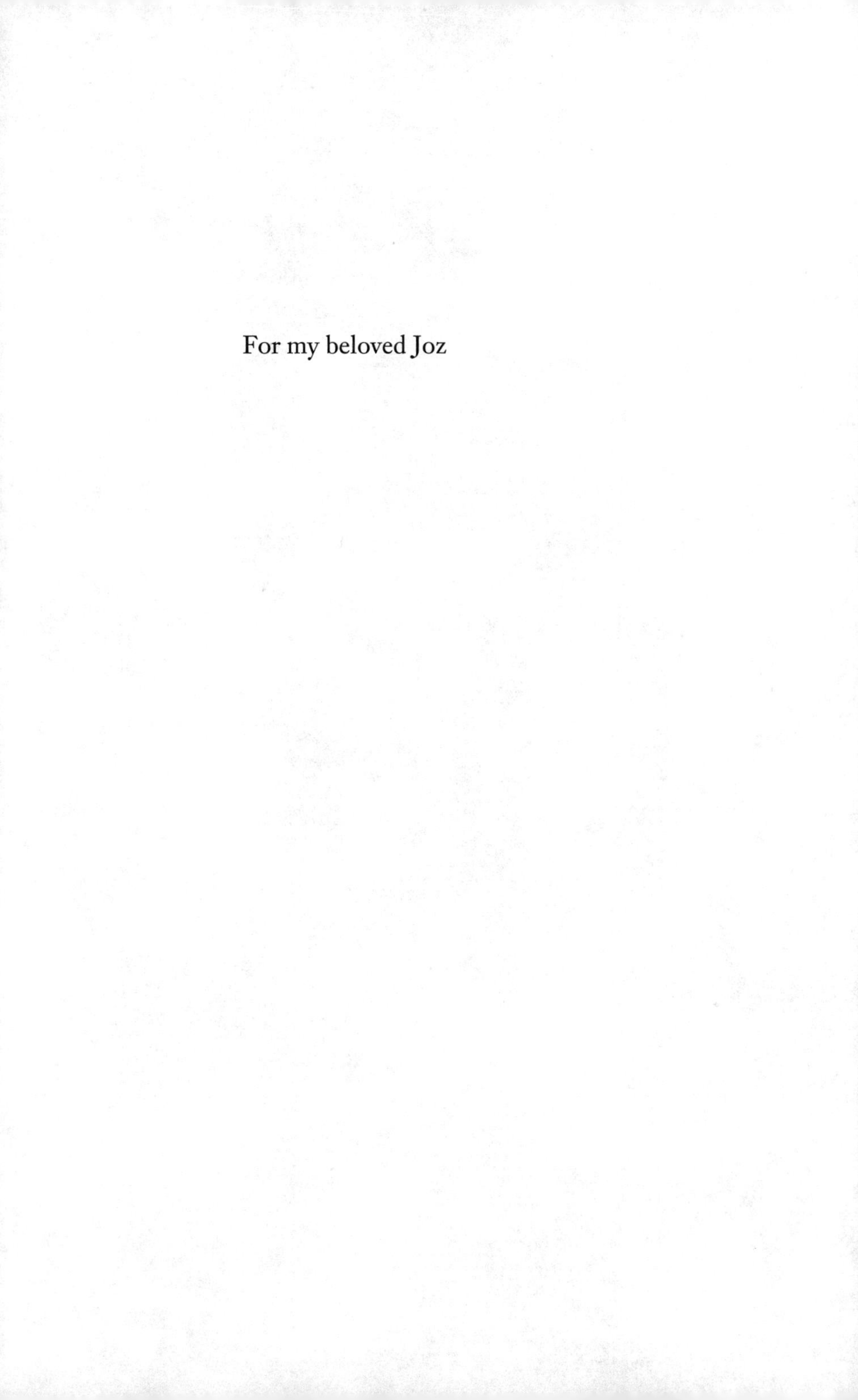

For my beloved Joz

CONTENTS

MORDECAI M. KAPLAN

Introduction

His friends likened him to a seismograph, his enemies to a heretic, his students to a holy terror. So strong was his presence, so formidable his reputation, that his was even a household name: Mordecai M. Kaplan. Stirring excitement and sowing controversy throughout his protean career as a rabbi, critic, author, thinker, and educator in twentieth-century America, he produced his own version of the Passover Haggadah and the Sabbath morning prayer book, fashioned a singular image of the Almighty, and redefined the meaning of Zionism. While each of these contributions made waves, lots of them, Kaplan's creation of a wholly American form of Judaism known as Reconstructionism—the first, and only, homegrown version of that ancient faith—was more audacious still, its impact transformative. At once a sensibility and a denomination, it changed how American Jews thought about, practiced, and expressed their Jewish identity.

Blessed with longevity—Mordecai Menachem was born in 1881 in Święciany, then a substantial town fifty miles outside of Vilna, and died in 1983 in New York—his 102 years encompassed, and paralleled, that of the modern Jewish experience in which he was an active participant. A restless soul if ever there was one, constantly "all a tingle with new projects," Kaplan never sat still, his inner turmoil fueling his capacity for innovation, for "concocting schemes" on the average of once a week, or so he claimed with only a smidgen of exaggeration: here a Zionist synagogue; there a student theatrical troupe called the "Institute Players"; and yonder, a Jewish religious order, *and* a Billy Graham–like crusade of "religious mobilization" for America's Jews, *and* a constitution for the Jewish people as a whole—*and* then, having set those ideas in motion, if only in his own mind, he'd start all over again. "Oh, the joy of activity," he'd say before coming up with yet another iteration of a synagogue, a fresh perspective on God, a reevaluation of the role of the Jewish people in history, a new twist on Zionism, and a battery of newfangled rituals. The Judaism he transmitted was an unusually expansive and fluid one, his understanding of faith unlike anyone else's.[1]

A self-styled theological maverick, Kaplan offered a brand-new, resolutely American form of Jewish identity, enlarging the meaning of religion in the United States of the twentieth century. Rooted in democratic sensibilities and in reason, in thinking ahead rather than looking back, on movement rather than stasis, it didn't so much reform, conserve, or preserve as reconstruct Judaism, altering its sensibility as well as its rhythms to fit the perquisites of a free and modern society. Just as we "cannot start a car by saying 'Giddup,' we can no longer rely on old assumptions," Kaplan explained. "Our way of life is as unlike the life of our grandparents as the automobile is unlike the buggy." What was needed was new machinery run on intellectual engagement, not on superstition or sentiment, with him at the helm, its chief engineer. "My ambition," he wrote, was "to get people to think," even if it meant slaying a passel of sacred cows along the way, among them the cherished belief in the chosen people, the primacy of the supernatural, and the inviolability of tradition. Kaplan had no truck with nostalgia either and railed against the "sickening sentimentalism" of Jewish life, determined to "break its spell"—along with the stranglehold of the past.[2]

If he had his druthers, American Jews would be "thinking Jews" who, through the give-and-take of intellectual discovery, embraced their identity instead of passively inhabiting it as a result of inheritance or because they had no other choice, a consequence of antisemitism. For Kaplan, intellection was an exercise in faith. Once American Jews could be made to understand that there was more, much more, to Judaism than either the treacly bits or its litany of demands; that it was composed of interlocking components—ideas, values, practices, customs, and "sense objects"—which, when toted up, constituted a commanding "religious civilization" all its own and which, like the best of civilizations, wasn't frozen in time but continually "evolving," they'd want to belong, to adopt a new calculus of commitment: to be "plus Jews" rather than "minus Jews."

A one-man "Jewish think tank," Kaplan was tireless in the promotion of Reconstructionism, making its presence felt from the pulpit, in the classroom, and through his many publications, including, most notably, *Judaism as a Civilization.* Still read ninety years after its publication in 1934, this whale of a volume has been hailed as a landmark of American Jewish literature as well as what "may be the most profound American text on modernity's test of religion generally." The best known of his works, it was hardly the only one. Book after book streamed from Kaplan's Parker pen, along with numerous magazine articles and editorials, pamphlets and resolutions, whose production kept him at his desk until the wee hours of the morning. During the day he liked to be out and about, in the thick of things. Making sure his ideas enjoyed an active life beyond the page, Kaplan sought, and found, a place at every communal table. Name an American Jewish enterprise of the twentieth century—synagogue life, Hebrew school, a training facility for Jewish social workers, a rabbinical seminary, charities, Zionist affairs, the Y—and there he'd be, stirring things up. Kaplan also made time for those who, seeking his counsel—congregants, students, fellow clergy, ordinary but troubled Jews—beat a path to his door, first at 1 West 89th Street and then, several blocks uptown, at 415 Central Park West, in the heart of Manhattan's Upper West Side, where he lived for most of his life. "It gives me a chance to view life at firsthand instead of through books," he once commented of his extracurricular pursuits.[3]

Accommodating such a full schedule was not easy on Kaplan's wife, Lena, and his four daughters—Judith, Hadassah, Naomi, and Selma—nor on his second wife, Rivkah Rieger, whom he married after Lena's demise. From time to time, each of them wondered about Kaplan's priorities, the object of his deepest affections: whom did he love more, the Jewish people or his family? It wasn't easy on him, either, provoking frequent mood swings as he toggled between exhilaration and despair. There'd be moments when Kaplan felt as though he "was walking on air at the thought of the tremendous significance of the attempt to bring about a metamorphosis in our entire Jewish being," and many more moments when he'd crash, experiencing his heightened Jewish consciousness as a form of physical distress much like an "exposed nerve of a tooth." Frequently ending up "in the dumps," with an acute case of the "blues" or the "mulligrubs," he thought he'd make a "good subject for a psychiatrist." Reconciling the "tic-toc of tradition" with the tempo of modern life, after all, was not for the faint of heart.[4]

In an effort to lighten her husband's mood, Lena prodded him into going to the theater, which he did grudgingly, grumbling all the way downtown at having been steered away from his study. With the exception of Noel Coward's plays, which he found "quite entertaining," and *The Diary of Anne Frank*, which he thought "marvelously well done," the Broadway stage did not leave him wanting more. By his lights, its actors were "all duds," and most theatrical productions "too stupid for words." Nor did Kaplan visit museums even though several of America's finest were within walking distance. "Despite all that I know about the stupidity of keeping one's nose to the grindstone, I can't help doing it day in and day out," he acknowledged. "Probably due to the same sense of insecurity [that] makes the miser fearful of losing a nickel makes me fearful of letting a minute of my time pass without leaving anything behind in work done."

Reading was the one activity Kaplan never begrudged himself. He always had time for a book, especially if it had to do with religion; no account about God or faith escaped his notice. Kaplan read William James, of course, and Josiah Royce; he "succumbed to the theological fashion of the time" by delving into Kierkegaard, Reinhold Niebuhr's *The Self and the Dramas of History*, and Paul Tillich's *The Theology of Culture*, but with the cavil that "it was seldom what Tillich said that I found acceptable. It was rather what he irritated me into thinking." Taking Plato along on vacation, Kaplan also cherished Ahad Ha'am, John Dewey, Ralph Waldo Emerson, Baruch Spinoza, Matthew Arnold, Emile Durkheim, William Hocking, and Yehezkel Kaufmann, whose four-volume *Golah ve-Nekhar* (Exile and the Alien Land) got him all riled up. Every author he read affected his thinking, but some influenced him more than others. "John Dewey together with Ahad Ha'am helped to mold my life more than any other person in the world, past or present," said he in 1955, saluting these two men for having furnished him with the respective intellectual frameworks of pragmatism and cultural nationalism in which to seed his own ideas. Nearly twenty years later, Kaplan gave pride of place to Durkheim, crediting that "forgotten sage" with helping him to "understand the difference between the God of Moses and the God of Aristotle."[5]

Much earlier in his career, he had found the Lynds' *Middletown* useful. "Have you read it?" he asked Ira Eisenstein, the assistant leader of the Society for the Advancement of Judaism, then in a funk over his quarrelsome congregants, adding that by comparison, the Society for the Advancement of Judaism looked like a "society of angels." Where *Middletown* comforted, Aldous Huxley's *Point Counterpoint* knocked him off his feet, and Henry Steele Commager's *The American Mind* prodded his imagination. *Madame Bovary* left him cold ("I didn't think much of it"), and despite Lena's urging—she thought he'd get a kick out of its familiar setting and cast of characters—Kaplan gave *Marjorie Morningstar* the cold shoulder, but he read Norman Mailer's *The Naked and the Dead* from end to end and enjoyed the occasional memoir such as Ben Hecht's *A Child of the Century*. Eager to find out what all the fuss was about, he also made his way through Dale Carnegie's *How to Win Friends and Influence People* and Norman Vincent Peale's *The Art of Positive Thinking*, though neither one made much of a dent.[6]

His worldview a distillation of different approaches and inspirations, one might think Kaplan indifferent to discipline, his disposition that of a magpie. Nothing could be further from the truth. By his own admission "discommoded by the least departure from Kantian regularity," he valued order, system, rationality, and control, extending their dominion over every aspect of his life. A series of pocket-sized notebooks in which he scribbled a daily to-do list, whose directives encompassed checking the supply of Alkaline tablets in the medicine cabinet to ordering Hermann Cohen's latest book, gave shape to his day; his desk served as a monument to order. When it was messy, complicating his search for an article, a letter, or his "good" pen, he'd be in a tizzy until he straightened it out, recovered the implement. He liked to keep his thoughts in order, too, by enumerating and tabulating them: 1, 2, 3, he'd write, or a, b, c.[7]

Kaplan kept an equally tight watch on his "bodily health," hewing to a regimen from which he rarely deviated, lest his "machinery" be thrown "out of gear": a good night's sleep, a cold shower, a breakfast consisting of orange juice diluted with hot water, one egg, one cup of coffee, and two rolls; a brisk, thirty-six-minute walk of two miles at least once and sometimes twice a day; a substantial lunch, preferably home-cooked; an afternoon nap if possible. He also made a point of weighing himself every day, watching what he ate and berating himself when he didn't. "No one, I dare say, could accuse me of not taking good care of myself," he crowed. As Kaplan grew older, he became more and more fretful about his physical well-being. "I don't shrink from every breeze," he noted, and "I don't think I am a hypochondriac." Even so, he worried about becoming one.

Kaplan's ordered existence led most people to think he was cut from different cloth. He certainly gave that impression. Smiley, easygoing, a man of the people he was not; reserved and distant was more like it. Ill-adept at making small talk, Kaplan kept his emotions to himself and only when pushed too far would he snap, revealing what was inside. He felt deeply—the destruction of European Jewry devastated him, the proclamation of the State of Israel touched him to his very quick, the atom bomb kept him up nights, the accomplishments of his grandchildren moved him to tears—but public displays of his feelings made him uncomfortable. So much so that Kaplan preferred to be anywhere other than at a wedding where saying a few good words to the happy couple made him as "nervous as a bar mitzvah boy," or at a funeral delivering a eulogy, which left him scrambling for *le mot juste.* No matter how much he tried, even attributing his reluctance to an "emotional bloc" that surfaced whenever he was "faced with the need of giving expression to an emotion," wriggling out of these commitments was never an option.[8]

Kaplan's physical appearance reinforced the public's perception of his emotional aloofness. Buttoned up, he was rarely out of a suit, or a formal shirt and dress pants, even when by the shore, in the country, or at summer camp where, one year, it took an extended heat wave to get him into a pair of shorts. "As a 'camper,' I am getting along swell, even to the extent of wearing my short pants on hot days, and there are many of them," Kaplan once told his daughter, Judith, when he was a "scholar in residence" at Cejwin Camps. But relaxed attire, much less a relaxed demeanor, was the exception rather than the rule. With a scowl rather than a smile usually affixed to his face, he seemed out of reach, adding to his mystique.[9]

Those who knew Kaplan only at a distance or through his ponderous publications and glowering sermons would be surprised by the Kaplan who, when writing to family and close friends, could be down-to-earth, chatty, and affectionate. He'd send kisses to his "dear ones," and respond with "goody, goody" when learning of a prospective visit from a family member. Although the man was familiar with the latest jingles like "I'd walk a mile for a Camel," and with popular expressions like "hot stuff," "boy, oh, boy," and "what fun," the voice most people heard was stiff and out of touch, the property of someone with his head in the clouds. For a more rounded Mordecai M. Kaplan, one has only to read his diary or journal, where he was most alive, his truest self. A ledger-sized account book went everywhere he did, accompanying him for nearly seventy years. Kaplan called it his alter ego, writing that when stuck, I'd "no sooner engage my Alter Ego in conversation than the thoughts marshalled themselves into excellent array. Each thought fell into its place like a well disciplined soldier." With the aid of his diary, he went on to note, "I am achieving no less a feat than the one ascribed to Rabbi Löw of Prague who is reported to have made a Golem." Kaplan had one, too: "my Golem," he called his daily entries, though unlike the fleshy original, his took the form of words.[10]

For a brief spell, there was talk of publishing Kaplan's diary in his lifetime, which would have enabled American Jews to get closer, to warm, to him. But its chronicler got cold feet and decided against doing so, fearful that some of his more sharp-tongued observations might get him into hot water. Another missed opportunity took place in 1941 when Eisenstein was invited by the *Universal Jewish Encyclopedia* to contribute a six-hundred-word profile of Kaplan. Sixty thousand words, let alone six hundred, wouldn't "begin to do justice to the man," he thought to himself, but he accepted the assignment nonetheless, submitting a text that was more résumé than biography. In preparation for the fuller, more accurate account that he might write someday—or maybe just for the fun of it—Eisenstein drew up a list of Kaplan's personal attributes, which he detailed as a "creative mind," "diligence," an "enjoyment of eating," "love of gadgets (if only for a day)," a "fear of illness," "conservatism in observance," a "way of frightening everyone," "unapproachability," "quick changes in belief," an "inability to judge people except by their acceptance of his ideas," a "tendency to resign and run away," "complete vagueness with respect to political action," "impetuousness," "etc., etc., etc."[11]

Whatever qualities Kaplan possessed and whatever name he went by—Max, Motl, Mordecai M., Grandpa Mark, Motele, Motti—he was a person to be reckoned with. Even the youngest member of the family knew that much. In the country one summer day in 1945, dressed in his customary armor of suit and tie, Kaplan was greeted by his grandchildren. No sooner did he welcome each one than six-year-old Miriam turned to him and said, "Why do you look so important?" Coming from out of nowhere and from one so young, the question struck Kaplan as eerily dybbuk-like. It so completely unnerved him that, for once, he had nothing to say. Miriam's unusually perspicacious question went unanswered.[12]

Why did Mordecai M. Kaplan look so important? Allow me to essay an answer.

1

The Sermon

Out of the blue one crisp autumn day in 1904, Mordecai Kaplan found himself in the eye of a storm, an unenviable position for a twenty-three-year-old, freshly minted rabbi to find himself, especially for something he didn't do: deliver a sermon. Though the junior clergyman had prepared a rousing speech in English to be given on the first day of Rosh Hashanah, the Jewish New Year, a time when, then as now, the pews of the American synagogue were filled to capacity, it ended up in his desk drawer. Even so, his words created a hullabaloo. Common, even humdrum today, a sermon was then a novelty within traditional American Jewish circles. A calling card, a herald of modernity, it appealed to those who prided themselves on being both traditional and forward-looking like the "fashionable" rising generation at Kehilath Jeshurun on Manhattan's Upper East Side. A year earlier, the aspiringly modern congregation, an exemplar of "prosperous Orthodox Judaism" housed in a brand-new, "architecturally ambitious" building on East 85th Street, had hired the young Kaplan, fresh out of the Jewish Theological Seminary's rabbinical school, to oversee its fledgling religious school and "to deliver lectures in the English language." Rumor had it that Kehilath Jeshurun sought a member of the cloth who would "complete the outfit" by being as "spacious" in his views as the synagogue's new digs. Mordecai M. Kaplan fit the bill.[1]

Acquitting himself well after only a few months on the job, Kaplan was quickly promoted, becoming the congregation's "minister," then a term which, among traditional Jews at least, denoted a clergyman of lesser standing than that of a bona fide "rabbi." That honorific, insisted the congregation's leaders, would have to wait, pending Kaplan's ordination, or *s'micha*, from a European rabbi of the old school, whose laying on of hands they deemed more authoritative, more authentic, than the certification granted by his alma mater. Usually quick to take umbrage, Kaplan could have easily read the conditions of his employment as a snub, an admission that neither he nor the Jewish Theological Seminary were good enough for Kehilath Jeshurun. In addition, he might well have viewed the terms of his employ as a formidable and unattainable hurdle. Given his limited resources, the chances of being able any time soon to travel to Europe to obtain the requisite imprimatur from "universally recognized Rabbis" were slender, at best. But with no other prospects on the horizon and with no leverage, either, Kaplan didn't balk, complain, or withdraw his candidacy in the face of Kehilath Jeshurun's lukewarm embrace. Instead, he acceded to the congregation's caveats. Had he insisted on negotiating better terms for himself, he might have seen the warning signs of a house divided, at odds with itself, but so eager was he to assume the pulpit at Kehilath Jeshurun that he missed those cues.[2]

In its indecisiveness over Kaplan's qualifications—was he or wasn't he fit to be its spiritual leader?—the congregation showed itself to be an unstable compound, home to both a young guard born in the United States, which relished change, and an old guard born in Eastern Europe, which fiercely resisted it. For those in the second camp, an English-language sermon, especially one slated for the holiest days of the Jewish calendar, was just not done. For one thing, the practice smacked of Reform Judaism, which Jews of their ilk anathematized; for another, vernacular preaching, they believed, set a bad precedent, opening the door to all manner of deviations. As the Slutzker Rav, Jacob David Willowski, would have it, English was a "profane" language, "unfitted for the word of God," whose presence in the sanctuary constituted a grave danger to Judaism. Better to leave the room, he counseled, than to be within earshot of an English-language sermon.[3]

A renowned East European scholar as well as a seasoned *maggid*, or preacher, the Slutzker Rav had been making the rounds of New York's synagogues in the fall of 1904 to raise funds for his various intellectual and institutional pursuits. Though a guest in town, he didn't hesitate to throw his weight around and publicly make known his fierce opposition to the English-language sermon. Nor did he hesitate to take his junior colleague's place in the pulpit where, reportedly at the invitation of Kehilath Jeshurun's president, he planned to deliver a fiery, old-fashioned Yiddish *drush*.

Despite Kaplan's conviction that sermonizing in English was an entirely kosher practice and good for the Jews, he deferred to the seniority and standing of the Slutzker Rav. Privately, Kaplan thought him a "bully" but, chastened, did as he was told and kept quiet—yet not before firing off a letter, in English, giving his congregants quite a tongue-lashing. Its tone one of disappointment laced with righteous indignation, Kaplan's text expressed dismay at Kehilath Jeshurun's "action in refusing me the pulpit on the most important days of our calendar," one made all the more inexplicable given that preaching in English was the reason he had been hired in the first place.[4]

Puzzled and hurt by the congregants' acquiescence to the preempting of their modern minister by a European *rav* from the Old World, Kaplan laced into them for remaining in the grip of "Ghetto manners," unable, or unwilling, to shake off the belief that the "Ghetto language" of Yiddish was the "only means whereby Judaism could be saved." Lest they miss the point, Kaplan concluded his remarks by stating unequivocally that he stood "for the very opposite belief. I believe that Judaism need not and must not be afraid to meet and absorb all that is good in modern culture. . . . I have faith and confidence in Judaism. You have no faith in Judaism's strengths nor confidence in me." So there! (It's not clear whether Kaplan actually sent the letter or if it stayed in the drawer alongside the contested sermon. He saved the document, though, which suggests how much he valued this early show of defiance.) Years later, Kaplan conceded that the "occidental" style of preaching could be "cold and unemotional," especially when compared with the "sad, plaintive singsong" of the old-fashioned, Yiddish-speaking *maggid.* But at the time, no such admission was forthcoming. Instead, he saw the ensuing brouhaha as a test of the congregation's commitment to him: Are you with me or not? Was Judaism to be a "living faith" or a dead letter?[5]

While Kehilath Jeshurun dithered, the public threw its support behind the American rabbi. As word of the congregational uproar spilled out into the Jewish civic square, developing into a cause célèbre, its more forward-looking inhabitants claimed that an "injustice" had been done Kaplan and called for "making reparation," though exactly what they had in mind—an apology? monetary compensation?—was never made clear, much less forthcoming. Another of Kaplan's champions, a fellow classmate and future brother-in-law with the unusual name of Phineas Israeli, took a slightly different tack, rendering the issue a referendum on the modern rabbinate. "Who in this country is anxious to hear a *maggid*?" Pitting his "aimless discourse" and lack of "concrete thought" against the "vigorous sermon" with its "really helpful" insights, he made the case that in the new world, the *maggid* (read the Slutzker Rav) was all washed up. Others, among them the editors of the *American Hebrew*, one of New York's leading English-language Jewish newspapers, took things further by characterizing the man as a "mischief-maker" who sowed discord and "stirred up enmity" wherever he went. The "sooner the Slutzker Rav gets out of the land, the better for Orthodox Judaism."[6]

The subject of these harsh remarks remained uncharacteristically silent. Not so his defenders, the most vocal of whom was J. D. Eisenstein, a learned businessman quick to take pen in hand and make known his strong opinions, of which he had many. In one of those curious twists with which history abounds, his grandson, Ira Eisenstein, became one of Kaplan's most devoted acolytes and his son-in-law, to boot. But all that was to come. At the time, J. D. Eisenstein insisted that the European rabbi had done nothing wrong. To prove his point, he offered a two-pronged analysis anchored in both linguistics and statistics. By his lights, the Slutzker Rav's denunciation of English had little to do with the perceived superiority of Yiddish, as some had erroneously maintained. "No rabbi ever claimed that Yiddish was the language of the Decalogue on Mount Sinai, or that it was ever sanctified," he pointed out, nor, he added, was a "conspiracy against the English language" in play. The issue was comprehension. Those in the pews at Kehilath Jeshurun knew enough English to conduct business but not nearly enough to comprehend the rhetorical flourishes of an English-language preacher. What they needed, wanted, and deserved, especially during the most sacred time of the year, Eisenstein explained at his most florid, was "something of substance; meat and wine in place of vegetables and water." An English-language sermon, he intimated, was thin gruel.[7]

And that was just the half of it. To ensure that his exoneration of the Slutzker Rav was irrefutable, Eisenstein went on to insist that, were heads to be counted, only a scant 10 percent of Kehilath Jeshurun's members and seat holders would understand what their English preacher had to say. One of Kaplan's champions, who mysteriously called herself a "woman of the synagogue," refused to let that remark go unchallenged. Marshalling her own set of competing statistics, she argued that Eisenstein, or whomever he had relied on for his information, had gotten it backwards: Ninety percent of the congregation understood, and delighted in, Kaplan's artfully crafted, lyrically worded sermons; only 10 percent, consisting of "very old men (may Heaven preserve them)," came up short.[8]

And round and round it went, until the flap ran its course and petered out. There was no grand denouement or dramatic resolution, no meeting of the minds, no truce. Eventually, the Slutsker Rav left the country, and Kaplan picked up where he left off, a bit dented but heartened all the same by the show of support he had received. As it turned out, this early twentieth-century incident would be the first, but hardly the last, time that controversy would cling to Kaplan's name: an augury of what lay in store. In the meantime, people at Kehilath Jeshurun and elsewhere were left wondering how things had so quickly come asunder.

Maybe it wasn't a marriage made in heaven, but the union between Kehilath Jeshurun and Mordecai M. Kaplan came awfully close. An immigrant like many of his congregants, Kaplan had moved from Eastern Europe to New York in 1889, following a brief stopover in Paris where, according to family lore, he played in the rubble of the Eiffel Tower, then under construction. Accompanied by his mother and his sister, Sophie—his father was already stateside—he was then eight years old. Along with many of his congregants, young Kaplan, known as Max on the street and Motl at home, grew up on the Lower East Side and attended the Eldridge Street Synagogue, where he held his bar mitzvah. Rabbi Israel, his pious and learned father, who for a spell worked with New York's chief rabbi, Jacob Joseph, as a *dayan*, an adjudicator of Jewish law—a position that made up in *yichus*, or pedigree, what it lacked in dollars—and who subsequently served as a ritual supervisor of the kosher meat business, saw to it that his only son was well educated in traditional Jewish subjects and in secular ones, too.

Shuttling between Public School No. 2 and Etz Chaim Yeshiva, City College and the Jewish Theological Seminary—then more preparatory school than college—Kaplan also studied Talmud with his father, honing his interpretive skills. Meanwhile, Anna, his exacting, fretful and superstitious mother, kept young Kaplan off the gritty streets, leaving him with few opportunities to experience the hijinks of an American boyhood and adolescence. A few months shy of his bar mitzvah, in 1894, the gifted, bookish Kaplan enrolled at the Jewish Theological Seminary where, ditching Max in favor of Mordecai, the name he would retain from here on, he took to his studies in Bible, Talmud, Jewish history, and codes (aka the *Shulchan Aruch*). Or he would have, had he not found the institution wanting: a "museum of fossils," he called it. Emphasizing memorization at the expense of critical engagement, its faculty, Kaplan related, was ill-attuned to modern modes of pedagogy. Joshua Jaffe, who taught Talmud, held classes at the ungodly hour of 6 a.m., when Kaplan and his fellow students were still asleep on their feet, while Bernard Drachman, whose classes in Bible met at three in the afternoon, was himself asleep on his feet by that low point in the day. When thinking back decades later on his unsatisfying stint at the Seminary, "I grow bitter," Kaplan recalled.[9]

Well aware at the time of his adolescent son's academic disappointments and concerned lest they prompt him to stray from the fold like many of his peers, Kaplan's father arranged for a series of supplementary tutors, his choice of instructors at once tactical and pedagogical. At great financial cost, he sought out two highly regarded, exemplary, and decidedly modern men to keep his disaffected, hungry-for-knowledge son on his toes and inside the tent. One was Arnold B. Ehrlich, a renowned Biblical exegete—the "greatest of living *m'forshim* [commentators]," crowed the *Hebrew Standard*, "America's leading Jewish family newspaper,"—and a longtime family friend. His exhortation to Kaplan, "*Bochur, bochur* [young man], how do you understand the verse?" was exactly the kind of intellectual provocation this fifteen-year-old *bochur* needed. Ehrlich's devotion to the life of the mind also inspired the teenager. "With a concentration which bordered on eccentricity, [Ehrlich's] whole being," one of his friends observed, was "wrapped up in the pursuit of his studies," demonstrating to the impressionable teen the value of ratiocination.[10]

Kaplan's other tutor was Joseph Sossnitz, a polymath as much at home in astronomy, chess, and mathematics as in Hebrew literature. Sitting side by side, the studious teenager and the middle-aged scholar, known as the "Socrates of the Jews," read through a number of difficult Jewish philosophical texts and studied Talmud, drawing on a more critical approach than that of Kaplan père. Though the time young Kaplan spent in the company of these two men was brief, they "exerted an influence" on his life, he later acknowledged, crediting Ehrlich with having "finally shattered my belief in *Torah min Hashomayim*," or divine revelation, and Sossnitz with having served as a model for how to be a modern Jew able to reconcile his ancient faith with the "spirit of progress."[11]

When not under their tutorial wing or in class at the Jewish Theological Seminary, Kaplan managed to acquire a general education in the humanities, first at City College, from which he graduated in 1900, and two years later at Columbia University, from which he obtained a master's degree in philosophy. His secular pursuits left a lot to be desired. With the exception of the philosopher Frederick James Eugene Woodbridge, an "original thinker who affects the thinking and beliefs of his pupils," Kaplan characterized his humanities instructors as a "poor lot," not nearly as demanding, or as exciting, as this eager beaver of a pupil who cherished the "sweet hope of attainment" would have liked. For that, he schooled himself, tackling Royce and Schopenhauer in his spare time.[12]

Transcending what he called his "inarticulate ancestry . . . and the worst kind of academic training to start me on my professional career," Kaplan was able to make of himself a person of substance, at once an "American in culture and tradition," and a "Talmudist and a scholar." His résumé attested to his striking ability to persevere, adapt, and synthesize the various elements of his upbringing. One might even say he possessed the perfect set of credentials or, as some of his Yiddish-speaking congregants were more likely to put it, *alle mayles.* He had *yichus*, knew his way around a *blatt gemara* (a page of Talmud), spoke Yiddish (when necessary), and understood what it was like to be an immigrant equally at home and at sea in America. Plus, he was well-versed in secular subjects; well-mannered, even courtly; exceedingly well-spoken, his English clear and unaccented, and in his neatly pressed and customary uniform of coat, tie, and vest, he cut a very good figure—qualities held in high esteem by his upwardly mobile congregants who placed a premium on appearance and the protocols of polite society.[13]

Mordecai Kaplan and Kehilath Jeshurun seemed destined for each other: a perfect *shidduch* (union). What could go wrong?

In the wake of the 1904 sermon upset—which just about everyone chalked up to a temporary setback—things at Kehilath

Jeshurun settled down into a comfortable rhythm; on the surface at least, the relationship between congregation and spiritual leader appeared to be harmonious. A proud example of the "word-juggling preacher of to-day," Kaplan spoke undisturbed every Sabbath morning and on every festival, holding forth on a wide-ranging array of subjects, from "The Drama of Israel—In Four Acts" to "Wanted—Jewish Leaders." Nothing if not purposeful, his repertoire had something for everyone. He taught a daily morning class in Mishnah to twenty members of the older set; successfully shepherded a hundred children through afternoon religious school, transforming a doleful experience into a pleasurable one; instituted a number of changes in the prayer service to render it more decorous; and secured the affection of the sisterhood ladies by encouraging their participation in synagogue affairs.[14]

Kehilath Jeshurun seemed happy enough with him and he, in turn, seemed happy enough with them. But were they really? Changes in the chain of command suggest that something was not quite right on East 85th Street. No sooner had the sermon snafu quieted down than the synagogue hired Moses Zevulun Margolies, a European rabbi of the old school who, for years, had been Boston's chief rabbi. Nearly twice Kaplan's age, Margolies was a gentle and kindly soul with a flowing beard who was said to look like his namesake "except that he wore gold-rimmed spectacles." Hoping to keep the ever-fractious old guard in line, Kehilath Jeshurun's leaders envisioned the older clergyman as a counterweight to the younger one: the *rav* to his minister. Privately, Kaplan was not pleased with having to share the pulpit, an arrangement that in his mind, if not in theirs, relegated him to second fiddle, dampening his enthusiasm for his ministerial responsibilities as well as for his congregants. But publicly, in a show of respect, the American-trained rabbi went along, making a point of working amicably with his more senior colleague, his discontent softened, perhaps, by commanding a larger salary.[15]

If shul politics wasn't enough to give Kaplan pause, an escalating series of internally generated doubts about what he did every day and why he did it pushed him beyond the pale, leaving him adrift. No longer was crafting a sermon a source of personal pride or intellectual satisfaction. "My sermons are mental tortures to me, for I have to wriggle so as not to offend. Enough," Kaplan related in 1906, without giving away the names or motivations of those whom he was trying diligently not to affront. Was he being muzzled, yet again, by the congregation's leadership? Or had Kaplan picked up on, and felt constrained by, his congregants' preference for "gushing sentimentality" rather than intellection, a predilection he believed was about as good for the soul as the "application of a poultice to a diseased part of the body which can only be cured by surgery." He never said.[16]

Kaplan did come clean, though, when it came to his waning belief in the merits of tradition, Orthodox Judaism, and the ways of his father and mother, all of which he braided together. "My heart is torn by conflict and all for the sake of parents!" he wrote on one occasion. On another, he went further still. "Oh God, what anguish of soul! How doubt tortures me." Souring on traditional Judaism, he increasingly questioned its sustainability in and value to modern America, his skepticism about the revelation at Sinai, the ongoing relevance of fifteen-hundred-year-old prayers, and the hold of the past on the present accelerating and ripening. To compound matters, "Judaism doesn't let us laugh enough," Kaplan declared. "Our festivals are dour and solemn."[17]

As one set of long-held ideas began to crumble, a set of new ones began to take shape and coalesce into something more than isolated instances of grumbling and finger-pointing: a "theology of Reconstruction," he called his emerging perspective in 1904; a "renaissance" a year later; and in 1907, resorting to a more blunt turn of phrase, he referred to wielding the "surgeon's knife upon the vital organ of Jewish life."[18]

Alternatively excited and troubled by ideas that kept him awake at night, Kaplan shared them with his parents who, in keeping with time-honored parental tradition, told him not to worry; he'd grow out of them in no time. That's not what their exercised son wanted to hear and, in keeping with the time-honored ways of disgruntled children, he told them so, insisting they were "slowly permitting my soul and spirit to die within me" and "deliberately allow[ing] that which is best and brightest within to waste away." Neither his mother nor his father took kindly to what their son had to say, dismissing rather than entertaining his concerns. "They heartened not," he poignantly noted. Burdened by the "widening gap" between himself and his parents and eager to narrow, if not close it altogether, Kaplan continued to study Talmud with his father until the latter's death in 1917. "Nothing could please parents more," he related. The ritual of Talmud study helped him, too, enabling him to find common ground at a time when father, mother, and son found "very little to talk about."[19]

When it came to coping mechanisms, Kaplan also took comfort from putting down his thoughts, observations, and feelings—"my ramblings"—on paper. In what would turn out to be a lifelong practice, he gave voice to and confided his "inward strife" and "mental acrobating" in a journal, its torrent of words a testament to a growing clash between thought and practice, creed and deed, congregant and clergy. Multipurpose, these diaries, spanning 1904 to 1907 and with a couple of sporadic entries from 1908, functioned both as a kind of theologian's blackboard, where Kaplan wrestled with big questions, and as an exercise in deflection, where he let off steam.[20]

The professional and the personal inhabited the same page, high-minded allusions to Kant sitting alongside his "abject whining" and "mewlings." Attending a wedding at which he found it difficult to mingle, Kaplan took himself to task.

"The fault is doubtless myself, a certain something acts like a barrier between me and other people. I am certainly not a misanthrope, and yet people have nothing to say to me and I have nothing to say to them." In another characteristic observation, he rued the absence of love in his life. "Of the vast lump of pleasure which exists in the world is there not just one little crumb for me? My life," he added, "lacks music."[21]

From time to time, Kaplan berated himself for indulging in such baroque statements: "Enough of this sighing and groaning. It is unmanly." But when that feeling passed, as it invariably did, he acknowledged to himself just how valuable the diary had become. More than a venue for venting or wrangling, it had developed into a powerful ritual device: "communings with the spirit" was how Kaplan described it, spelling out these four words in a flowery hand on the title page of his very first diary. Are my entries "not each more truly prayer and confession than the infinite repetition of daily prayers?"[22]

Beset and wrung out by internal conflict—what, he wondered, would "Kehilath Jeshurun have to say to the above line?"—Kaplan resolved to leave his position and in 1906 submitted his resignation. What took him so long? He asked himself the same question: "Why do I stay where I am, you will ask. Well, I did send in my resignation and it nearly broke my parents' hearts." Nicely put but only partially true. Filial devotion went only so far in keeping him at Kehilath Jeshurun; the board's rejection of his request and its subsequent battery of propitiating gestures kept him in place and in line for the time being.[23]

How fortuitous that Kaplan remained at Kehilath Jeshurun for it was within its ranks that, in 1908, he found himself a beautiful young wife: Lena (née Lillian) Rubin, who came from a very large family—she was the youngest of nine children—that attended the 85th Street congregation. As the story goes,

Newlyweds, Lena and Mordecai, 1908.
The Collection of Hadassah K. Musher, New York.

one Sabbath morning, while seated on the pulpit, the handsome, young minister just happened to look up into the women's gallery where Lena was sitting; their blue eyes locked and, well, you know the rest. Their betrothal made the news, circulating throughout Kehilath Jeshurun's pews and beyond. It was first announced in late February of that year in the *American Hebrew*, followed by an additional flurry of announcements in the *Hebrew Standard*.[24]

A few months later, in June, the bride aged twenty-two, occupation "none," and the groom, aged twenty-six, occupation "rabbi," were married at her widowed mother's brownstone home, 150 East 81st in Manhattan, by Rabbi Margolies who, in honor of the occasion, signed his name on the civil certificate of marriage as "Morrish Margolies." Standing under the huppah (wedding canopy) with Lena was the "happiest day of my life," Kaplan related. It may also have been one of the most lavish, for the nuptials were marked by an elaborate wedding dinner, whose bill of fare was unlike anything the groom had ever consumed. The festive repast opened with "Orange Fantaise," followed by "Consomme Nudel" and a cascade of enticing, if misspelled, French dishes that included "Filet de Boef," "Sauce la Truffle," "Sorbet a la Buckingham," "Royal Squabs on Toast," and Long Island duck. Still hungry? A "Wedding Cake in Satin Boxes," "Petit fours," "Bon Bons," "Fruits of Season," and cigars awaited.[25]

With full hearts and bellies, the young couple set out a week later on a honeymoon to Europe, stopping in Paris long enough to take in the Folies Bergère and the Eiffel Tower, the source of one of Kaplan's most cherished childhood memories. The newlyweds then traveled on to Heidelberg and Frankfurt, not for the purposes of sightseeing, as one might expect, but for professional reasons. Kaplan was eager to obtain the long-deferred *s'micha* (ordination) from Rabbi Israel Jacob Reines, the innovative educator, religious Zionist, and much respected rabbinic authority. From the get-go, the couple's travel plans were incongruous. Given Kaplan's growing estrangement from orthodoxy, one would think it unlikely that his being credentialized by an echt Orthodox rabbinic authority remained a career objective. Yet, the newly married

A honeymoon souvenir, 1908.
The Collection of Hadassah K. Musher, New York.

minister went out of his way—and on his honeymoon no less—to secure the requisite bona fides. It's almost as if he was determined at all costs to prove his worth to those who had discounted it. Then again, Rabbi Reines's imprimatur, his official *s'micha*, was a form of insurance: money in the bank, so to speak. Henceforth, Kaplan needn't worry lest someone question his qualifications for the Orthodox rabbinate. He now had Reines's blessing.

And Lena's, too. From the very outset of their marriage, she and Mordecai established a pattern of behavior that would hold fast throughout the course of their fifty-year-long relationship: he would come first in all things. For half a century, Lena saw to it that her "darling" had what he needed to get through the day: three square meals, an afternoon nap, a restorative cup of tea with jam and a plate of homemade cookies, a daily constitutional or two, his clothes always in good repair, his briefcase at the ready. Though she was unable to get him to come to bed when, at two in the morning, he was still fine-tuning a phrase, hashing out an idea, writing in his journal, correcting proofs, or preparing for class, it wasn't for want of trying.[26]

Level-headed, sure-footed, and with a keen sense of what made people tick, Lena kept Mordecai from making rash mistakes, staying his hand when he was tempted to fire off (yet another) intemperate letter, miss a meeting, or avoid a social gathering. His biggest fan and most honest critic, she would tell him whether at synagogue services he had spoken for too long or too loftily and if the proceedings dragged and lacked warmth. It was she who calmed him down in the wake of frequent upsets, listened attentively to his litany of woes, proffered advice and propped him up when he was low. A boon companion, Lena was also the mother of Kaplan's four daughters—Judith, Hadassah, Naomi, and Selma—who were born in quick succession between 1909 and 1915. Their "Papa" (he also went by "darling Pops") was a loving, if demanding, presence in their lives, but it was Lena who, day to day, saw to their welfare. She fussed over her daughters, sometimes to excess; encouraged their writing letters to their father whenever he was on the road or the high seas; and made sure they piped down when he was at home and in his study. At the dinner table, should the household erupt in hostilities—as it frequently did once the "kiddies" grew into adolescents, prompting the lone male in the family to throw up his hands and exclaim, "Girls in the home, girls in the school. That is too much for me"—Lena kept the peace.[27]

Mordecai was utterly dependent on her. The words of "I Love to Lean on Lena," a family-composed ditty, had their relationship down pat.

In time of strife, I need my wife
I always lean on Lena
In time of peace, my need don't cease
I love to lean on Lena.

She'll protect me from an importuning guest
Who is likely to become an awful pest
And when the text is troubling me
She'll bring cherries and hot tea
To restore to me my intellectual zest.[28]

A person in her own right—a stalwart of the synagogue sisterhood and an influential member of Hadassah, the Zionist women's organization, where, among other things, she was "chairman of the trees," a reference to her service on the committee that promoted the forestation of the Holy Land; an active faculty wife; a sweet singer—Lena did all this and more while presiding over a busy household. She even learned to type so that she might prepare her husband's manuscripts, draft after draft, as well as his lecture notes, public addresses, and sermons, tidily arranging his words either on long sheets of paper or on four-by-six index cards, which could be placed within easy reach in one of his many pockets.[29]

At his best and most relaxed when prepared, Kaplan preferred to rely on notes, outlines, and a fully elaborated text when giving an address. No matter the venue—classroom, sanctuary, huppah, banquet, cemetery, faculty meeting—or the subject matter—student affairs, the biblical portion of the week, God, Zionism, love or death—his peace of mind insisted on advance preparation. Speaking off the cuff, extemporaneously, was not for him. Troubled by his inability to go from "sentence to sentence" on the fly, he was tempted now and then to give it a whirl, but winging it made him too anxious—his palms became sweaty, his heart pounded—lest he meander or forget an important point.[30]

It's not that Kaplan didn't trust himself or lacked faith in what he had to say; that was never it. Rather, he trusted too much in the power of the pulpit, in speech and in words, to treat them casually. With a rich, plummy, booming voice like that of Basil Rathbone, or so it was said, he'd propel volleys of intricate sentences into the air. Bursting with ideas and "more than two syllable words," they enthralled his audiences, especially those whose "grammar creaked."[31]

Kaplan-the-preacher took great pains with his verbal presentations, subjecting them to multiple revisions and often resenting the amount of time and midnight oil it took him to get them into tiptop shape so that their contents might leap off the page. "What a nuisance preaching is! I feel it in my bones every time I have to work on a sermon," he acknowledged, wondering whether it was worth the effort. It was. Though he might not want to admit it, Kaplan relished delivering sermons—the practice sustained and kept him in circulation—preaching long after most of his colleagues had called it quits. Eulogies and cheery salutes to the bride and groom, though, were something else again: de rigueur but disdained. It was of little moment whether the invitation to speak came at the behest of a family member, a congregant, the board of trustees, a colleague, or even a friend, the prospect of having to indulge in sentiment rather than substance, in pieties rather than ideas, made Kaplan uncomfortable, ill at ease. He was none too keen, either, on ceremonial remarks, especially the kind he dubbed "after-dinner speeches without the dinner." Though he delivered more than his fair share, the genre's characteristically fleet and glib sentiments left him cold. "I am absolutely unable to repeat platitudes," Kaplan once confessed. "My memory simply rebels against them."[32]

Monitoring his words, Kaplan also monitored the size of his audience. As if a contestant in a popularity contest, he routinely took note of whether he drew a full house, a decent crowd, or a meager one. He even recorded the number of those who showed up: "about 400," "over 500," "under 110," or "at least 125." Behind the lectern, his sociological imagination was also in full swing, prompting him to pay close attention to the audience's composition, to its gender, age, physical appearance, and literacy, and on how these variables affected their reception of him. Were his listeners held rapt? Or bored silly? Nodding along or nodding off? Time after time, Kaplan believed that his performances were not up to snuff, his manner too stilted and preachy, his remarks more rant than balm. He worried that he had overdone it, speaking so fast "as almost to bowl people over," and acknowledged that in the course of one speech he had "stormed and raged and thumped the pulpit with such vigor that my hand hurt me all day."[33]

But then Kaplan was just as quick, and eager, to share the blame with his listeners, especially American Jews at the grass roots. In his estimation, they rarely rose to the occasion—their knowledge too shallow, their perspective too frivolous—testing his resolve. "I might as well have tried to talk on higher mathematics to six-year-olds," he lamented shortly after delivering a speech on American Jewish life to the members of a Midwestern synagogue in the 1940s.[34]

Kaplan's audiences may not have understood him, but they were inspired all the same by his delivery, erudition, and passion. (His banging away at the pulpit "seemed to have made an impression," he recalled.) At other moments, they understood him all too well, cringing in their seats as he exhorted the men among them to "read the Bible or some other serious book instead of playing cards all the time that they were at leisure" and the women to "do less talking about the price of potatoes, onions and gasoline" and to "take up reading now and then a chapter from the Bible." And just as often, in what Kaplan called the "worst possible reaction," one or two listeners would invariably come up to him after services to say, "Don't you think it was over the heads of the people? I, of course, understood the sermon, but I am afraid the others couldn't follow you." On at least one occasion, Kaplan had the last word: "Anyone but a moron, it seems to me, ought to have been able to understand what I had to say."[35]

While these exchanges left Kaplan cranky and out of sorts, he still felt as if he retained the upper hand. A less than rapturous audience response, though, got the better of him, which is exactly what happened at the Baltimore Hebrew Congregation in 1918, during the height of the war effort. Instead of hanging on his every word, a largely all-female audience ("about seventy-five people") knitted away, the clacking of their needles throwing him off his game. "It took me a few minutes to adjust myself," he observed at the time, adding gratuitously, "sometimes the women do get me tired with their brainstorms and fads."[36]

Kaplan's agility as a preacher got him into trouble. It also secured his reputation as well as a lifelong position at the Jewish Theological Seminary—and in the nick of time. In 1909, a year after his wedding and now a brand-new father, Kaplan was about to resign as Kehilath Jeshurun's rabbi and to reestablish himself as a lawyer or an insurance agent. While exploring his options, he received an invitation from the alumni organization of the Jewish Theological Seminary to give a talk. Some might call it divine intervention; others, serendipity; and still others, *mazal.* No matter. That unexpected collegial overture saved the day—and Kaplan from having to "throw the whole thing overboard once and for all."[37]

In mulling over what to talk about, Kaplan decided it'd be a "wonderful opportunity to formulate my new perspective on Judaism," which held that its "focal point was not its theology but the Jewish People." He anticipated a hullabaloo but, much to his surprise, was showered with hosannas instead. No sooner had the applause died down than Kaplan was summoned by the Seminary's president, Solomon Schechter, who had been in the audience. Expecting a reprimand, the guest speaker received his second surprise of the day when Schechter invited him to "undertake to organize the Teachers Institute" and to do for Jewish educators what the Seminary was doing for rabbis: professionalize them and establish a field. "I think we have found the right man," Schechter wrote expectantly to Cyrus Adler, his close friend, confidante, and later successor, of his decision to hire young Kaplan.[38]

With that appealing offer in hand, Kaplan was able to resign from Kehilath Jeshurun with no second thoughts. Appointed principal of the Teachers Institute, he joined the Seminary rabbinical faculty a year later, a position he would retain for more than half a century, teaching midrash, homiletics, and Religious Philosophies A and B to would-be rabbis. Set for life, Kaplan was set free. No wonder he pronounced the day he came to speak at the Seminary the "second of the happiest moments in my life."[39]

2

The Blueprint

"I FIND MYSELF AT the beginning of a new spiritual enterprise which holds out great promise," Kaplan declared in April 1915. "For the present at least the very opening up of a new vista of possibilities is exhilarating." An opportunity to make good on, and formalize, what had been on his mind for years was now in the offing: the creation from scratch of a new kind of Jewish institution that would make the case for a maximum kind of Jewish commitment, one that affected every aspect of daily life, not just Shabbos morning services or giving a donation. Had mantras been as popular in American circles as they are today, Kaplan's would have been "Before Judaism, Jewishness," the first a faith, the second a culture, or, as he would later put it, a "civilization."[1]

The timing of this venture couldn't have been better. Ever since leaving Kehilath Jeshurun, Kaplan had gathered unto himself a handful of like-minded American Jews, including the occasional luminary, such as Dr. Judah Magnes and Henrietta Szold, organizing them into informal study groups to consider the "economy of the Jewish soul." Meeting on Saturday afternoons or Sunday mornings, these convenings over the years addressed such lofty philosophical issues as the essence of Judaism while also wrestling with more immediate concerns like remaining Jewish in modern America.[2]

Identifying the problem was easy. Current expressions of American Jewish identity, it was clear, were no longer viable. Orthodox Judaism was too rigid, Reform Judaism too austere, and Conservative Judaism, then in its infancy, too much in love with history for its own good. And everywhere "committees and sub-committees" cluttered the landscape, making for chaos.[3]

Finding a solution turned out to be more elusive, challenging Kaplan and his followers to consider different kinds of institutions. What kind of enterprise might best revitalize Jewish life? A new kind of synagogue, perhaps? Or a literary society? Maybe a social club just for intellectuals? They tossed around names, too. How about a "Zionist synagogue"? Kaplan ventured, deploying Zionism as a synonym for a bold, adventurous, and fresh undertaking rather than the designation of a philanthropic venture or a shorthand for a "sulking, sullen Chauvinism." When that suggestion was tabled on the grounds that an adjective like "Zionist"—or any adjective, for that matter—might put off rather than attract potential recruits, he put forth another. What say you to "Jewish cultural society"? That didn't fly, either; it was a hard sell among some of the participants who thought "cultural" sounded too snooty, even cold. Enlivening but inconclusive, these discussions went nowhere fast.[4]

When not bandying about names and notions, Kaplan took to the pulpit and the dais, preaching and lecturing so widely that, during the second decade of the century it often seemed as if, in the greater New York area, no cornerstone was laid or Jewish edifice dedicated without Kaplan on hand. These dutiful, lengthy proceedings might bore guests to tears, but his evocative language made them sit up a bit straighter. How could audiences not pay attention when, in speaking about modern notions of God, he told them that they could no longer "expect God to come leaping over the mountains"?[5]

A whirlwind of ideas, Kaplan also made sure to commit his ideas to paper. In 1915 in the *Menorah Journal*, then American Jewry's leading journal of arts and letters, he laid his views before a discerning public. In bracing prose, Kaplan likened contemporary notions of Judaism to "a long drawn-out yawn" and lamented the absence of "living energy." Without singling out any particular denomination by name, he decried the "language of theology" and advocated replacing its abstract principles and dogmas with a "language of concrete and verifiable experiences."[6]

Sounding a wake-up call, Kaplan encouraged young American Jews to "do some very hard thinking," to go beyond dictionary definitions of Judaism and vague claims of "heritage," and to grapple with what living a Jewish life in twentieth-century America entailed. "We Jews must know not so much what Judaism meant twenty centuries ago, nor even a century ago, but what it is to mean to us of today," he charged. If that meant retiring the term "Judaism" and throwing it onto the "scrap-heap of obsolete terminology," so be it, just as long as what replaced it—"Jewishness," say—would mean "Jewish consciousness, and not merely 'gefilte fish,' or some other Jewish dish."

Volumes of words and scads of talk may have fulfilled Kaplan in the short term, but in the absence of realization they remained inert: more of a conceit than an instrument of change. That probably would have been their fate had Kaplan not been approached in 1913 by a small band of *baalbatim*, well-heeled and well-intentioned Jewish lay leaders, some of whom had known and kept up with him since his Kehilath Jeshurun days. Taken with Kaplan's big, bold, and fresh views on modern Jewish life, his capacity to see things from a variety of perspectives, and his singular gifts—there was no one quite like him—they sounded him out: Would he consider working with them to develop a novel Jewish institution in the heart of the Upper West Side, Manhattan's newest and most prosperous Jewish neighborhood? If he'd come up with and develop the concept, they'd find the money.

The answer to his prayers, this tempting proposition was not one Kaplan could turn down. He agreed to it, waiting patiently in the wings while funds were being raised and a plot of land purchased on West 86th Street. When two years later, in 1915, the project finally got off the ground, Kaplan joined with Joseph Henry Cohen (aka J. H.), William Fischman, Abraham Rothstein, and Judge Otto Rosalsky in what they ambitiously called the "Center movement."[7]

Different personalities all—Cohen, the group's leader, was strong-willed and intellectually curious; Fischman not too troubled by abstraction but alive to new ideas; Rosalsky liked to hear himself talk; Rothstein soft spoken and kind—they constituted a distinctive cohort of Jews: second-generation Americans, the children of Russian Jewish immigrants, and with the exception of Rosalsky, who sat on New York City's criminal bench, successful garment manufacturers. Content with their lot, they were known derisively, in Yiddish, as *alrightniks*, which means exactly what it sounds like. Feeling flush and expansive in the years immediately preceding World War I, these men and their families had recently forsaken the east for the west, drawn by the Upper West Side's broad avenues and substantial apartment houses with their "abundant closet space," "scientifically arranged" layouts, and array of the "latest conveniences." Once a neighborhood of small private homes, it had been recently transformed into a mecca of "high class," twelve-story apartment buildings, a change described by the *Real Estate Record and Builders Guide* as a "reconstruction." As modern as could be, the Upper West Side met the needs of this group of well-heeled American Jews in every way but one: it lacked a synagogue that appealed to them. With the exception of Shearith Israel, an imposing Sephardic congregation on Central Park West, the local Ashkenazic orthodox synagogues were not only few in number but also "small in size . . . and in mind." These Upper West Siders, emboldened by their surroundings and their good fortune, hankered for something else: a "spiritual laboratory" rather than a shul.[8]

As smart and up-to-date as West 86th Street itself, of a piece with its commodious and stately apartment buildings, especially in its verticality, the physical plant that the Center's promoters and Kaplan envisioned had many floors and many rooms: a sanctuary, library, classrooms and clubrooms, gymnasium, natatorium (swimming pool), showers, steam, vapor and electric baths, a lounge, dining facilities, and an auditorium that doubled as a ballroom and a movie theater, as well as a kindergarten where five year olds would "gambol their way into Judaism." With classes and lectures and afternoon teas and Saturday night dances and Sunday morning breakfasts and, and, and . . . the building would thrum like the motors of the newfangled cars that few Center members were without.[9]

Running with a concept that was very much in the air at the time—a house of worship that offered more than worship—Kaplan gave it an additional push. His was as much a conceptual statement as a physical construct. Valued on its own terms for its spaciousness, the Center was also designed with a new kind of Jewish sensibility in mind, one animated by pleasure as well as responsibility. Although Kaplan stopped short of using the word "fun," its elements—delight, enjoyment, laughter, good cheer, bonhomie—were woven throughout his grand scheme. The Jewishness he envisioned was amiable rather than dour, buoyant rather than weighty; it beckoned rather than deterred. Above all, the Jewish identity Kaplan wanted to see at the Center was thoughtful rather than knee-jerk, a reckoning with heritage not just its transmission. By his lights, the flimsy, half-hearted Judaism practiced by the sons and daughters of immigrant Jews had little to do with commitment or comprehension and everything to do with parental obedience, with not ruffling the family feathers. "They consider the routine performance of what their mammas and poppas expect them to do as the sum and substance of spirituality," Kaplan observed, adding that it rarely occurred to them that there might be more to Judaism than the "domestic traditions to which they had always considered it confined." If he could make his mark, there'd be no room at the Center for complacency or its cousin, sentimentality. The building at 132–135 West 86th Street would be the site of an intentional, full-throttled Jewishness.[10]

Over the span of three years between 1915 and 1918, Kaplan met frequently with J. H. Cohen, the project's prime mover, at his 35th Street loft, where they chatted away amid a sea of packing boxes and the clamor of sewing machines. He also lunched with the manufacturer at the nearby Waldorf Astoria Hotel where, lifting an eyebrow, he observed his host perform the traditional mealtime rituals of hand washing, blessing the bread, and reciting the post-prandial grace in a decidedly secular, non-kosher setting. He also attended a series of meetings at the midtown Hotel McAlpin. (In a curious twist of fate, that facility would be the site of Kaplan's excommunication thirty years later.) The two men, along with Fischman, the third member of the triumvirate, even took off for a long weekend retreat in Tannersville, New York, in 1917 where, undisturbed by the demands of family and the pressures of business, the three talked a different kind of shop. A multipage outline that

When in the country, Kaplan liked to work outdoors, n.d.
The Collection of Hadassah K. Musher, New York.

Kaplan prepared for the occasion provided talking points. Top heavy with allusions to God, memory, the "social mind of the Jewish people," and the "Jewish organism," the conversation it engendered, he noted in his journal, was "most enjoyable."[11]

Whatever the venue, Kaplan was on the ground floor, meeting often with Louis Allen Abramson, the Center's architect, then in his twenties, who many years later would become famous for designing Horn & Hardart's Automat. The two reviewed and refined the building's blueprints so many times that Kaplan couldn't resist comparing these documents to a "prima donna who was forever making her final appearance." Kaplan also served on the Constitution Committee, for which he penned the document's "preamble"; chaired the Plan and Scope Committee; and composed the "principles" of the Center for use in a promotional pamphlet. The prize for his labors—he worked pro bono—was the Center rabbinate. Though that position wouldn't officially be his until the building was up and running, this arrangement suited Kaplan just fine. For the time being, he was content with being an éminence grise rather than an eminence.[12]

Throughout the protracted process of institution building, Kaplan made clear to Cohen, or thought he had, that his religious views were "heterodoxical." Lest that ten-dollar word escape the manufacturer's grasp, Kaplan told him explicitly—and repeatedly—that he wasn't orthodox in his heart or in his head, though when it came to ritual observance, he still kept the faith. For now. He also made explicit, or thought he had, his unwillingness to bestow a denominational label, especially that of "Orthodox," on the new enterprise, preferring to "keep an open house." More pointedly still, Kaplan repeatedly expressed his reluctance to consider the *Shulchan Aruch*, the authoritative sixteenth-century ritual compendium, as the ultimate arbiter. While he wouldn't knowingly violate any of its provisions, he wasn't prepared to defer unhesitatingly to them, either; sometimes "discretion" would have to rule the roost.[13]

Taking things even further, Kaplan made clear, or thought he had, what kind of spiritual leader he envisioned—be it himself or someone else—at the helm of the Jewish Center. In lieu of regarding the rabbi as the congregation's "spokesman or mouthpiece," he advocated that the spiritual leader be "one who is working out the true interpretation of Judaism in light of modern thought." "Under these circumstances," Kaplan continued presciently, "the organization must be prepared to hear things from him that its individual members would have not been in the habit of hearing till now."[14]

To which Cohen and Fischman, Rothstein and Rosalsky, and the small but growing number of families who contributed the lofty sum of $200 or $250 to become members of the Jewish Center rousingly said "amen."

It didn't take long before Kaplan was in a bind, increasingly unsettled by growing doubts about the Jewish Center; his ambitions for himself and the project tempered by anxiety over its viability. "I have grown cold to the idea of my having anything whatever to do" with this enterprise, he wrote only a year later, in 1916, increasingly reluctant to associate with it.[15]

Busy teaching at the Jewish Theological Seminary; superintending its Teachers Institute; lecturing here, there, and everywhere while also actively involved—a "public factor"—in a wide range of Jewish communal activities, from Jewish education to Zionist affairs, Kaplan didn't need to add more to his plate. Walking away from the Jewish Center would have been a completely understandable decision, even the sensible thing to do. But staring down a long list of tasks wasn't what cooled him on the project; where others faltered when their workload was too heavy, Kaplan flourished.[16]

What curbed his enthusiasm were doubts that the venture would ever get off the ground: its costs were too high, the responsibility too heavy for any one or two or even three people to shoulder, and potential members, near as he could tell, took their religion much too lightly. Kaplan's faith in the ability of the Center's champions to pull it off wavered, especially when months went by without his hearing a word about it. And when, finally, there was good news—things were moving apace—Cohen, a one-man band accustomed to having his way, induced second thoughts. The lay leader was increasingly ill-disposed to make good on Kaplan's vision; either that, or he didn't fully understand what it amounted to, confounded by the distinction that Kaplan drew between inner belief and outer practice. Whatever his rationale, Cohen insisted, when it came to the design of the sanctuary, that it be traditional in every way: separate seating, no organ, the reader's desk facing away rather than toward the congregation. "I am at a loss whether it is better to be as stubborn and determined as he is . . . or to resort to compromise as by temperament I am always inclined to do," Kaplan reflected, before deciding to let Cohen have his way this time around. Holding his tongue as well as his nose, he went along with the businessman's unilateral decision, conceding the sanctuary to him. "There were more important issues than these in Judaism," he rationalized. "If I were to insist on these lesser issues, the more important ones would be obscured." Still, Cohen's efforts to "sway" him rankled.[17]

If that wasn't disturbing enough, a set of increasingly insistent doubts about the future of Judaism in America, not just on the Upper West Side of Manhattan, further weakened Kaplan's resolve to stay the course. In the grip of despair throughout the summer of 1916, he now thought it a fool's errand to proceed any further with the Jewish Center when, given the nature of American Jewish life, to him it seemed doomed from the start. The community's youth were aimless, its communal professionals inept, and its rabbis, especially those who hailed from the Old World, spent most of their time "giving a heksher [ritual approval] on washing powder." Add to the mix Kaplan's theological doubts, of which he still had many, and his casting off of the hypnotic spell of age-old ideals, one by one, and it's a wonder he remained on board for as long as he did.[18]

Somehow, by force of will, Kaplan kept everything in check and humming until one day in March 1918 when, just weeks before the Jewish Center's dedication ceremony, his pent-up accumulation of grievances and disappointments tumbled forth. The trigger: J. H. Cohen. Again. For reasons known only to himself, the Center's tireless champion decided that now was the perfect moment to insist once more that the *Shulchan Aruch* be the law of the land at 132–135 West 86th Street. Taken aback, rendered "quite miserable" by his associate's intransigence, Kaplan wrote in his diary of feeling "adrift again, tossed hither and thither by contrary gusts of passionate anger and disappointment." This time, though, he resolved to "cut loose" once and for all and to sever all ties with the Center. Finis.[19]

Cohen, caught off guard by this dramatic, unanticipated turn of events, made a beeline for Kaplan's West 89th Street apartment, wanting to know "wherein he sinned." To which, Kaplan unequivocally responded, "You are ruining my soul." Despite such a definitive statement, the two men had at one another for a few more rounds until it was clear that neither one would budge, at which point Cohen "froze up as I had never seen him before," Kaplan recalled at the time. " 'That settled it,' is what his bearing implied." Cohen's next move did more than imply. Without missing a beat, he prodded the Center powers that be to cast about at once for another rabbi.[20]

When the designated candidate failed to pass muster—"he was not the man for them"—they returned, hat in hand, to Kaplan, beseeching him to come back, please. A delegation composed of Rothstein and Rosalsky, both of whom Kaplan admired, came to his home to "inveigle" him into the fold and onto the pulpit. Telling him how much they were invested in his ideas and how when the going got rough only the thought of having him in their corner kept things afloat, they played to his considerable ego.[21]

Against his better judgment, Kaplan let himself be won over and agreed to sign on the dotted line; he had invested too much in the enterprise to call it quits. But he did so with one proviso: he would not draw a salary or in any way be considered an employee, a hired hand. To sweeten the deal, at least in his own mind, Kaplan insisted that he receive no compensation; instead, a substantial chunk—some $5,000—of his putative salary would be donated to the Teachers Institute to be used for scholarships.[22]

A strategic move, a signal to Cohen and the others that he wouldn't be bossed around, Kaplan's calculation was also an internal safety valve, allowing him in good conscience to assume the position of the Center's rabbi. Had he drawn a salary, he wrote in his diary, "I could not be true to myself. I would feel morally cramped, and once I would feel that way, all my spiritual strength would be gone." And then, for good measure, Kaplan allowed how Jewish communal leaders must set an example and "display something of the spirit of sacrifice."[23]

The Center's lay leaders, seasoned and tough-minded businessmen, went along with Kaplan's proposal, but they didn't like it one bit; his not being a salaried employee ran counter to their way of doing things. As Cohen crudely put it, Kaplan's refusal to accept remuneration was akin "to a man who lived with a woman to whom he wasn't married." The Center rabbi might couch his financial arrangement in high-minded terms, but those at the top read it as a declaration of independence, an expression of defiance.[24]

With dedication ceremonies right around the corner, everyone put on a good face and went on with the show. Literally. Everything about Sunday, March 24, 1918, "Jewish Center Day," was a performance. The festivities opened with *The Land of the Aleph Bes*, a play put on by the Jewish Center's children. The formal dedication exercises, a composite of song, prayer, ritual (the lighting of the Eternal Light, placing the Torah scrolls in the Ark), and far too many speeches, followed later that afternoon and went on for hours. After a brief interval, celebrants returned to their seats for *The House of the Jew*, a "pantomime-allegory" performed by the Center's young adults and a recital of Jewish folk songs and then (finally!) social dancing.[25]

An elaborate production from start to finish, Jewish Center Day signaled an institutional commitment to what Kaplan, in his exuberant dedicatory remarks, called a "Judaism of the five senses." Exhilarating, alive, "big and heroic," the Jewish Center's version of the ancestral faith, he affirmed, was sure to thrill, delight, and command attention. If the celebration was any indication, the Jewish Center also promised to be an exercise in participatory democracy. Getting it off the ground called for the membership to field an unusually large and varied number of committees, among them the Entertainment Committee and the Floral Committee, the ushers' Arrangements Committee, the Costuming Committee, the Festival Program Committee, and the Souvenir Program Committee. By all accounts—in the *New York Times* and the Anglo-language Jewish press, among many others—the Jewish Center's dedication was a triumph, a herald of good things to come. With great delight mingled with relief, Kaplan settled in for the long haul.[26]

Once open for business, it didn't take long before cracks marred the Jewish Center's handsome appearance. Congregational interest in its affairs seemed to have peaked on March 24. From that point on, hardly anyone responded to Kaplan's calls to read a Jewish book, drop a suggestion into the "Contributor's Box," or ask a question. Only the "T.B.M," as Kaplan colorfully put it, referring to "tired businessmen," showed up for Bible study on Wednesday evenings, while the younger set were "entirely unapproachable." Surveying his kingdom, Kaplan concluded that it was about as "dead as a door nail."[27]

To make matters worse, when Rosh Hashanah and Yom Kippur rolled around in 1918, only a handful of Center members expressed any interest in attending services in their new facility. That year, the High Holidays came "very early," when most members were still happily ensconced in their summer redoubts and planning on celebrating the holidays right where they were. At Cohen's urging, Kaplan made his way to Far Rockaway, the seaside Long Island town that many Centerites called a second home, to persuade them to bestir themselves. Appealing to their better selves, he spoke of their responsibility to the Center and of how their collective absence on the holiest days of the Jewish calendar might prove fatal to its viability. "All right," they said. "We'll come for Yom Kippur."[28]

His congregants' grudging response made him feel he was wasting his time and energy for a "lot of people who are spiritually and Jewishly beyond redemption . . . too far gone to be shaken out of their spiritual self-complacency." It wasn't just that they were "too intoxicated with the joy of their newly acquired wealth" to be concerned with otherworldly matters. Self-centered, demanding, and boorish, the Center people were hard to like. "God knows how rude most of them are," an exasperated Kaplan noted to himself. The men didn't think twice about making their annoyance publicly known when they were given a lesser communal honor than an aliyah [a call to the Torah]. Time and again, the Center's male congregants insisted on being humored and placated when, according to Kaplan, they should be disciplined, called to account. Their wives were no better. With a keen sense of the amour propre these newly affluent women assiduously cultivated, he caricatured them as "their highnesses," who couldn't be bothered to tear themselves away from whist parties, "automobiling," and shopping. As for their offspring, especially the adolescents among them, what a pampered bunch they turned out to be, the girls "foolish gigglers, the boys uncultured, rich boobs."[29]

What disappointed the Center's spiritual leader even more than his self-absorbed constituents was their tottering commitment to investing in the Center as a multistoried structure. Fundraising had stalled; even the chair of the Building Committee had run out of steam. It was looking more and more as if, having grown to three stories, the building had reached its limit and the congregants, theirs. They appeared ready to "rest on their oars," to make do with a lot less. But not Kaplan. To him, the difference between a three- and a nine-story building was not just a matter of height; scale was pivotal to his agenda. "These other stories," he explained, "were the motor. I could not be expected to pilot the new social mechanism with the motor left out." Eventually, Kaplan prevailed and fundraising resumed, but it took a while—until July 1920—before the Jewish Center reached its mature height of nine stories.[30]

Meanwhile, at the close of his first few months as rabbi, Kaplan took stock and came up short. "On the whole, I feel that my contact with the Center has not meant anything for my mental or spiritual development. It is a sacrifice unrelieved by the conviction that the cause for which it is made is worthwhile." Put more simply, he wondered whether it was worth it.[31]

Still, the man stayed. And stayed and stayed through multiple rounds of slings and arrows, his forbearance even giving him pause. "I am really surprised at myself that I have held on to the Center so long," Kaplan acknowledged in a July 1919 journal entry. At first, he tolerated the well-aimed barbs. Falling within the orbit of shul politics, they were not anything he hadn't experienced before. As is their wont, members took umbrage at some of Kaplan's sermons, especially those in which, his finger pointed squarely at the pews, he held forth on business ethics and the five-day work week. The Jewish Center's rabbi was well aware that his sermons "rubbed the fur the wrong way," an especially witty observation given the number of Center folks involved in the fur business, but he persisted all the same.[32]

Some of the Center's congregants, especially its leadership, felt Kaplan was taking a crack at them personally and tried to contain him by suggesting that he and the community he served would be better off by convening a kitchen cabinet, a team of advisors, to vet his speeches and point out what might fall flat and what might leave everyone cheering. Kaplan nixed the idea, of course, and continued saying what was on his mind, no matter whom he might offend. But only up to a point. By 1920, the nit-picking, second-guessing, needling, and mudslinging had taken on lives of their own, their momentum threatening the integrity of the entire enterprise and Kaplan's role within it, destabilizing both. Throwing the rabbi's words and "newfangled" concepts in his face, Cohen and his confreres accused him of tricking them into adopting a " 'new Judaism' " and refused to let themselves "be experimented with" any longer.[33]

In his defense, Kaplan argued that Cohen had gotten it all wrong, his interpretation a strange brew of well-intentioned blunders and willful misreading. For starters, Cohen was under the impression that when Kaplan accepted the position as the Center's rabbi he had "pledged to make it 100% Jewish according to the 'Din Shulhan Aruch.' " Not true; that never happened. For another thing, having helped to craft the text, Kaplan could attest to the fact that there was "nothing in the Constitution which says that the Center must be Orthodox." As for the wounding charge that Kaplan sought all along to deceive the Center community, he said this: "It was not a new Judaism that I was trying to formulate, but on the contrary. . . . I was doing all in my power to enable traditional Judaism to live."[34]

What set off these fireworks were back-to-back publications, the first an essay titled "A Program for the Reconstruction of Judaism," which Kaplan published in the August 1920 issue of the *Menorah Journal*, and the second an article titled "Society of the Jewish Renascence," in the November issue of *The Maccabaean*, a Zionist monthly. One alone created a stir; two, a commotion. While much of what Kaplan had to say would have been familiar to those American Jews who had been paying attention, something about these two essays—their timing, resolute tone, clarity of purpose—was provocative enough to make folks on and off West 86th Street see red.[35]

Dense and at times hard to follow, there was no mistaking the thrust of the *Menorah Journal* piece: if Judaism were to survive, it had to be thoroughly "revitalized," and "reconstructed." Although its author stopped short of calling for a new denomination, he maintained that American Jews could no longer look to either Reform or Orthodoxy for spiritual sustenance; both had had their day. (Conservative Judaism, for its part, didn't even merit a sentence.) A stinging rebuke, a no-holds-barred denunciation of both denominations—neither one showed the "least sign of being able to perpetuate itself"—Kaplan was at his fiercest when it came to traditional Judaism. He upbraided it for its blinkered approach to authority, wrongheaded belief in the "infallibility of tradition," and for putting its head in the sand by ignoring just how difficult it was for the majority of American Jews to keep the Sabbath, maintain the dietary laws, and sit through lengthy prayer services whose liturgy no longer made much sense to them. "Orthodoxy," he declaimed, "is altogether out of keeping with the march of human thought."

Something had to be done. And fast. "The ship of Judaism is bound to be wrecked upon the dangerous shoals towards which it is drifting unless we immediately take hold of the helm and try to steer it to safety," Kaplan dramatically intoned, before proffering a lifeboat: a "program for the reconstruction of Judaism." Its tenets included, among other things, "the interpretation of Jewish tradition in terms of present-day thought," active support for the upbuilding of Palestine, and the "formulation of a code of Jewish practice so that every Jew may know definitely what constitutes loyalty to Judaism." Impassioned rather than definitive, even a tad vague and open-ended, Kaplan's words were more of a clarion call, a rallying of the troops, than the stuff of a concrete program. They were initially intended for the members of the Society of the Jewish Renascence, a recently established, loose coalition of kindred souls, of disgruntled Seminary-trained rabbis and Jews at the grass roots, to whom Kaplan now entrusted the mighty task of reconstruction, or renascence. (Though some among them were not sure what "renascence" meant, or what it had to do with Judaism, those familiar with the word thought it offered a more appealing way of putting things than "reconstruction.") The society's dues-paying members, a vanguard of young committed American Jews, were at the ready, prepared to see to it that Judaism was "capable of dropping old forms and taking on new ones, of clothing itself in new thoughts as soon as the old thoughts grow obsolete."

A new "spiritual adventure," the Society of the Jewish Renascence renewed Kaplan's faith. Newly energized by its possibilities, he was eager to spread the word, to acquaint a broader Jewish public with the opportunities it presented and to garner new recruits. The *Maccabaean* article marked the society's public debut.[36]

Right off the bat, it made clear that the group's intention was not to "create a Judaism *de novo*," or to offer a "new abbreviated Schulchan Arukh." It had other goals, lots of them: to study Jewish history and literature; to endorse Halakah (Jewish law) as the "norm of Jewish life" while also being ready to "interpret and develop the body of Jewish law in accordance with the actual conditions and spiritual needs of modern life"; to affiliate actively with a synagogue; to attend religious services; and to cultivate close ties, through correspondence and pilgrimage, with the Jews of Palestine. Every one of these activities was designed to ensure that the society "not degenerate into a mere discussion group." Those who signed on took to heart the idea that "to further the Jewish Renascence in others, they have to give evidence of the Jewish Renascence in their own lives."[37]

Knowing what he did about the workings of the American Jewish community—how elements within were quick to kick up a fuss, fume, and even demonize—Kaplan had to be aware that some of the statements contained within these two articles would anger and threaten those, both within and without the Jewish Center, whose orthodoxy was cherished and nonnegotiable. Still, buoyed by his association with the Society of the Jewish Renascence, he thought it worth the risk to declare himself, to make clear where he stood and what he stood for; his abiding belief in intellectual honesty demanded no less. Besides, what better way to generate a conversation?

If creating a buzz and shaking things up was Kaplan's intention, he succeeded well beyond his expectations. His remarks gave rise to dark murmurings on the *yidishe gas*—the traditional side of the Jewish street—that is, where he was branded a heretic and his views a "brazen piece of blasphemy." Writing to the editor of the *Hebrew Standard*, one unhappy American Jew, speaking for his traditional coreligionists, put it this way: "Behold! He's here. Who? None other than Mordecai M. Kaplan. What is it this time? you ask." And with that facetious opening, he was off on a tear, asserting that Kaplan posed far more of a danger to American Jews than the antisemitic Henry Ford; that he was working "energetically to chloroform us, then to break us, spiritually speaking"; that he would go down in American Jewish history as a "black traitor";

and that in years gone by, someone like Kaplan would have "brought himself excommunication, anathema, public condemnation. Today one can get away with anything." Well, almost anything. Henceforth, the Jewish Center, the letter writer concluded, dare not "call itself 'Orthodox.' "[38]

A more sharply defined and slightly more measured critique in the form of an editorial and a detailed "consideration" took shape within the pages of the *Jewish Forum*, a magazine designed to serve as a "lighthouse" of traditional Judaism. "It is hard to find words with which fitly to characterize such views on the part of an ostensibly religious leader without becoming guilty of unparliamentary expression," Rabbi Bernard Drachman, its managing editor and Kaplan's former teacher, noted in his opening salvo.[39]

For Drachman there was no shortage of words: shocking, disturbing, subversive, pernicious, and un-Jewish were just some of the adjectives strewn throughout his seven-page account. The only word Drachman managed not to use was "rabbi." At no point did he call Kaplan a fellow clergyman; instead, he consistently made use of "Prof.," cutting his colleague—and student—down to size. The substance of Drachman's remarks was that traditional Judaism, which he conflated with "Judaism," had been maligned by Kaplan, whose perspective "fairly swarmed with misconceptions, half-truths, incorrect assumptions, and illogical conclusions." Yes, contemporary Jewish life was in a tight spot, the number of "indifferent, disloyal and actively hostile [Jews]" on the rise. But Kaplan made it seem as if Judaism was the problem, when the real culprits lay elsewhere, with modern life. "Judaism is in no way responsible for these conditions, has nothing to do with them. . . . Judaism is all right, though the Jews may be all wrong."

Warming to his subject, Drachman went on to explain how Kaplan, in his rejection of tradition, was as radical as any reformer, even if he distanced himself from that association. "Tradition is the *conditio sine qua non* of Judaism," the critique's author declared with a rhetorical flourish. "All that we know or have of Judaism we owe to tradition. If tradition cannot be believed, nothing is left of the Jewish faith of which we can be sure." Everything central to the Jewish faith—the commandments, the Hebrew language, the calendar, identity—was bound up with tradition. "Take away tradition from Judaism and the whole structure falls in ruins." In loosening its grip on modern American Jews, Kaplan had made a "fatal mistake." Were his ideas to take hold, "it would be an extraordinary calamity."

Comments like these enjoining traditional Jews at the Jewish Center and elsewhere to look upon Kaplan's views with "feelings of horror" blackened his good name and tarnished the reputation of the 86th Street enterprise, upsetting those associated with it. "In every corner you would meet groups of Centerites discussing theology as though they had to pass the next examination at the Seminary," Kaplan recalled with a touch of good humor, while in a register more pained than lighthearted, he also acknowledged the shouting and yelling, the "howls" and the "abuse," that emanated from behind the closed doors of the Center's boardroom.[40]

Calls for Kaplan to do the "honorable and manly thing" by resigning soon filled the air. He did no such thing. Though "very despondent," Kaplan stayed put and turned the other cheek. Not because he fancied himself a latter-day Jesus, or a masochist who enjoyed being pummeled and bad-mouthed. There were moments in his long career when Kaplan relished stirring the pot and acting as the gadfly, the bad boy, in the room, but this was not one of them. Nor did economics account for his decision to weather the storm. Though he and his growing family, which by now consisted of four small children, could use the money, owing to the terms of Kaplan's contract, he would not derive a penny from the Center's coffers.[41]

Kaplan remained at the Jewish Center because he wanted to see it through; his belief that it held out "more promise of enabling Judaism to strike root in this country than any other" undertaking remained intact. It had been only a few months, after all, since the building had been completed, and he was eager to put all of its programs to the test and measure the results. Kaplan was well aware that an experiment like this took time and that his subjects needed to adjust to the notion that a " 'thus said the Lord,' that is three years old, pronounced by a man whom they can see and hear," was just as, or even more, valid an approach as a " 'thus said the Lord,' that is thousands of years old." To leave now would be premature, even irresponsible, much less a blow to his ego. "I am human and have sufficient pride not to allow Cohen and Fischman to compel me to resign," he would later admit when accounting for his foot-dragging. "I want to resign from the Center, but I don't want anybody to make me do it." "Anybody" also included his mother who, writing to her "dear Motl," encouraged him to "make Judaism happy by *kiddush Hashem* instead of *chillul Hashem*," the first Hebrew phrase referring to the sanctification of God's name, the second to its desecration. "Make peace with the crazy Cohen and his company. Do I need to tell you the importance of peace?" Just in case her advice did not hit home, she went on to urge her son to "change, give up some of your ideas you don't have too many followers, better try to work with Cohen. . . . Your mother."[42]

With so much at stake, Kaplan did seek peace, though not as his mother would have it. He hoped to avert what, by the winter of 1921, some congregants, mindful of American history, likened to a "civil war." By then, the Jewish Center had split into two distinct factions, one that refused to function with Dr. Kaplan at the helm and the other that refused to function without him. The two parties and their respective followers were arrayed along a fault line with the Center leadership and some of the membership on one edge of the precipice and Kaplan and his devotees on the other.[43]

Someone or something had to give.

Kaplan was determined it wouldn't be he. In February 1921, in an effort to lower the temperature, reestablish trust, and get back on track, Kaplan convened a public meeting of the Center membership; today, one would describe it as an attempt at damage control, or even as a Hail Mary pass. He called it a "get-together gathering," an opportunity for a "heart-to-heart talk," as if it were just a group of friends casually meeting on an ordinary Wednesday evening. (That a stenographer was on hand to take down every, or nearly every, word, suggested it was a lot more than that.) For over two hours, Kaplan sought to dispel the "misunderstandings" that had recently arisen and distorted his words, having gone through "at least ten to fifteen media," or versions. "Here's your chance to hear the truth from me, not your neighbor," he told the hundred or so people who made a point of attending despite inclement weather.[44]

Before opening the floor for discussion, Kaplan laid his cards on the table. "I am saying exactly the same things now and teaching the same things from the pulpit and the lecture platform that I have been teaching for the last fifteen years." In case that point didn't resonate, he made it again a few minutes later. "I want to disabuse your minds of the impression that I have come with a new revelation and that I am advocating anything that is contrary to historical or traditional Judaism," he asserted. "I want to make clear to you that historical/traditional Judaism—Judaism in its continuity—is what I stand for and what I work for." Delving into specifics, the Center's spiritual leader went on to claim that he never, ever said that kashruth was to be discarded, that it was no longer necessary to have two sets of dishes, or that, given the difficulties of observing the Sabbath in America, Shabbos had become optional.[45]

How, then, did it come to pass that people maintained that Kaplan "preaches a new kind of Judaism which does not demand any more duties?" He explained away that misguided perception by saying that his description of a problem was erroneously taken to be its solution; that in encouraging his congregants who could not keep the Sabbath 100 percent to "keep it seventy-five percent; if you cannot keep it seventy-five percent, keep it fifty percent," he appeared to license them to do as little as possible. Nothing could be further from the truth: I "stand on tradition and on history."[46]

Responding cannily to some charges but not others, Kaplan avoided the use of the term "orthodoxy" and left open, perhaps for another day, a discussion of what constituted religious faith, especially the elements of traditional Judaism. Was it a sensibility? A way of being in the world? A set of devotional practices? He didn't say. What Kaplan did offer that wintry February evening in 1921 was assurance. No, he wasn't leaving the Jewish Center for something else, nor was he up to something new. A bit bruised, battered, and worse for wear, he was still the same Mordecai M. Kaplan, who, three years earlier, had cast his lot with the Jewish Center—and they with him.

Both the substance of his remarks and the open, candid, conciliatory manner in which he shared them won over his audience, who greeted his explanations with "applause," "hearty applause," "great applause," "prolonged applause," and, ultimately, a standing ovation. "We stand by him," declared Judge Rosalsky, Kaplan's most steadfast champion, summing up the audience's sentiments. "There has been nothing said by Doctor Kaplan that is incompatible with any of the provisions of this Constitution." His penchant for speechifying in full flower, the magistrate went on to say that the "Center owes it to him to stand by him not because he is Doctor Kaplan, but because he stands for conviction, for principle." To those who defame him and "stab him behind his back, the nearer will we draw to him, the more will we hold up his hands as the hands of Moses had to be held up." With a rousing plea to "stand unitedly now and forever behind the man who is leading us," Rosalsky finally sat down to "prolonged applause."[47]

Kaplan may have faced the opposition "like a man" and carried the day, but not for long. In the weeks that followed, the politicking and jockeying, the maneuvering and outflanking continued with renewed vigor, variously calling to mind a duel or a chess match: thrust and parry, check and check again. Neither side gave an inch. One faction insisted that it would "only consider peace at the sacrifice of Dr. Kaplan," adding "he is too big a man for the Center and we don't want him." The other, no less adamant, would not consider peace without him. "The Center without the Ideals that Dr. Kaplan tried to infuse into it was a big building with expensive furniture inside, but as empty as a drum. A body without a soul."[48]

Meanwhile, rhetoric escalated, becoming progressively nastier:

KAPLAN: "Cohen is out after my scalp."
COHEN: Further discussion will take place "over my dead body."
KAPLAN: "They made my life hell."
COHEN'S WIFE: "Kaplan will be the death of him if he doesn't resign."[49]

As 1921 drew to a close, even the estimable Rabbi Judah Magnes, who, skilled in the art of mediation, had been brought in to calm the waters, "threw up his hands" in frustration. At an impasse, there was only one way out: in a decision he called "heartrending," Kaplan resigned.[50]

Tendering his resignation "forthwith," on a piece of Jewish Theological Seminary stationery dated January 16, 1922, the Center's rabbi began by expressing his regrets: "I could hardly have dreamt . . . it would come to this." He then briefly summarized the history of his relationship with the Center, especially with Cohen, before arriving at the clincher: "I find myself hampered at every step by the Board of Trustees. I find it necessary to discontinue my services at the Center." And with that, Kaplan took his leave.[51]

Of the sixteen sentences in the lengthy paragraph that comprised this letter, one that reads "he knew me as well as I know myself" stands out. This poignant passage, a reference to Cohen, underscored the extent to which the Center contretemps was as much personal as institutional. What made the rift especially bitter was that it hinged on the souring of a once-valued friendship. When Cohen and Kaplan first met, each thought quite highly of the other. Kaplan, who wasn't given to complimenting American Jewish lay leaders, characterized Cohen as a "most stimulating person" and enjoyed spending time in his company; Cohen, who delighted in parrying with the young rabbi, eagerly sought him out, too. But once their relationship foundered, Kaplan came to see the Center's chief mover and shaker as a "self-deluded hypocrite," while Cohen regarded the Center's rabbi as a renegade.[52]

The relationship between the two men and, ultimately, with the Jewish Center, came aground on a misreading of one another and of the institution they thought they were building together. For his part, Cohen didn't know his rabbi as well as he thought he did. Taken with Kaplan's vivid, engrossing ideas, he didn't fully comprehend them. By the time it dawned on him, in April 1921, that what Kaplan "meant by saying [his] conception of Judaism involved shifting the center of gravity from the Torah to the people," things had spun out of control.[53]

What's more, Cohen undoubtedly thought that Kaplan would, as a matter of course, defer to him and the other *baalbatim* as every other rabbi did; that he would be able to control him and modulate, even neutralize, some of his more outré ideas; and that, like Kaplan's parents before him, once the Jewish Center in all of its nine-story glory became a reality, his protégé would simmer down. Wrong on all counts. Cohen had made a colossal mistake.

Nor did Kaplan know himself as well as he thought he did. He believed his pronouncements to be crystal clear when murky was more like it; he let himself be repeatedly outmaneuvered, thinking he retained the upper hand; and he profoundly underestimated the degree to which Cohen and his confreres were invested in keeping Orthodox Judaism a going concern. One way or another, the rabbi of the Jewish Center had badly misconstrued and mishandled the situation.

No one came out ahead. Not the Center, or Cohen, or Kaplan, or American Judaism.

What had started out auspiciously ended in failure, haunting the Jewish Center's ex-rabbi for the rest of his life.

3

Musical Chairs

How DO YOU FEEL about dark mahogany chairs upholstered in dark green imitation leather, sample number 4001? Or a lighter shade of mahogany chairs upholstered in brown imitation leather, sample number 74-a? For an extra fifty cents per chair, you can have a book rack on the back of a chair. Interested? Once you've made your selection, would you prefer stationary or mobile chairs? Or perhaps wooden benches might be an even better, and simpler, choice? Lest readers think that in turning the page, and starting a new chapter, they've wandered into another book—one having to do with furniture—imagine how disoriented Kaplan must have felt when he had to entertain these very same questions and resolve issues that related to interior design rather than the state of one's soul.[1]

No, he didn't make good on his threats to leave the rabbinate by becoming a furniture salesman. Swept along by the enthusiasm of his Jewish Center supporters, Kaplan found himself enmeshed in a new enterprise that called for chairs as well as a place in which to put them: the creation of a "new organization to carry on the ideals of the old," without in any way duplicating "in method or point of view any other existing synagogue, including the Jewish Center."[2]

With barely enough time to catch his breath and recover his equilibrium, Kaplan jumped from the frying pan into the fire. Though Lena emphatically cautioned him against further "entanglements," as did many of his friends who encouraged him to devote all of his time exclusively to teaching and writing, he couldn't resist the siren call of public adulation.[3]

It turned out that as Kaplan's relationship with the Jewish Center was coming to a dramatic close, a behind-the-scenes drama of another sort was underway. His supporters—by some accounts over thirty families, or at least half the congregational membership—banded together in the fall of 1921 to plot their next move. What form that might take generated heated discussion, which went on for hours, sometimes into the early hours of the morning. Should they remain at the Center without Kaplan, or resign, en masse, as a unified bloc? If they did leave, what of their financial contributions? Should they cut their losses and walk away, or hire a lawyer to get back their "investment"? Maybe the best solution might be to wrest control from the board of trustees, "install all our own people," and stay put? If, however, they were to secede, then what? "Do we want to continue the original purpose of the Centre [*sic*] and start anew?" And would Kaplan come with them? If not, where would they go?[4]

After much give-and-take, a strong consensus emerged in favor of exiting the Jewish Center as a unit and regrouping as a "new institution" with Kaplan in charge. As they tentatively looked toward the future, some of his champions thought big. "To leave the Jewish Centre [*sic*] and go into a small synagogue seems ridiculous. Dr. Kaplan should not leave a beautiful place and go into anything small. We should build a bigger, better and beautiful Center," Mr. Katcher declared. To which Mr. Unterberg suggested a different course of action: "Let us start with those who want to follow Dr. Kaplan and organize in a modest way. We can start small." Others thought it altogether premature to resolve the scale of the enterprise then and there and instead limited their remarks, and intentions, to expressing unbridled support of their rabbi. "I am heart and soul for Dr. Kaplan," a proxy for Mr. Lubell noted, while Mrs. Samuels, in person, passionately declared that she was "more than 100% with Dr. Kaplan. Not only I but the lives of my children are dedicated to Dr. Kaplan. I will follow him into any organization."[5]

The object of their affection not only kept abreast of what his followers were up to in the months leading up to his resignation but was also an active participant, a co-conspirator, in the proceedings. Kaplan's journal, usually full of lively details, went silent as things took a turn for the worse at the Center, leaving the impression that he was in the dark about these rump meetings. But an undated transcript of one such gathering, whose time frame situates it sometime between the fall of 1921 and the onset of 1922, revealed that Kaplan was in the room on at least one occasion and directly involved in the deliberations.

Galvanized by the currents of enthusiasm that coursed through the crowd, he agreed to be its spiritual leader but only if everyone present went into the project with their "eyes open," mindful both of the criticism that was likely to come their way and of the kinds of activities that lay in store. "There should never be an occasion afterwards for anyone to say that there was any cause for misunderstanding," Kaplan cautioned. Once that acknowledgment was out of the way, things began to move quickly. By the time the new year rolled around, the Lubells and the Samuels, the Unterbergs and the Katchers, the M. H. Rubins and the J. H. Rubins (Kaplan's brothers-in-law), the Lubetkins, the Levys, and the Liebovitzs, among others, had resigned their membership in the Jewish Center. They reconstituted themselves on January 17, 1922, as members of a new entity called "the American Synagogue." Leasing what had previously been a private family residence at 41 West 86th Street, they held their first Friday night services ten days later. The group's new home was only a stone's throw away from the Jewish Center, a detail lost on no one.[6]

Kaplan liked to think that his latest undertaking "came as near to being my own creation as I could ever expect." Certainly, the vision he advanced had a familiar ring, drawing on phrases and concepts that he had promoted in print and at the Jewish Center: a democratic and "living" Judaism, a steadfast, unusually robust commitment to the "idea of Palestine as a spiritual center," and an approach to tradition that seesawed between the past and the present. Those who followed him out of the Center expecting a clean break with traditional Judaism would have been disappointed. What they found instead was Kaplan's characteristic equivocation on Jewish ritual matters, especially in relation to the *Shulchan Aruch.* Once again, he hemmed and hawed. "I do not say here that I shall live up to the Shulkun Arukh [*sic*] but I will go by that code because it is the only code to go by, but I cannot follow it out to every letter. I must use my common-sense." What that meant in practice was anyone's guess. Temporizing as well as equivocating, Kaplan put it this way: "Later, we can decide on the ritual and the mode of carrying on the services, which may be a departure from orthodoxy." Or maybe not.[7]

Where the religious identity of the new venture was purposefully left vague and open-ended, its name was clear as a bell. Calling it "the American Synagogue" heralded its origins as a "synagogue which shall strike its roots in American life, which shall show to this country that there is a future, not only a past." It also signaled Kaplan's intention to think nationally rather than locally, more in terms of a "movement embracing large numbers" than a "small local institution."[8]

Understandable, maybe; compelling, less so. The name lasted barely a month before Kaplan retired it, telling those who attended the very first members' meeting on January 24, 1922, that "the American Synagogue" seemed to be "open to misunderstanding and misinterpretation." Consequently, the name was scrapped in favor of "the Society for the Advancement of Judaism," a title which, by his lights (if no one else's), more adequately expressed the "true purpose of the organization": a "society of searchers," not just a congregation. The new designation, Kaplan explained, would have the added benefit of putting us "on record as a Society, similar to the various other organizations which realized their aims in getting large number of adherents and followers, and were not limited to the local community."[9]

On the page "the Society for the Advancement of Judaism" seemed to be a sensible and even dignified choice. Saying the name out loud, in the context of speech, was a different matter entirely: a mouthful of a title, it didn't exactly roll off the tongue. Little wonder, then, that its adherents at the grass roots took to calling it, simply, "SAJ." Kaplan met them halfway, insisting on "the S.A.J.," at least when referring to it on paper, his way of emphasizing that this designation was an abbreviation, a shorthand, rather than a nickname, a corruption of the original.

Concepts came easily to Kaplan; titles consistently eluded him. Whether casting about for a name for this new enterprise or, a few years earlier, figuring out what to call what eventually became the Society for the Jewish Renascence—an opaque and lumbering title if ever there was one—he typically opted for the grandiose when a straightforward, less cumbersome option was also at hand. Consider that group's flailing attempts in July 1920 to come up with a name; the minutes of their efforts reads like a comic routine, an onomastic version of "Who's on First." Should they call themselves a movement, a society, or a league? Should their name convey all of their aims; be "non-committal," short, and to the point; or "picturesque," perhaps even "biblical," whatever that meant? At one juncture in the conversation, Kaplan, who favored the use of "society," hailing it as a "good word," proposed "the Society for the Advancement of Progressive Judaism." He barely finished speaking when a fierce discussion erupted over whether "progressive" was a "misused" and "abused" word or one whose meaning was stable and positive. When that roundelay went nowhere, it was decided that the only way to resolve the impasse was to refer the naming process to a specially designated committee with the admonition, voiced by Kaplan, that ultimately he and his colleagues were most "interested in the aim, and not in the name."[10]

It wasn't easy in 1920 or in 1922 to find an appropriate designation for what Kaplan had in mind. "Center," now a tainted word in his book, was clearly off the table; "synagogue" was too limited and limiting; "temple," too dated and even compromised a term. A traditional Hebrew appellation like "Kehilath Jeshurun" didn't fit the bill either; it clashed with the organization's decidedly American orientation. And so, "the Society for the Advancement of Judaism" it became and SAJ it remained. If nothing else, the awkward-sounding name effectively conveyed its distinctiveness. No one would mistake 41 West 86th Street for a "run of the mill" congregation.[11]

Its humble quarters made sure of it. In a hurry to establish a physical presence on the Upper West Side, Kaplan's followers rented an unoccupied rowhouse, which like many structures on West 86th Street and throughout the neighborhood was probably slated for demolition and hence available for a nominal rental fee. "Instead of a great big building empty all the time with a terrific overhead," the group's new, and admittedly modest, home was more than "ample," at least for the foreseeable future. It "needs no apology from any of us," those responsible for this hastily cobbled together real estate deal were quick to point out, alluding sideways to the site's association with George M. Cohan, the legendary Broadway impresario, rumored to have once been a former occupant.[12]

Much was made of that connection, as if Cohan's cachet would rub off on them, easing their difficult transition from the modernity and grandeur of the Jewish Center to this tumbledown, old-fashioned, dark, and cramped space. No amount of cheerleading could disguise the fact that the site of the Society for the Advancement of Judaism had seen better days. Its followers, having grown accustomed, both in their own homes and in the public spaces they frequented, to the *dernier cri* of stylishness, were now called on to adjust their sights and lower their expectations, to make do with very little. In contrast to the shiny and spacious Jewish Center, where everything was new and in its proper place, 41 West 86th Street was a study in improvisation, its parlor refashioned as a sanctuary, its bedrooms repurposed as classrooms. To cushion the blow, Kaplan made a point of translating the rough-and-tumble of their new circumstances into a virtue, a badge of distinction. It's the spirit, not the surroundings, that matter, he reassured his followers, making those members who lived on West End Avenue feel as pioneering and intrepid as those who had ventured out West.[13]

To make up for its lack of physical amenities, the Society for the Advancement of Judaism embraced the most modern forms of presentation and promotion. The house on 86th Street dated to the late nineteenth century, but its newest occupant was up-to-the-minute in every other respect. Through advertisements positioned on local subway platforms and on the screens of the district's "large moving picture houses," it actively recruited prospective members; to ascertain how many school-age children lived in the area, it hired professional canvassers to go from house to house. Eager to get underway, the SAJ made particularly effective use of the latest office machinery. Under the watchful eye of Hannah Machlowitz, the keeper of a mimeograph machine that cranked out a barrage of publications—songbooks, supplementary readings, the text of a "Junior Service," and a weekly bulletin-cum-magazine known first as the *S.A.J. Bulletin* and then as the *S.A.J. Review*—it kicked into high gear, forging a distinctive personality. When writing about postwar American Jewry's newfound interest in traditional Jewish cuisine, Ruth Glazer, *Commentary*'s in-house expert on "informal Judaica," noted that its proponents might have us believing that "the eggbeater is today the most effective weapon for propagating the faith." More than thirty years earlier much the same could be said of the mimeograph, which provided "speed where speed is needed." Without its fast-paced, inexpensive capacity for duplication, SAJ would not have gotten off the ground as swiftly and as energetically as it did.[14]

Within a matter of weeks, a number of standing committees—among them, one on social activities, another on membership and publicity, a third on "house administration"—sprung into being, along with a constitution, by-laws, and a board of trustees. Acting as if there was no time to waste, Kaplan held a series of members' meetings, sometimes as many as two a month, at which he brought both his followers and prospective members up to speed on what he hoped immediately to accomplish: meaningful religious services, an active lecture program, and the cultivation of a resolutely Hebraic sensibility. "Hebrew should not be Greek to the Jew," he told his congregants, hoping to engender among them a commitment to Zionism that was active rather than passive, inhabited rather than gestural.[15]

And that was just for starters. In his capacity as SAJ's "leader," a term Kaplan now happily assumed, finding it preferable to "rabbi" and much more in keeping with the group's identity as a society rather than a shul, he contemplated a sweeping array of ritual changes, some of which he instituted right away and others he kept to himself until he felt the time was right. Kaplan's wish list, or, better yet, his targets, included the Sabbath morning prayer service, which he felt went on for far too long, generating boredom rather than reverence; separate seating in the sanctuary (an "absurd" practice in this day and age), calendar reform (eliminating the burdensome second day of the "overabundant" two-day Jewish festival), rethinking the hitherto mandatory practice of kashruth ("there's no question that sooner or later Judaism will have to get along without dietary laws"), and abolishing the Kol Nidre prayer on the grounds that it was "incompatible with present day life." From time to time, Kaplan augmented his wish list, adding, somewhat whimsically, in 1924, that he hoped to "improve" the Passover Haggadah "to such an extent that it will be more important even than the 'kneidlach.' "[16]

Anyone familiar with both Kaplan's views and strong-willed personality would have anticipated that once freed of constraints, he would make good on his long-standing ambition to contemporize and rejuvenate whatever he felt needed to be contemporized and rejuvenated. But his introduction of a brand-new ceremony, the bat mitzvah (or bas mitzvah, as it was then called) and when SAJ was a mere infant, only a few months old, took everyone by surprise. After all, there was no inkling either in his private musings or in his public statements that the ritual life of adolescent Jewish girls was of any concern, let alone so pressing a matter that it had to be quickly addressed. Granting women the right to vote in general elections as well as in congregational affairs was of interest to him, as was providing every Jewish daughter with access to Jewish education, but a special coming-of-age ritual for girls?

To avoid any unnecessary friction, especially at this early stage in SAJ's life, Kaplan presented the idea to the board in February 1922. One would think its novelty, if nothing else, would call for a lengthy disquisition on his part and at least a semblance of to-ing and fro-ing on theirs. Instead, the minutes tersely record that Dr. Kaplan "suggested" that a bas mitzvah ceremony be introduced at SAJ so that every twelve-year-old girl would be "formerly [*sic*] initiated into the fold of the Jewish people." He then "asked permission to have the privilege of allowing his daughter, Judith, [to] inaugurate this custom." The minutes record that his proposal was "met with the hearty approval of the members of the Board." And that was that.[17]

The event itself, which took place the following month, also occasioned no waves. In retrospect, Judith Kaplan's 1922 bas mitzvah has come to be seen as a landmark in the history of American Judaism, but at the time it passed without much notice. Everything about it was low-key. Introduced with no fanfare and without much advance preparation by the bas mitzvah girl herself—according to family lore, she was informed only the night before that her bas mitzvah would take place the very next morning, a detail that makes for a better, more dramatic story, but one which, given the family dynamic, seems inexplicably cruel and most unlikely—the event hardly registered outside the immediate precincts of the family and those of the SAJ.[18]

The ceremony was a modest, circumscribed affair, whose rhythm set it apart from the traditional bar mitzvah. While the bar mitzvah boy would be called up during the actual reading of the Torah, Judith was called up only after that portion of the service had ended. What's more, after reciting the customary blessings, she read from a printed text in lieu of chanting from a Torah scroll, which lay just a few feet away, wrapped up tight and ready for its return to the Ark.[19]

The spirit of the occasion was equally restrained, more in keeping with the modest bar mitzvah of Eastern Europe than with the big shebang, the increasingly outsized, extravagantly scaled affair characteristic of modern American Jews: it took the form of a *kiddush*, a collation at the synagogue following services, and a celebratory dinner at home later that evening.

A newfangled ritual like this one, especially given its association with the controversial Mordecai M. Kaplan, surely would have occasioned a raised eyebrow or at the very least generated a sentence or two in the press. But no one batted an eye. Or paid attention. Or seemed to care. Even the bas mitzvah girl's father and originator of the ceremony played it down, casually and succinctly noting the event in his diary ten days after the fact: "Last Sabbath a week ago (March 18), I inaugurated the ceremony of the *bas mizvah* [the last two words written in Hebrew] at the S.A.J. Meeting House (41 West 86th Street)—about which more details later," he wrote in a March 28, 1922, entry. "My daughter Judith was the first one to have her *bas mizvah* celebrated there."[20]

If everything went according to plan, Judith's bas mitzvah would be the first, but not the last, such celebration. In 1923, SAJ published a handsome booklet with deckled edges to commemorate its first anniversary. (Mindful of the occasion's significance, the board authorized the extra expense; a mimeographed text would just not do.) Under the rubric of "Our Activities," which included religious services, Hebrew School, and lectures, the text read as follows: "Bas Mizvah Ceremony: Realizing the important service the Jewish woman is capable of rendering in a revival of Jewish life, we have introduced the ceremony of formally initiating the young Jewess into the Jewish fold." The promotional gambit continued: "The young girl thus becomes a Bas Mizvah on the Sabbath following her twelfth birthday through an impressive ceremony similar to that by which the Jewish lad becomes a Bar Mitzvah." Together with her male counterpart, she was also expected to sign a pledge to continue her Jewish education for several years, in return for which each one received a "beautifully engraved" certificate.[21]

Despite the institutional seal of approval, the bas mitzvah was slow to take off at SAJ, its practice occasional and intermittent. By 1933, interest in the ritual, never too pronounced to begin with, seemed to have slackened dramatically, prompting Kaplan to relate that it had "fallen into desuetude of late." Many were the forces that militated against its adoption: too few twelve-year-old Jewesses were on hand at SAJ to render it a going concern; the pledge was too onerous a responsibility for teenage girls to take on; and the realization that the bas mitzvah's import was more symbolic than actual, affecting little in the way of woman's religious opportunities, also got in its way. Still, Kaplan resignedly expressed the hope that the bas mitzvah ceremony might be "kept up regularly."[22]

It wasn't. The bas mitzvah may have arrived on the scene like a bolt out of the blue, but it remained a subdued presence well into the postwar era when it finally came into its own at SAJ and in synagogues throughout the country.

Inaugurating the bas mitzvah was an unusually bold move on Kaplan's part. When augmenting or tinkering with ritual practice, SAJ's spiritual leader typically proceeded cautiously, even sub rosa, so much so that the more scrupulously observant men who had followed him from the Jewish Center had nothing to complain about, at least not at first. When, in April 1922, Kaplan amended a long-standing element of the Sabbath liturgy having to do with the restoration of ritual sacrifice so that it now read as an ancient, historical practice rather than an ongoing aspiration, he admitted to doing so "in a manner that might be characterized as surreptitious." Instead of announcing the alteration ahead of time, he instructed the cantor to go ahead and "read the service with these changes."[23]

In this instance, as in several others, Kaplan relied on the behavior of his constituents, praying that since "most of the people have their minds on other things while the cantor recites the Amidah, [they are] therefore really unaware of what I have done with the text" and none the wiser. On another occasion, he mischievously acknowledged his dependence on the congregation's complicity. He had tried all sorts of schemes to make the services seem short, he told his audience at a members' meeting. Many of his congregants assisted him by resorting to a simple device: "They come late."[24]

For a while there was talk of introducing an organ, and with it instrumental music, into the services, but that idea was quickly quashed for fear that SAJ would be associated with Reform Judaism, a recurrent concern of some board members determined to safeguard their reputation, and that of SAJ, as traditionalists. Vocal music, on the other hand, was warmly encouraged. Congregational singing and, later on, a congregational choir, of which Lena was a member, contributed to the "singy-ness" of the service, especially once the gifted and keen Moshe Nathanson, an enthusiast of the latest melodies from the land of Israel, became SAJ's long-running cantor in 1924. Thanks to him, Kaplan related on the occasion of Nathanson's thirty-five years of "unforgettable" service, SAJ was "not reduced to a passive audience listening to a musical performance, but joins in lustily with all the verve, but without the antics, of a Hasidic service." A source of pride, SAJ's musicality gave rise to its reputation as the "only Jewish organization of a religious character that had college spirit."[25]

Like the organ, mixed seating in the sanctuary remained a big no-no. Though nothing untoward resulted—no mass exodus, no thunderbolts from on high—when High Holiday services that year (and the one after that and the one after that) were conducted in a much more commodious rented facility known as the Leslie Rooms, where mixed seating prevailed,

SAJ refrained from instituting the practice on its home turf for a number of years. Every time the issue came up, which it frequently did in those early days, "protest" stayed Kaplan's hand. From where he sat, there was "no reasonable excuse for continuing the custom of separating the sexes during prayer when men and women sit promiscuously at all other functions, social and educational." But some of his earliest, staunchest, and most steadfast supporters—men like Joseph Levy and Abe Liebovitz—felt that abrogating that tradition would identify them as "reformed Jews," and that simply wouldn't do, especially at such an early, fluid moment in SAJ's existence. Rather than risk alienating his biggest fans, and upsetting his mother as well as his mother-in-law, both of whom added their voice to the chorus of naysayers, strongly making known their disapproval of mixed seating, Kaplan heeded what its opponents had to say and resolved to bide his time until everyone, or nearly everyone, was on board.[26]

Not everyone would be. Within a few years of SAJ's formation, a number of members, including Isaac Polstein, a prosperous "real estate operator," the developer of Upper West Side apartment buildings, who had followed Kaplan from the Jewish Center and now chaired the SAJ's Committee on Seats, chafed more and more under his rabbi's increasingly liberal tilt. First, the omission of several prayers from the Yom Kippur *Ne'ilah* or closing service upset him; then it was the ever-looming prospect of mixed seating in the sanctuary. No shrinking violet, the businessman made known his discontent, threatening to resign and prompting Kaplan to reminiscence, none too fondly, about the " 'good' old days" at the Center. When Polstein came by Kaplan's home one Saturday afternoon to have it out with him, "this time I no longer beat about the bush," Kaplan recalled. "I told him outright that the S.A.J. was outspokenly unorthodox." (For his part, Polstein responded by saying that he would have to consider his options and asked Kaplan to bear him no ill will should he take his leave from SAJ. Kaplan assured him of their "continued friendship." He stayed.)[27]

Polstein was right to worry that his more traditional orientation increasingly rendered him a fish out of water, especially when Kaplan's intention to do away with the much beloved Kol Nidre prayer, a staple of the Yom Kippur liturgy since the ninth century, became more widely known. Key to his evolving master plan—the "necessary reconstruction of Judaism"—its abolition was among the very first items he took up with the SAJ's board of trustees. As early as May 1922, Kaplan informed them of his plans to observe the coming Yom Kippur, SAJ's first, without it. By his account more of a legal formula calling for the dismissal of vows than a heavenly petition, Kol Nidre struck him as unseemly, ill-suited to the holiness of the day, much less the spirit of the times, and hence warranting its very own disavowal. SAJ's leadership, determined not to rock the boat—it was much too soon for any show of discord—went along, despite having qualms that it was not the right thing to do, and agreed to the following resolution:

> Whereas we, as Jews, who take our religion seriously, cannot permit ourselves to enter upon this solemn day [of Yom Kippur] with an avowal that is not compatible with present day life and is likely to be misinterpreted and misunderstood, therefore be it
>
> Resolved that Dr. M. M. Kaplan, our spiritual leader, be asked to formulate a prayer compatible with our conscience as Jews in place of Kol Nidre, and further
>
> Resolved that we retain the present melody of Kol Nidre.[28]

A few months later, Kaplan tabled the idea, telling the board that he had "reconsidered the recommendation" and "for the present [would] allow the Kol Nidre to be sung." The SAJ's spiritual leader had backed down when some of his colleagues, whose opinion he valued, counseled against it. "Tampering" with Kol Nidre, they cautioned, was ill-advised. "Let that prayer alone."[29]

Kaplan's change of heart was short-lived. No sooner had Yom Kippur 5683 come and gone than he brought up the issue, again and again. Between 1923 and 1930, reconsidering the recitation of Kol Nidre became as regular an occurrence as the solemn day itself. For SAJ's spiritual leader, the age-old Aramaic prayer was a symptom of what was wrong with American Judaism and had to go. "People have no idea of what it is about," he complained. "The pious emotions that it evokes, if it does that at all, have nothing to do with the contents. Such a state of affairs is deplorable in any religion since it makes for mummery and hypocrisy," all the more at SAJ where intellectual honesty was touted as the coin of the realm. If anything put to the test Kaplan's vision of a modern Judaism in which the head ruled the heart and intentionality triumphed over sentimentality, Kol Nidre was it.[30]

Nothing if not insistent, Kaplan kept hammering away, only to encounter stiffening resistance on the part of the board, the membership, and his mother, all of whom found the prospect of a Yom Kippur without Kol Nidre inconceivable. "I hope you will not be angry with me but I can tell you that for your dead father's sake you should not make surely a *chillul hashem* [desecration of God's name]," Anna Kaplan anxiously wrote her son. "I cannot understand why you have to announce before the whole world that you do not believe." As for Kaplan's congregants, even if they barely understood a word of the text, or, worse still, misconstrued its meaning, Kol Nidre meant a lot to them: its doleful melody and ancient words ushered them into the twenty-five-hour fast, held lovely memories of Yom Kippur past, and connected them with both their forebears and contemporary Jews around the world. What they didn't say, at least not directly, was that it would not look good if SAJ were to retire Kol Nidre just as the prayer had come in for a considerable amount of favorable public attention: the Victor Talking Machine Company's 1923 release of a recording of Kol Nidre by the storied cantor Yosele Rosenblatt, followed a few years later by *The Jazz Singer*, in which the words and melody had a starring role, had everyone talking.[31]

Kaplan usually had his ear to the ground, but here he missed, or chose to ignore, the rumblings of dismay. He failed to reckon with, or refused to acknowledge, the emotional hold that Kol Nidre, and Judaism more generally, had on its adherents, deriding it as little more than an "irrational attachment, with all the earmarks of the kind of devotion that primitives entertain toward a fetish." His obtuseness in full swing, Kaplan responded characteristically at first: bridling at what he took to be an instance of congregational interference, he was quick to dismiss it as "pestering." Slowly it dawned on him that the fate of Kol Nidre threatened the stability of the house he had just built and, as he would later recall, was the only problem that had ever truly "agitated the S.A.J."[32]

In an attempt to smooth things over, Kaplan retained the melody, adjusting its cadences to fit those of Psalm 130, which he substituted for the Aramaic text. When that strategy didn't work, he came up with another: those who wanted to could recite the Kol Nidre to themselves, silently, but only after the cantor had recited Psalm 130. That solution also left a lot to be desired, infuriating SAJ's spiritual leader. "Is Jewish life so poverty stricken that a measly practice like that deserves having a fuss made over it? I am simply flabbergasted." He was also flummoxed. Unsure of how to proceed, Kaplan swung between giving in and holding out, until 1930 when he entered into the High Holiday season confident that, at long last, the battle was now behind him and "K.N." consigned to history, the question of its role in the Yom Kippur services "closed" for good.[33]

For him maybe, but not for his congregants, a representative quorum of whom came to see him right before Yom Kippur to plead yet again for its restoration. As storm clouds gathered for the umpteenth time, Kaplan documented what ensued, recording his impressions in his journal just in case he might need to jog his memory in the future. After belittling each and every member of the delegation (one was a "confirmed moron who rolls in wealth," another as "full of sophistries as a dog with fleas"), he detailed how each man "went at me hammer and tongs for over two hours. They bullied, they cajoled, they flattered me to get me to yield. I held out to the end." Proud of his win, as if at a sports match, Kaplan concluded his account by crowing, "Nothing would move me from that decision."[34]

Famous last words. Only a few days later something did: an exchange with J. D. Eisenstein. The attentive reader may recognize his name in connection with the 1904 sermon imbroglio. Over twenty-five years later, the man surfaced again, this time in defense of Kol Nidre rather than the Slutzker Rav and, not so coincidentally, acting in a personal capacity as the grandfather of Ira Eisenstein, SAJ's recently hired executive director and one of Kaplan's former students as well as his eventual son-in-law. In a lengthy letter dated October 5, 1930, the seventy-six-year-old devotee of tradition sought to persuade Kaplan to reinstate the Kol Nidre, an "essential" component of Yom Kippur, by emphasizing that its purpose was to "soften our hearts and make us feel better towards our fellowmen." With goodwill at its core, it sought to "make the road clear for forgiveness." Building his case brick by brick, Eisenstein went on to chide Kaplan for retaining the melody but not the words, an approach, he wrote, that "appears to me as playing Hamlet and leaving out the Prince of Denmark." And then, in a last-ditch appeal, he pointed out that "there is no man, no matter how great he may be, who can persuade the worshipping masses to exclude it from the service. So why create dissensions when unity is so essential to our national existence?"[35]

Eisenstein's letter hit its mark. "Believe it or not, there is a possibility of my changing my mind about the Kol Nidre and advocating its restoration in the Yom Kippur service," Kaplan declared (to himself) in his October 8 diary entry, clarifying that J. D. Eisenstein's intervention might enable him to see the "question in an entirely new light." With its emphasis on people and their social interaction, it recast the prayer as an exercise in community rather than a religiously sanctioned excuse for casting off responsibility, an interpretation Kaplan found "plausible."[36]

But not all that plausible. A month later, having come to the conclusion that it was "never with this rendering in mind that the mass of Jews ever recited the Kol Nidre," Kaplan was back where he started, as committed as ever to its abrogation. Still, something about Eisenstein's rendition continued to tug at him, inspiring him to reconsider. By the time 1930 came to a close, Kaplan had not only reassessed, he had arrived at a "peaceful settlement" that simultaneously appealed to his congregants, assuaged his conscience, and allowed him to save face, too. In the future, Kol Nidre would be restored in full as long as the following words were inserted into the text: "All vows uttered in anger or undue provocation intended as punishment or revenge, these and only these vows should be null and void."[37]

And with that, the issue was laid to rest. At SAJ, Kaplan's version of the Kol Nidre prevailed.

As it happened, SAJ's very first Yom Kippur did not go well, but not because Kol Nidre was recited or the setting with its "improvised ark on the stage and its camp chairs on the floor" represented a "come down" from the Jewish Center's dignified and orderly sanctuary. It didn't go well because Kaplan found the behavior of his congregants deeply upsetting, a mockery of everything he had hoped the Society for the Advancement of Judaism would advance. The "leisureliness" with which they gathered for services troubled him, as did the "lackadaisical" manner in which they attended to their prayers, not even bothering to answer "amen" at the appropriate time. Unnerved by the spectacle of several hundred disengaged Jews, he lashed out at them. At the holiest moment of the Jewish year, when discipline, restraint, and community building were the order of the day, Kaplan gave in to his emotions and yelled.[38]

A rabbinic faux pas, if ever there was one, and bad for business, too, or as one of his pragmatically oriented brothers-in-law had it, Kaplan was "driving away customers with [his] rough treatment." He subsequently felt a pang or two of regret at his ill-considered actions. His Yom Kippur outburst, though, was no one-off, an isolated expression of unhappiness. It was symptomatic of a deep well of frustration. Keenly aware that SAJ was a work in progress, Kaplan was unable all the same to hold back his disappointment at what he adjudged to be the sluggish pace of change. Despite everything he had accomplished in less than a year—a new community, a new home, a new position, the bas mitzvah, a modified prayer service—things on the ground didn't move fast enough for him. "I have in fact been feeling very uncomfortable at the slowness with which the Society has been progressing toward that goal that I have in mind," he noted as early as April 1922, regretting the "impulsiveness" that drove him to it in the first place. If only his followers possessed more than the vaguest idea of what he was trying to do. "Most of them still fail to see the difference between my conception of Judaism and the Orthodox point of view."[39]

For that, Kaplan blamed everyone but himself. Once again, he held his people to account, prompting H. L. Simmons, chairman of the SAJ board and another of his earliest and most stalwart champions, to rebuke him for being much too demanding. Simmons's assessment was spot-on. No congregation was more financially and emotionally generous, more eager to do right by the man they had appointed "leader for life" than SAJ. Determined to give him the widest possible "latitude" for his work and to develop a new model of comity between clergy and congregant, Kaplan's people not only tolerated his distemper, choosing to see it as a virtue, a mark of his singularity, but also deferred to him at nearly every turn. As May Lamport, another of Kaplan's fans, put it at a members' meeting very early on, "We are on trial, not Dr. Kaplan. Let us first show Dr. Kaplan during the next five years that we are worthy of his leadership."[40]

Plaudits like these went in one ear and out the other. They made only the slightest impression on Kaplan, who continued to believe that his congregants' investment in SAJ, and in him, was limited. They might talk a good game, but on Yom Kippur and throughout the rest of the year their behavior suggested their heart wasn't in it. The members of SAJ came late to Shabbos services, when they came at all, and either talked incessantly throughout or fell asleep; they had to be cajoled into attending lectures, Hebrew classes, and other public programs, and they were espied buying a newspaper from a local newsstand only moments after Shabbos services had wound down or lighting up and smoking a cigar on the way home, a pronounced breach of Shabbos etiquette. The final straw was a celebratory dinner and dance in May 1922 intended to show the colors, to demonstrate how warmly the membership felt toward SAJ. The event backfired as far as Kaplan was concerned. Attendance was paltry and not one person among the few who did show up wanted to discuss the new society or listen to exhortatory speeches. All anyone wanted to do was to

This 1928 pencil sketch of Mordecai Kaplan by Joseph Tepper was a gift from a grateful congregant. Courtesy, The Reconstructionist Archives, Philadelphia.

talk about golf and dance. A disheartened Kaplan returned home to "bury my disappointment in my pillows."[41]

A few months later, he took a trip. Together with Lena, Kaplan returned to Europe for the first time since their honeymoon fourteen years earlier. This overseas adventure, seven and a half weeks in duration, was made possible thanks to the largesse of a congregant, Harold Spiegelberg, who gave the Kaplans free passage on the S.S. *Philadelphia*, which he had just transformed from a wartime transport ship into a peacetime luxury liner. As an additional testament to the affection in which they were held, the SAJ community not only encouraged the couple to set sail, it also showered them with gifts, including a hefty check (which, in good conscience, Kaplan couldn't, or wouldn't, accept).

Temporarily freed from institutional and domestic responsibilities, Kaplan found a new outlet: tourism and its "mishaps." He fretted over the inevitable delays in getting from one place to another, the seaworthiness of their vessel (for which he had cause: the boiler kept acting up), and the possibility that when he and Lena visited Naples, Vesuvius might erupt at any moment (which it did not). "Not being much of a traveler there were moments during this trip when my heart was in my mouth," he noted at the start of their journey, adding at its close, "I never recited the prayer '*haskevanu*,' [which calls on God for shelter and safekeeping] every time I went to bed with such intensity as I have been doing it the last few weeks. Has it helped in any way? I am not sure. I certainly wish it would."[42]

For all his travel-induced anxieties, Kaplan didn't wait too long before taking off again. Nearly a year later, in late June 1923, he went abroad once more, this time without Lena and on business, to attend a Zionist congress in Karlsbad. A funny thing happened on the way to the confab: while crossing the Atlantic, Kaplan was presented with the opportunity to jump ship by joining the faculty of the newly established Jewish Institute of Religion (JIR), the determinedly nondenominational rabbinical school just launched by Stephen S. Wise, the controversial, outspoken Reform rabbi, whom most of those within Kaplan's circles regarded as the "last word in Jewish heterodoxy."[43]

One of Kaplan's fellow travelers on board the S.S. *George Washington*, also headed for Karlsbad, was Judge Julian Mack, a committed Zionist and ardent Wise supporter. Not given to beating around the bush, he put it to Kaplan directly: "What are your intentions vis-à-vis the Jewish Institute of Religion? Are you ready to join the faculty this coming Fall?" Taken aback by Mack's abruptness, Kaplan was also aware that the opportunity the judge presented him might represent his last chance of "being emancipated" from the environment in which he found himself. And even though the exact nature of the offer had not yet been made clear—Would he be given a chair? And if so, in what?—he said yes, surprising himself by the firmness of his response.

At that point in the story, things began to move quickly, thanks, in part, to Mack having radioed the good news to Wise and, in part, to the long-running tango between the two rabbis; they had history. Three years earlier, in a July 1920 meeting brokered by Irma Lindheim, a member of Wise's Free Synagogue and a supporter of Kaplan's, Wise told Kaplan that were he able to raise the funds for a rabbinical school, he'd put him in charge. In the meantime, would he consider teaching a year-long course on the "social interpretation of religion"? On the spot and eager to oblige, Kaplan agreed, only to change his mind a few days later, citing the extra workload he had to carry at the Seminary in the wake of the untimely and tragic death of his colleague Israel Friedlander.[44]

The very next year, as his feelings toward the Jewish Center and the Seminary grew increasingly frosty, Kaplan initiated a conversation with his Reform colleague, sounding him out on various options and actively contemplating the prospect of "throw[ing] myself into the arms of Wise's following." But once again, he stopped short and didn't follow through, claiming to be "oppressed by misgiving, lest my expectations of true spiritual revival in that direction turn out to be but dust and ashes."[45]

Another year, another dance. Throughout the spring of 1922, Kaplan and Wise continued to circle each other. No sooner had Kaplan closed one door and entered another than he seriously considered opening a third: the Jewish Institute of Religion. "I would have grabbed the opportunity with both hands if it had come last January before I organized the Society for the Advancement of Judaism," he admitted. But it wasn't too late: opportunity still knocked. Kaplan visited with Wise in April 1922, when SAJ was just getting off the ground, to see if his offer to join the JIR faculty might still be good.[46]

Reassured that it was, he gave the proposition much thought—"Will I have the courage to cross the Rubicon of my career?"—even going so far as to consult some of his "closest friends" on SAJ's board. Some cautioned him against associating himself with Wise, lest he be seen "in the mind of everybody as extremely radical." Others "heartily" approved but warned of dire consequences for the SAJ, and still others had no hesitation whatsoever in favoring the alliance. Then again, as Kaplan noted in his journal, since the men who fell into the latter camp "would not mind seeing Judaism reduced to a minimum," their counsel had to be discounted.[47]

After weighing the pros and cons for several weeks, Kaplan decided against taking the steps that "might emancipate me for the larger life and the greater contribution that I might make to the cause of Judaism." Fear that were he to link arms with Wise, the SAJ, along with a number of valued friendships, would be "wrecked" and that he'd end up feeling as if he had "betrayed" his followers held him back. But that's not what Kaplan told Wise. Instead he made some noise about the fate of the Teachers Institute and how duty to the students compelled him "to stay where I was." He also made sure to let

Wise know that this wasn't his final word on the subject and that he "considered the matter of acceptance as suspended rather than concluded in the negative."[48]

Nothing if not a good sport and a patient one, too, Wise agreed to keep the door open; after all, he had nothing to lose and everything to gain. "I do want him if I can get him," he told Rabbi Solomon Goldman, one of Kaplan's oldest friends, adding, "He and you and I are very nearly of one mind. There is no fundamental or unbridgeable gulf between us. We are bent upon doing the same thing." Kaplan, meanwhile, was awash in regret, observing of himself, "I am apparently doomed to go through life like Hamlet, a victim of weak will and indecision." This damning self-assessment hit the bull's-eye. Equivocation was his lot. Even more of a doubting Thomas than a lily-livered Hamlet, he second-guessed his way through most situations, always eyeing some other shore, thinking it a safer harbor.[49]

It's not surprising, then, that when the opportunity to revisit Wise's offer flared up anew in 1923, Kaplan moved with all due speed. "You know how long I have been hesitating and wavering," he wrote to Lena. "I only hope it meets with your approval. Should the change materialize it would seem to have come about providentially." His "darling love" didn't share his belief in fate. "Disapprove proposition," the sensible wife cabled her impetuous husband, urging him not to make any rash decisions until they had a chance to talk face-to-face. He stood his ground. Trapped, feeling unappreciated, Kaplan saw the Jewish Institute of Religion as an escape hatch. Repeatedly invoking the language of emancipation, of being freed of the burden of pretending to be more of a traditional Jew than he actually was, he was even prepared to overlook his long-standing antipathy to Reform Judaism, to claim Wise as a kindred soul, a fellow mover and shaker who, like Kaplan, was big on ideas, short on labels, and a Zionist, too. That the Jewish Institute of Religion favored a less "rigidly patterned" and more pluralist approach to modern Jewish life sealed the deal, assuaging any lingering concerns Kaplan might have had.[50]

Possessed of both motive and opportunity, he did everything but sign on the dotted line, authorizing Mack to "radio to Wise," who, several anxiously awaited days later, cabled back: "If Kaplan ready we are pleased to offer him chair religious education and homiletics." Kaplan was ready. "I need not tell you how keenly I appreciate the honor and value the confidence of your repose in me," he told Wise shortly thereafter, expressing an interest in getting together in a few weeks' time to "go over with you in detail . . . the courses that I will have to give, the number of hours per week that I shall have to teach and other matters of a similar nature."[51]

In short order, Wise responded with an effusive three-page letter in which he emphasized how mutually beneficial this new arrangement would be and how much he looked forward to ironing out all of the details. "I welcome you with all my heart," he wrote, adding for good measure that he would do "everything that lies in my power to move you always to rejoice in the decision that you have reached."[52]

Heartened by Wise's expression of "whole-souled friendship," Kaplan felt good about his decision. But once on dry land and about to begin negotiations, he experienced bouts of "uneasiness," leading him to question his decision. Was Wise truly in a position to act on his promises? Perhaps he underestimated the difficulties in selling his faculty on the idea of Kaplan joining their ranks? And what to make of all that talk, courtesy of the grapevine, that the Jewish Institute of Religion was too disorganized to be effective, of faculty coming and going, of a marked absence of direction? "Was I then going to waste my time?"[53]

Unable to arrive at a decision, Kaplan once again sought the counsel of his friends on and off the SAJ board, but they, too, were of divided mind, clouding his. The board gave the proposition its "unqualified approval"; even those who, at first, had been "unalterably opposed," came around and "relented in their opposition," much to Kaplan's surprise and relief. Green light. Go. The very next day, however, after taking a long walk with Samson Benderly, his "father confessor," the green light turned red. His longtime friend and fellow educator told him that resigning from the Seminary and relinquishing his hold on SAJ might be the right move, but aligning himself with Wise was not. Stop. "At last my mind was made up," Kaplan wrote in his diary, determined this time around to decline Wise's offer and, concomitantly, to cut loose from the Seminary; he ended up carrying out the first act but not the second.[54]

Wise couldn't have been more gracious and accepting of Kaplan's decision, so much so that he was tempted to change his mind yet again. "On the whole I must say that [Wise's] conduct that evening put a doubt in my mind as to whether or not I acted wisely," Kaplan noted in his journal after the two had a face-to-face talk. But he held firm and stayed the course, closing the book on this chapter of his life. Or did he? It certainly looked as if this most recent exchange spelled "finis" to any future alliance. Hadn't Wise had his fill of Kaplan's vacillations by now? Hadn't Kaplan, for his part, learned a painful lesson?[55]

Kaplan wasn't the only one at the Society for the Advancement of Judaism to feel hemmed in. Most of its members felt that way, too, but theirs was born of spatial limitations rather than existential ones: the appeal of 41 West 86th Street had begun to wear off; the shelf life of their can-do spirit, their tolerance for the jerry-built space in which they found themselves, about to expire. Accustomed to the finer things in life, SAJ's people couldn't hold out much longer. By 1924, momentum for a dignified, permanent home with all the trimmings began to build, especially when it became clear that without one recruiting new members was unlikely, and that without new members SAJ's future looked shaky. Besides, the lease on its current property was about to run out. "If the S.A.J. is to continue we have to secure new quarters," Kaplan proclaimed in November of that year, reiterating two weeks later that members "must proceed at once with the putting up of a building." He was so eager to move forward that H. L. Simmons rapped his knuckles once again, berating Kaplan this time for being much too impatient, too eager to seize the first opportunity that came SAJ's way.[56]

Simmons needn't have cautioned Kaplan to slow down. A number of external factors—rising property values, for one—would have done the job for him. With the Upper West Side's development in full swing throughout the 1920s, real estate was a precious commodity, hard to come by and harder to afford even for those with hefty bank accounts. True, many of SAJ's members were in a position to dig deep, but having recently invested a considerable amount of money in the Jewish Center, they were reluctant to loosen the purse strings for yet another building project. Much to Kaplan's frustration, even some of SAJ's trustees held back, "looking for reasons why we should not build so that they should not have to contribute to a building fund." Institutional indecision about whether to renovate an existing building or construct one from scratch also complicated matters, giving rise to prolonged discussions about the more prudent, fiscally responsible way to proceed. And then, there was Kaplan, who, being Kaplan, was of two minds. On one hand, for SAJ to have a series of well-designed rooms of its own would undoubtedly be a real boon, ensuring its stability. On the other, owning a building with all of its attendant problems might compromise the Society's larger vision of itself, entangling it in financial and logistical problems which, inevitably, would narrow its focus. Wouldn't worrying about the bills that came with a permanent and much larger facility make SAJ like every other synagogue on the West Side?[57]

What to do? Why, form a committee of course: a building committee, whose members were empowered to find suitable quarters, preferably an already existing structure on the Upper West Side so the renovation wouldn't unduly tax SAJ's budget or the goodwill of its members. Like anxious suitors, Joseph Levy, the committee's chair, and his fellow committee members found most prospective candidates wanting. One site was too wide, another too narrow, a third too near a noisy intersection, a fourth too far west. Or else a potential property was too expensive, needed too much work, the carrying costs of securing outside financing more than SAJ could comfortably sustain. Eventually, Levy and his committee settled on the quaintly numbered 11½–13–15 West 86th Street, just up the block from the SAJ's present location. The four-story property, home of the Alcuin School, a small private facility for girls with classes from kindergarten through high school, consisted of two late nineteenth-century brownstones, which conjoined gave the appearance of a unified structure and one, moreover, whose renovation wouldn't be too extensive or costly. And the price was right: $175,00 for the plot and the structures on it. Louis Abramson, the architect who years earlier had worked amicably with Kaplan on the design of the Jewish Center, was hired early in 1925 to come up with plans for a fireproofed space with a gymnasium and a capacious auditorium that would double as a sanctuary on the Sabbath and festivals and as a multipurpose space at other times during the year, which he did. But when the architect submitted a $50,000 estimate, he was replaced forthwith by the well-known and highly regarded architectural and engineering firm of Deutsch & Schneider, which came in with a much lower and more pleasing bid of nearly half that amount.[58]

SAJ then set about raising the necessary funds to purchase the land and remodel the building, including the removal of its old-fashioned stoop and several "intervening walls," but neither the renovation nor the fundraising went smoothly. The project's renovation costs soon ballooned to $43,000, but the building fund's coffers did not keep pace. Members were less than forthcoming when it came to making a contribution, compelling the Society to secure outside funding and embroiling it in considerable debt. Leaving 41 West 86th Street might not have been such a good idea after all.[59]

In March of 1925, smack in the middle of all this activity, not to mention the spring semester at JTS and the impending holiday of Passover, Kaplan took off again, this time bound for Jerusalem, where, as a representative of both the Zionist Organization of America and the Seminary, he was to participate in the dedication ceremonies of the Hebrew University and give a speech or two. Though the trip—his first to the Holy Land—meant leaving his family, congregants, and students for weeks on end and couldn't have come at a more inopportune time—it was a not-to-be-missed occasion, both for the Zionist project and for him personally. Kaplan would also not miss the headaches that came with SAJ's renovation; leaving them behind was an added incentive for taking flight when he did.

The dedication ceremony for the Hebrew University, held in the amphitheater on Jerusalem's Mount Scopus, was quite something. Between the spectacular setting overlooking the Judean Hills and the thousands gathered in celebration, some of whom, for want of space, perched in trees, Kaplan's expectations ran high and were met, at first. The initial moments of the opening day ceremony were so stirring that he "cried like a baby." But his emotional mood soon evaporated. Too many speeches, including one from Hayim Nahman Bialik, the revered Hebrew poet, that ran "as long as the exile," got in the way. Still, nothing could diminish Kaplan's excitement at being in the poet's company as well as that of Ahad Ha'am, one of his long-standing cultural heroes, and for being on hand to witness this turning point in Jewish history. His own formal address, which he delivered a few days later, reflected his high spirits. Full of stirring biblical phrases and extravagant hopes for the Hebrew University as the "worthy successor to Israel's ancient sanctuary," it went off well enough to please this most exacting of critics, adding to his good humor. "I played my little part in the proceedings with satisfaction to everybody concerned," he duly noted.[60]

When not giving celebratory speeches or socializing, Kaplan toured the country, taking a side trip to Damascus and Baalbek. Sometimes he traveled on foot, at other moments by automobile, and at still others in a "hay wagon without the hay." Much more affected by modern-day sites than by age-old ones, inspired more by the "outstanding activity" of Hadassah, the women's Zionist organization, than by the mystics of Safed, Kaplan detailed what he saw and when and with whom in Hebrew. A point of pride, a neat and tidy Hebrew script filled the pages of his journal from edge to edge. "I try to use every opportunity I can to speak Hebrew. I am at present at that stage when one is inarticulate because I have unlearned to think in English and have not yet learned to think in Hebrew, which fact means that I cannot think at all," Kaplan told Lena.[61]

He exaggerated, of course. His letters to his wife, which he wrote almost weekly, were models of structure, clarity, and texture. They're also great fun to read, not so much for their details, though these are juicy and compelling, as for their buoyant, light-hearted, and affectionate tone—a far cry from his usual captious and dolorous self. In his element while in the Holy Land, Kaplan became upbeat and effusive, describing his experiences as "glorious" and "thrilling." He had so much to impart, he told his "sweet love," that he looked forward eagerly to sharing the details "when we shall be able to punctuate our talks with kisses and hugs." Kaplan also looked forward to satisfying her desire for an antique silk rug and some etchings to hang near the piano by going shopping, yes, shopping! ("Remember it must be antique," Lena reminded him, "otherwise you will have to pay duty.") In the meantime, he missed her and the "kiddies" terribly, signing off as "your yearning Mordecai."[62]

By the time Kaplan returned to New York two months later, in mid-June, both renewed and tuckered out by his overseas exertions, he hoped that the bulk of SAJ's renovation would be done. No such luck. The "process of reconstruction" dragged on for several more months, into the summer and fall. Despite numerous assurances from the contractor that the building would be ready in time for Rosh Hashanah 1925, it wasn't. "Everything is an awful mess," Kaplan observed, determined all the same to hold holiday services in the unfinished space, even if it meant going home in the middle of the Torah reading to put on an extra pair of socks to ward off the "chill in the air."[63]

The congregants were also none too thrilled with their new quarters. Reading between the lines of a September issue of the *S.A.J. Review*, one gets the sense that once the dust had cleared and the scaffolding had been removed, they were less than enthralled by their new home. "It should be unnecessary to tell you that we have not gone in for the building of a magnificent edifice of worship," Kaplan wrote, intimating that it was, in fact, quite necessary to explain why they hadn't chosen that option. "If we were to measure the structure by the standards of noble architecture . . . we are sure to be disappointed. But," he hastened to add, "if all that we aim for is to have a modest, inviting home for our Society, a home that would be conducive to friendship on a high plane, and to the interchange of ideas about things that matter, then we shall find the building which we are about to occupy completely adequate to our needs."[64]

Kaplan required as much convincing as his congregants. Despite a spanking new home and the promise of a fresh start, his spirits "drooped," his repertoire of discontents expanding rather than contracting. When on one of their evening walks Kaplan told Lena of his current state of unhappiness, she, in true wifely fashion, hinted that he had only himself to blame. "Why had you gone ahead with buying a site and renovating the buildings when, at that juncture, you could have freed yourself entirely of SAJ?" she asked him directly. "Logically she was right," Kaplan reflected. "I was stumped for the moment. But the fact is that the very desire of the S.A.J. to go ahead . . . was to me an indication that they were interested in the aims for which the S.A.J. stood." How could he have been so mistaken?[65]

The new quarters of the "S.A.J. House" had much to do with Kaplan's malaise. For all the money expended on it, the space was not quite right, more "makeshift" than polished. Only a small sign squeezed in between two bays of windows indicated what went on inside; otherwise, passersby were liable to think it was another school or a private home. Things weren't much better within. The corridors didn't align so much as slope toward one another, the auditorium-cum-sanctuary required constant tweaking—including the construction of a new Ark and a platform to house it—and even the addition of a motion picture booth and projector did little to brighten an otherwise dull and dreary space. Surveying his new surroundings, Kaplan concluded bleakly that the "fit name for the S.A.J. House as far as I am concerned is 'Heartbreak House.' "[66]

In the years that followed, numerous attempts to render the space more attractive were undertaken, including a major do-over in 1938 that resulted in reorienting the interior; reclaiming the auditorium as a sanctuary and relegating its more frivolous functions to an upstairs social hall; installing casement windows; and fashioning a brand-new exterior that hid all traces of the building's late nineteenth-century origins behind a façade. Its use of terra-cotta, cast stone, and ochre-colored brick like that of the recently constructed apartment building next door spelled modernity—or more to the point perhaps—Moderne. Gilding the lily, SAJ's latest architect, Albert Goldhammer, affixed a series of decorative flourishes to the façade. They ranged, somewhat incongruously, from wooden doors with metal clasps that brought to mind Tudor England to a pair of geometric bronze lighting fixtures perched atop two classically styled columns that flanked the entranceway. Up above, a series of Gothic-styled letters spelled out the words "The Society for the Advancement of Judaism." They were not hard to miss, though a Magen David inscribed in a circle above them required a fair amount of squinting to be seen. More of a hodgepodge than a unified whole, the entire composition, observed Edward Schachner, an architectural historian who oversaw SAJ's most recent renovation in the early 2000s, "looks as if the architect rummaged through a catalogue of historical references and threw them all at the building." Not sure what to call the resulting mix, New York City's Landmarks Commission came up with "Modern Semitic," as if that designation lay the matter to rest. It didn't. But no matter. If SAJ's visual strategy was intended to signal its rootedness in history, announce itself on the street, and confound expectations in one fell swoop, it succeeded on all three fronts. From here on, no one would mistake 15 West 86th Street for anything other than a Jewish institution. Of some sort.[67]

Once inside, visitors encountered an equally incongruous, brightly colored, tightly packed mural in an otherwise "drab and ugly" sanctuary. Composed of three pieces, its central panel—a horizontal composition, twenty feet long and five feet high—depicted, among other things, heaps of oranges, abundant greenery, and clusters of bronzed, healthy *halutzim* (pioneers) clad in shorts and bright white, short-sleeved shirts working the land of Palestine. It was flanked on either side by two vertical panels, each eight feet high and five feet wide, one of which represented the "old elements" that could still be found throughout the country (an Arab oarsman, ecstatic Hasidim, a Bukharian woman, "all glowing and rosy," and, of course, the Western Wall). The other, the "direct opposite of its sister panel," showcased the country's "newer elements," including the Ruttenberg Electrical Works and the Technion. The creation of Kaplan's former student, Temima Nimtzowitz, who as Temima Gezari subsequently enjoyed a distinguished career as a painter, sculptor, and arts educator, *Old and New Elements in Modern Palestine* had been commissioned in 1934 as a memorial to Israel Unterberg, one of SAJ's founders and a longtime champion of its leader. The mural had other purposes, too. A visual testament to, and perhaps even a reminder of, the allure of Zionism, it did double duty as the centerpiece of Kaplan's efforts to have every nook and corner of modern Jewish life "breathe Jewishness."[68]

Kaplan heralded Gezari's three-pronged mural, but it met with a chilly reception when initially proposed and again, a year later, when unveiled. The board of SAJ, which had to be prodded and coaxed into awarding the commission in the first place, continued to have reservations, as did some of its members, none of whom were the least bit shy about airing them. "A few dopes," recalled Rabbi Ira Eisenstein, by then SAJ's associate leader, objected to the artwork's figurations, claiming they violated the Second Commandment; others maintained that the "thick arms of the laborers" violated their aesthetic sensibilities. Even Kaplan acknowledged the mural's limitations, yet he attributed them entirely to its setting—over the entrance to the sanctuary—which did the work no favors: during services, it didn't face the worshippers in their plush seats but sat behind them, out of sight. The artwork's unfortunate location, he went on to relate dismissively, was "paralleled by the reaction of the members themselves who have no appreciation of [the mural's] significance and beauty." After a number of years, *Old and New Elements in Modern Palestine* was moved from the sanctuary to the social hall where, amid platters of cake, urns of coffee, and the resulting commotion of hungry congregants it got lost, yet again.[69]

The building was the least of Kaplan's worries. The foibles and shortcomings of its occupants troubled him more. Consider Isaac Polstein, for instance. As chair of the Committee on Seats responsible for furnishing the sanctuary, he took his assignment so seriously that it was all he could think about, prompting Kaplan peevishly to remark that the man's "idea of a synagogue is not one apparently that appeals to the head but that provides comfort to the bottom." At least Polstein took an interest in SAJ. With the exception of a few others like Harry Liebovitz who worked like a "trojan" on its behalf, and May Lamport who headed up the Women's Division, most members, regardless of gender, remained "spectators" who disappeared once the High Holidays had come and gone. By the time Succoth set in, Kaplan noted, "over 70% become invisible to me."[70]

No amount of scolding or "pummeling"—and there was a lot of that—could prompt the remaining 30 percent to commit wholeheartedly to SAJ. Their tireless leader couldn't even get them to read the *S.A.J. Review*, much less grasp his larger (and admittedly elusive) vision of a "chain of societies in congregations, Zionist organizations and similar bodies . . . ready to subscribe to the principles I have formulated as those for which the S.A.J. stands." In the absence of a robust response, the Society for the Advancement of Judaism was well on its way to becoming what Kaplan had feared: a typical house of worship with its usual array of petty crochets and a reputation for being cold and cliquish.[71]

Even the top 1 percent of the leadership chain, those presumably closest to him, were a source of exasperation. Drawing a wry and telling portrait of those in charge, Kaplan observed how the acting chairman of SAJ's board was given to making "interminable speeches," the head of the Building Committee sulked, a third trustee invariably missed the point, a fourth never spoke, and a fifth was hard of hearing: "These are the people with whom I tried to save the ship of the S.A.J."[72]

Dragged down by this "lot of Babbitts"; tired of "jogging along like a drayhorse" amid a constant round of funerals, shivah calls, weddings, and congregational complaints; frustrated by the necessity of coming up with something new to say every Shabbat morning only to discover that his wisdom fell on deaf ears, "as though I haven't said a word"; and disturbed to find himself in the position of a scold with a permanent frown on his face, Kaplan was at his wits' end. "Whew!" he wrote in his diary, which was fast becoming his very own book of lamentations. "This is more than I bargained for."[73]

With no letup in sight, Kaplan took to "daydreaming" about an exit strategy or, in his words, a "really free field." One sleepless night, he wrote in his diary, "I lay awake . . . picturing to myself what I would do if Wise were to telephone to me the next morning." A few weeks later, in December 1926, Kaplan decided to take matters into his own hands by giving his colleague a call. The first time the line was busy; on the second try, he no sooner dialed Wise's number than chickened out and quickly returned the receiver to its cradle. End of story. But then, a day or so after Kaplan's nerve had failed, he bumped into George Kohut, another of Wise's close associates, while taking his evening constitutional. Screwing up his courage, Kaplan sounded him out on the possibility of reopening negotiations with the Jewish Institute of Religion. "I imagine [Kohut] was throwing out a bait," he recalled, when Kohut responded with enthusiasm. "I did bite."[74]

So did Wise. Before you could spell "T-o-r-a-h," JIR's acting president was back in touch in January 1927, inviting Kaplan to join the faculty, pending the approval of the board and the faculty. After some dithering, Kaplan said yes, proud of having finally made the leap. "Thank God that I need no longer accuse myself of being cowardly and vacillating," he wrote. "The Rubicon has been crossed." In his mind, maybe, but he still had to bring round his SAJ supporters as well as the Seminary's officialdom, which wasn't going to be easy. To the first group he explained "that besides [his] inability to carry out many projects in the S.A.J. . . . there was complete indifference on the part of the Seminary authorities to the Teachers Institute," a sign that it was time to go. After considerable discussion of the merits, they gave Kaplan their blessing but with the warning that moving to the JIR would surely be seen as his having "broken not only with Orthodoxy but with Conservatism." On the contrary, Kaplan retorted. It would put him in a "position to define Conservatism more fully."[75]

His Seminary colleagues were not likely to agree, nor were they about to greet word of his resignation with equanimity, or so Kaplan feared, confiding in his diary that "how to resign from the Seminary without leaving behind any ill-feelings" would be tricky. Toward that end, he wrote Cyrus Adler, its president, a very long letter spelling out his reasons for leaving, the long and short of which was that due to what Kaplan took to be its "drift toward Orthodoxy," the Seminary atmosphere was no longer conducive to the kind of "creative work" he wanted to do. "I need to be free to voice my opinions concerning the spiritual needs of Jewish life without almost continually having in mind that I might be jeopardizing the interests of the Seminary."[76]

Adler's written response could be boiled down into two words: bye, bye. Since leaving it at that would have been awkward and not in keeping with his bureaucratic sensibility, the Seminary president covered the one and one-half pages of his letter (and himself) with words. He made it seem as if whatever unpleasantness Kaplan experienced was a function of the give-and-take of academic life, insinuating that the issue at hand was Kaplan's thin skin, not the Seminary's inhospitality to liberal ideas and diverse opinions. "Of course, I am the last person to dissuade you if you have a feeling of restraint in your present association," Adler wrote in conclusion, keeping his true feelings in check. "Since you have not consulted with me as to the proposed step I assume it to represent a matured judgement on your part about which you did not wish to confer."[77]

Kaplan, expecting a mild show of resistance, a squeak of protest, from Adler was surprised and even a tad disappointed by the "suave and cold" tone of his response. But the impassioned reaction of the students, along with that of the Teachers Institute faculty and the members of the Rabbinical Assembly (RA), the official representative of the Conservative rabbinate, to news of his resignation more than made up for it. The students protested, using the occasion to draw up a "declaration of grievances" against the Seminary and to insist on "official assurances" that Kaplan would be granted "absolute academic freedom" were he to stay where he was and had been for nearly two decades. Singing his praises loud enough for Adler to hear, they singled out Kaplan for being "preeminently [the] one man among our teachers who is responsible for what faith, and courage, and vision we may lay claim to." For their part, Kaplan's colleagues at the Teachers Institute, their hearts filled with "sorrow and despair," were "staggered" by his decision to move on and pleaded with him not to act on it, and the RA unanimously adopted a resolution saying it would do "everything within reason" to prevent his departure.

The equivalent of a full court press, calls from these different elements of the Seminary community not to resign heartened Kaplan enormously, restoring his faith in the institution, even though, as he would later observe, "when he took the plunge, [he] was fully aware of the price that [he] would have to pay for it."[78]

Little did he know that it wasn't exactly smooth sailing over on West 68th Street, home to the Jewish Institute of Religion. Kaplan wanted the academic chair he would soon occupy to bear the title of "Philosophy of Judaism." The JIR faculty balked. Some among them didn't think it a "happy" or even a sensible choice. From where the dean sat, for instance, bestowing on Kaplan the title of "professor of the Philosophy of Judaism" was most unfortunate, "as there is no such thing."[79]

Despite assurances from Wise that what to call the chair was a minor issue and, the dean notwithstanding, an easily resolved one at that, the faculty's response bothered Kaplan once he heard about it, suggesting to him that conditions at the Jewish Institute of Religion might not be a bed of roses and leading him to make his title a sticking point in the negotiations. It's almost as if the Seminary's professor of homiletics and midrash was looking for reasons to back out; he found plenty. The foot-dragging of JIR's faculty provided him with one, the Seminary's embrace another. And in the wake of a two-hour meeting with Adler in mid-February, in which the Seminary president made clear just how upset he was by Kaplan's imminent departure and reassured him that he was a valued member of the faculty and that, it went without saying, academic freedom was the rule, he now had a third.

One can see where this is headed. It should come as no surprise that once again Kaplan left Wise at the altar, declining the latter's invitation to join the JIR and withdrawing his own resignation from JTS in February, only a few short weeks after he had first reopened this Pandora's box. As Kaplan explained to

Wise in person and to Judge Mack in a detailed letter, he was under "tremendous pressure" to stay at the Seminary and found it hard to resist. "You can well understand my predicament."[80]

Mack certainly did, telling Wise that while he was keenly disappointed at the outcome, he had seen it coming, given Kaplan's history and makeup. "He is essentially judicially minded," the distinguished judge observed, "and one of the penalties of this sort of mind (as I know all too well) is to see all sides . . . a passion to reach the best conclusion even though it involves changes of view back and forth several times." Where Mack put a positive spin on the proceedings, Wise grumbled at what he took to be the "latest of [Kaplan's] flirtations with us." Whereas his judicial colleague was inclined to be generous in his assessment of Kaplan's character, Wise described him as "pitifully and even tragically weak," cursed with a will that was little more than a "rope of sand." Still, JIR's founder wasn't prepared to write off Kaplan completely. "I have no bitterness or anger in my heart against him. I like him too much."[81]

The tectonic shift in circumstance Kaplan thought would be his had he decamped for the Jewish Institute of Religion never materialized, but something else, only a little less groundbreaking, did: a decision on how to conduct the rest of his life. Feeling that he had little to show for all the years spent preaching and teaching, Kaplan resolved to spend more time summoning a book into being. He didn't have one and lamented its absence. Despite a loving and dedicated wife, four children whom he cherished, a good job (two, in fact), and a steady stream of people who sought his company and counsel, he felt incomplete without a book to his name. Without one, he worried lest his grand ideas would amount to little more than a "will o' wisp." And, boy, did he have a grand idea. "Whenever I get a chance to concentrate on the problem of Judaism as a civilization," Kaplan wrote as early as December

1924, "I see more and more light. . . . I am quite certain that if I could go on working uninterruptedly I might at least realize the dream of my life—to work out a clear formula for Judaism as a civilization, both in Palestine and in the Diaspora, before my mental powers will began to wane, which I understand is normally the case at 55."[82]

Kaplan expressed that sentiment when he was forty-four.

Tick-tock.

4

Fighting Words

As a young man Kaplan had big plans. "With G's help," he confided in his diary in 1904, "I have in mind, viz., first of writing a work which shall be a kind of 'Guide to the Perplexed,' and, secondly, of purging the 'Shulchan Arukh.' " By the 1920s he'd spend much of his career going head-to-head with Joseph Karo's authoritative text without ever successfully compiling a purged version. He had much better luck with Maimonides, whose bold "reconstruction" of the Judaism of his time and "reconciliation between Jewish tradition and Aristotelian philosophy" inspired Kaplan to follow in his footsteps. Though it took him thirty years to make good on his youthful ambition, Kaplan eventually came up with a guide to the perplexed of his day. After mulling over the possibility of calling it "Whither Judaism?" he named it *Judaism as a Civilization: Toward a Reconstruction of American-Jewish Life.*[1]

The book Kaplan wrote was unlike anything American Jews had ever seen: *curiosa Judaica* was how one of their number aptly put it. At once a manifesto, a proclamation, a prospectus, a critique, an exposé, a history, and a cri de coeur, it represented Kaplan's attempt to "spin a Jewish utopia out of the frailest cobweb of possibilities." Shuttling between past and present, history and sociology, Kaplan's magnum opus not only situated American Jewry within the *longue durée* of the European Jewish experience, it also provided a road map for the future.[2]

Judaism as a Civilization opened with a stunning sentence—one of Kaplan's best—and didn't let up for over five hundred pages. "Before the beginning of the nineteenth century," he wrote, "all Jews regarded Judaism as a privilege; since then, Jews have come to regard it as a burden." And with that he was off. A *tour d'horizon* of the modern Jewish landscape, Kaplan's account, by turns urgent and breathless, thoughtful and considered, made the case that were Judaism, and with it the Jewish people, to survive into the next century, nothing less than a top-to-bottom overhaul of every one of its time-honored, long-held assumptions, priorities, and practices was imperative. "The sooner Jews realize how little they can save Judaism by the means and methods of former times, the better," he cautioned, adding that "blind habit" would not help, either.[3]

What would? Well, if you thought Judaism was just a religion, think again, Kaplan told his readers, encouraging them to conceive of its constellation of beliefs and rituals as elements of a civilization rather than the lineaments of a faith. If you maintained that Zionism affected only benighted Jews from overseas, it was high time, said Kaplan, to retire that perspective in favor of one that acknowledged the indispensability of the Zionist project to the well-cushioned life in the Diaspora. If you believed that rituals such as kashruth or the

Sabbath had had their moment in the sun, give them another try by thinking of them as human folkways rather than divine commandments. On and on went the bold, hard-hitting text, upending and subverting the most regnant notions of the day, supplanting them with a brand-new, expansive approach to all things Jewish, one rooted in the here and now of twentieth-century America.

When published in 1934, this sprawling book was no one's idea of bedtime reading, and yet it came to be seen as the definitive account of modern American Jewish life and thought, the yardstick against which all others were measured. If your family's bookshelf contained only one volume about Jews, chances are that *Judaism as a Civilization* was it. Even the White House library owned a copy.

Judaism as a Civilization brought together much of what Kaplan had been teaching, preaching, and writing about for decades. Though he didn't actually sit down and begin work on the book until the mid-1920s, its silhouette is readily discernible within the pages of his journal, the content of his sermons and speeches, the bones of his lecture notes, and his musings in print, including, most especially, a 1927 *Menorah Journal* article entitled "Toward a Reconstruction of Judaism." From its title through its pointed observations about recasting one's Jewish inheritance from a "liability" into an "indispensable asset," it's all there: a streamlined version, an adumbration, in unusually lively, even lyrical prose of what he'd eventually detail in several hundred dense pages. "To reduce a civilization to a philosophy," Kaplan wrote, "is like changing a rosebush into a bottle of perfume"; to "preserve any of [its] elements without the others is like trying to cultivate roses in a vase." Moving from horticultural references to geological ones, he likened Emancipation to an earthquake and the Enlightenment to a tidal wave, sweeping everything in its wake. Lest the

Jewish people become the "Humpty Dumpty of the nations . . . [which] all the king's horses and all the king's men will not be able to put [back] together again," he called for a commitment to "social engineering."[4]

Arresting ideas couched in effective prose leap off the page, leaving no doubt that the man could write and had something to say. What, then, took him so long to write the book? Circumstances, for one. So full were his days that Kaplan, "thwarted" by his responsibilities at SAJ and JTS, was hard-pressed to set aside a chunk of time for work on a book. When he did pick up his pen, he directed it toward his journal rather than a blank piece of paper. "This is not meant to be literature and does not deserve that mental strain and concentration which I ought to reserve for more serious tasks," he acknowledged after his eldest daughter Judith prodded him into putting away the diary and focusing on the book. Easier said than done: the conjuring up of incident, observation, and personality was more immediately gratifying, and considerably less taxing, than reckoning with complicated ideas. Meanwhile, as word of the Nazi rise to power penetrated the secluded walls of his study, giving rise to anxiety about what lay ahead for his German Jewish coreligionists, Kaplan found it even harder to make headway: "I feel like a polar bear on an ice floe that is drifting into warmer zones as he watches with growling impotence the steady dwindling of his home." Writing a book animated by a vision of the future seemed pointless.[5]

Lack of confidence also slowed Kaplan's progress. Despite abundant evidence to the contrary, he felt he was not up to the task, lacking the requisite writerly skills to bring a book into being. "I have a great deal of poetry in me, but it is absolutely inarticulate," he once wrote, summing up his literary shortcomings. On another occasion, he lamented his inability to stay the course. "No steady light is mine. I haven't the fuel to keep it burning. I have to be content with the momentary flare and sputter of fireworks." And were that not enough to stay his hand, Kaplan constantly looked over his shoulder. Comparing himself to other writers, especially to such eloquent men of the cloth as Harry Emerson Fosdick and John Hayes Holmes, who to his mind tossed off one sentence after another with ease, he'd come up short every time, convinced he was cursed with an inability to come alive on the page.[6]

Kaplan was too hard on himself. More than capable of turning a pretty phrase, sustaining a narrative, and distilling complicated ideas, he could hold his own with the best of them. But he found writing a struggle, an ongoing test of his capacity to commit to one idea at a time. A penchant for abstraction, for getting bogged down in argument and exposition, also got in the way, dulling even his most trenchant insights. Though Kaplan valued "color and form," insisting that Jewish life "must be redeemed from mere abstractness," he ended up mired in the abstruse and the opaque. A tendency toward abstract reasoning "runs away with me," he admitted.[7]

Many writers get stuck as they toggle between the circumstantial and the personal; Kaplan was no exception. What distinguished, and complicated, his getting the right words in the right order on the right page was a different kind of struggle: an honest-to-goodness essay contest that both catalyzed and impeded the gestation and birth of his book.

Attentive readers might have noticed a small, inconspicuous article announcing an essay contest in the *New York Times* or the *Chicago Daily Tribune* of October 7, 1929. This kind of forum was commonplace in the United States of the time, but one devoted to the "Future of American Judaism" and sponsored by Julius Rosenwald of Sears Roebuck & Co. fame and fortune was not. Offering a $10,000 award for the best essay of between fifteen to one hundred thousand words on how Jewish life might "adjust itself to and influence modern Jewish life," and promising to "publish and circulate [it] as widely as possible," the contest hoped to act as a "leaven upon the intelligent minds in American Jewry," encouraging the American public, as well as its Jewish cultural elite, to come up with some bright ideas. Though the competition fit Kaplan to a T, he wasn't among those who saw the announcement. Had his brother-in-law Phineas Israeli not told him of the contest, he would have missed out, and history would have taken a different turn.[8]

Energized by both the size of the pot and the challenge of winning it, Kaplan decided to throw his hat in the ring, well aware that if he were to "stand a chance of trying for the prize," he'd have to buckle down, to "be up and doing." The contest gave shape to his day—an incentive to spend it writing. But writing did not come easily. For more than a year, Kaplan struggled, his frustrations mounting the longer it took "beating into shape the substance of the book." First, it was a matter of finding the peg, the interpretive device, on which to hang his argument. It took him months to come up with its "ariadne's thread," as he evocatively put it. With that piece in place, Kaplan expressed his relief—and pleasure—by noting "I felt as though I walked on air." But not for long. Several months later, another lament. "So far I have on my hands merely a good metaphor," Kaplan noted in October 1930, referring to the conceit of Judaism as a civilization. "My problem is how to have that metaphor strike fire." As fall gave way to winter, he was still complaining about the difficulties of finding the right words. "There is no end to the number of times I have to rewrite a passage before it expresses what I have in mind." When, in the summer of 1931, it was time to send off the manuscript, he was glad to have it "off my chest," even as he wondered whether it might be "fifteen or twenty years too late."[9]

Kaplan's anonymous submission, along with dozens of others, including one from his brother-in-law and another from his close colleague Rabbi Eugene Kohn, was sorted first by Samson Benderly, who served as the contest's administrator, before being handed over to a panel of six judges. A Noah's ark of modern-day Jews, the panel consisted of two from the Orthodox community, two from the Reform community, and two Zionists. With the aid of directives that asked them to consider whether it "is possible to pilot [American Jewry's] course" and "to what extent can the process be controlled," culling the submissions took no time at all. The judges made quick work of separating the wheat from the chaff, the substantive from the oddball. Kaplan's essay rose quickly to the top of the pile and was labeled "Entry Number 1."[10]

Declaring a winner, though, turned out to be a protracted process; it took the panel more than two years to arrive at a decision. The many outside responsibilities the panel members shouldered as academics, businessmen, lawyers, and judges, respectively, slowed things down. The group's inability to reach a consensus further complicated the proceedings. At an impasse, the panelists couldn't agree among themselves which entry merited the award, their reasons for either embracing or rejecting Entry Number 1 as the winner mirroring the particular perspective each man brought to the table. The Orthodox members of the panel found Kaplan's contribution too unorthodox, too radical; its rejection of revelation hard for them to swallow, much less validate. The judges at the opposite end of the spectrum found its suggestions on how to live a modern Jewish life unrealistic in the extreme. "You can't expect Guggenheim to sing z'mirot on the Sabbath," one of them reportedly said. The remaining judges, with varying degrees of enthusiasm, leaned toward Entry Number 1, but wavered when taking into account its ardent waving of the Zionist flag, concerned that this posture might antagonize the Rosenwalds by threatening their patriotism. Back and forth it went, the panelists' hardened stances reflecting the internal divisions, the unhealthy fragmentation, that Kaplan's contribution sought to overcome.[11]

As the decision-making process dragged on, Kaplan-the-contestant grew more "agitated," fretful, and irritable. Time and again, he'd complain of experiencing a "malaise both physical and mental which is taking all the effervescence out of me and leaving me vapid and stale." In a constant state of suspense, he couldn't put the contest out of his mind. Consumed by its outcome—would he or wouldn't he win?—Kaplan thundered against the judges for their "slipshod and dilatory" behavior, castigating them for their insensitivity to those who, like himself, anxiously awaited a "yea" or a "nay."[12]

Kaplan didn't leave it at that: he sought to find out what he could of the committee's deliberations. Repeatedly besieging Benderly, his longtime friend, to give him a crumb, a hint, something, anything to hold on to, he also waylaid people he knew to be close to the contest's judges, hoping for scraps of information. On "tenterhooks," Kaplan came very close to crossing the line. But why? What prompted him to compromise a long-standing friendship, to make himself look weaselly and desperate? Why lose sleep over something so inconsequential as an essay contest? Yes, the prize money would come in handy as a subvention when seeking a publisher, but it wasn't as if he didn't have other funding sources. Besides, his livelihood, much less his reputation, did not rest on its outcome.[13]

Try telling that to Kaplan, who insisted that he had to win. Losing was tantamount to branding him and everything he had worked on over the past three decades as "hopelessly irredeemable." Others, including most of his contemporaries, considered the essay contest a side show, but not Kaplan. Ratcheting up the stakes, he chose to see it as a vindication of his life's work, a referendum on its viability. "Failure to win the prize would prove to me that I have been mistaken," he told himself. "If six men of the type who have been appointed as judges . . . cannot be convinced of the validity of my proposed version of Judaism, what likelihood is there that other Jews would find it acceptable? I would therefore be deprived of the faith which I have had in the philosophy of Judaism as a civilization and be bereft of the chief stimulus and inspiration in my thinking about and planning for the future of our people." Under those circumstances, were his foundation to crumble and "Judaism as a civilization goes to pieces," Kaplan hoped he'd be able to come up with something else to do so that "I might not go to pieces with it."[14]

Fortunately, neither he nor his beliefs crumbled. After much dillydallying, the contest's judges came up with a solution in the spring of 1933. Since they couldn't see their way clear to picking a winner, they reframed the prize money as a grant, or more precisely, as three grants, and scaled back the size of the awards. That way, no one proposal could be said to have won the day nor the Rosenwald family's approbation; the entries that were singled out were commended for their scholarship and analysis rather than for their winning strategies: A for effort. Kaplan took home the largest grant, $3,500, while Rabbi Lee Levinger, the Hillel director at Ohio State University (Essay Number 3), and Rabbi Eugene Kohn (Essay Number 7) received $1,500 and $1,000, respectively. Lest the recipients—the "three 'Marrano' prize winners," as Abba Hillel Silver, a member of the advisory committee, called them—be tempted to crow about their good fortune, they were enjoined from publicly acknowledging how they came by the extra cash, a provision that ran counter to the committee's initial enthusiasm about publishing the results far and wide.[15]

How did Kaplan feel about the contest's outcome? Mum's the word. He honored its stipulation of silence, even going so far as to avoid any mention of the contest's denouement in his diary. One moment, he was twisting in the wind, bemoaning his fate; the next, he was about to send off a manuscript along with a check to pay for the costs of publication to the Macmillan Company, leaving nary a clue as to what had transpired in between. Nor did the finished product, of which 1,500 copies were initially released, make any mention of the Rosenwald contest, dropping not even the tiniest hint of how the book came to be. And yet, somehow, word got out of Kaplan's involvement and before you could say "mazal tov," the grapevine—and history—cast Mordecai M. Kaplan as the winner.

Once *Judaism as a Civilization* was published, it didn't take long before its author was inundated with invitations to give a talk or two about it. Eager to spread the word and sell books, Kaplan took "*Judaism etc.*," his nickname for his magnum opus, on the road; no place was too out-of-the-way or too unprepossessing. In one notable instance, at the Jewish Community Center of Troy, New York, whose audience Kaplan characterized as being "of the usual sub-normal kind," *Judaism as a Civilization* was introduced as the "greatest work of its kind since Spinoza's Guide to the Perplexed." Though the details were incorrect—Maimonides, not Spinoza, was responsible for that storied text—the comparison was intended as a compliment. Hungry for hosannas, Kaplan took it in that spirit, even as he winced at this whopper of a gaffe.[16]

It's not that words of praise for the book and its author were in short supply. Hailed for the "almost surgical precision of his thinking," his astute grasp of history, fierce honesty, and "uniquely clarifying and positive analysis," Kaplan was also applauded for providing the "most dignified and well-thought-through program" for contemporary Jews. And yet, torrents of negative criticism from every quarter of the American Jewish community threatened to overwhelm the book's positive reception. Reform Jews maintained that it gave short shrift to the "exalted" role of religion; secular Jews that it contained too much "God-stuff." Orthodox Jews denounced the book as "dangerous," a "new *Shulchan Aruch*," certain to lead American Jews astray. Zionists, for their part, thought its emphasis on cultural nationalism minimized the geopolitical significance of a Jewish homeland in situ; non-Zionists thought it "barnacled with meanings of state-craft and politics"; devotees of Marx faulted its sparse treatment of left-wing alternatives. Still others, among them Cyrus Adler, the Seminary's president, believed that Kaplan's characterization of the Jews as a national entity gave aid and comfort to their enemies and publicly made that point in a speech at JTS graduation exercises, embarrassing Kaplan, though not for the first time nor the last. And then there were those who relished the analysis but thought little of the book's proposals to reconstruct Jewish life, dismissing them as pie in the sky, too redolent of the midnight oil. "It may be a perfect blue-print in [Kaplan's] study but it will not work in the American environment and it will not be acceptable to the American Jew," one sharp-eyed reader declared. All this—and more—was the stuff of conversation on the street, the sanctuary, around the dining room table, in the classroom, and within the pages of numerous newspapers and magazines.[17]

When first released, *Judaism as a Civilization* was reviewed by "practically everybody else in the world" except the *New York Times*, the one venue that mattered most to Kaplan. Made miserable by its lack of attention, he resorted to a conspiratorially minded interpretation to account for the absence of a review. How else to explain it? Clearly, not on the merits. According to this theory, or rumor, which someone had first whispered in his ear, Cyrus Adler was to blame. No fan of the book or of its author, the Seminary president had reportedly buttonholed the paper's publisher, to whom he was related, persuading him to give it the cold shoulder lest it tarnish the Seminary's reputation.[18]

Fifteen months later, on July 21, 1935, after what one imagines was considerable nudging from the publishers, who, in turn, had been repeatedly nudged by Kaplan, the *Times* published a review. Its appearance during the summer, when the public's attention sagged, and its placement on page 14 of the Sunday literary section were unlikely to buoy its author's spirits, nor were its contents. More summary than analysis, the review added nothing to the conversation, not even a usable adjective or two. Worse still, *Judaism as a Civilization* shared the page with another volume under consideration. Called *Judaism—An Analysis and an Interpretation*, it not only bore a similar title to Kaplan's creation, confusing readers, but was written by Rabbi Israel Levinthal, a Seminary colleague whom Kaplan held in low regard. Sometimes, when Kaplan was bitterly aggrieved, he wrote nothing in his diary. This was one of those moments.[19]

Years of bearing the brunt of controversy did little to thicken Kaplan's skin or blunt the edge of criticism. He bristled at the slightest hint of disagreement with, much less critique of, his book. When, on more than several occasions, his hosts balked at having to purchase twenty-five copies of his book (at $1.65 a piece, less than half the retail price) in lieu of a customary speaker's fee, claiming that while there were more than enough potential listeners on hand to warrant sponsoring a lecture, there weren't enough potential readers to warrant any kind of fiscal commitment, no matter how modest, Kaplan interpreted the response as a first-class snub, sourly noting it in his journal. At other moments, he railed against the thickheadedness of audiences who didn't much like what he had to say, preferring a "sugarcoated pill that would work magic."[20]

Now and again, Kaplan conceded that some of his critics had got it right. By his own admission, he was insufficiently attentive to the appeal of Communism, particularly among the younger generation, and he agreed with those who claimed that he missed an opportunity to reconcile his vision with that promoted by Marx—or to repudiate it. Kaplan also trained his sights on himself, lamenting the inelegance of his prose and the clumsiness of his word choices. At other moments, though, he'd take on the naysayers, itching for a fight. In May 1935, for instance, at a session of the Rabbinical Assembly's annual convention given over to "Dr. Kaplan's Philosophy of Judaism," Dr. Kaplan didn't wilt under a barrage of attacks by one of his rabbinical colleagues, he put up his dukes. "I countered his attack with body blows that sent him reeling," he proudly recalled.[21]

It was a momentary triumph. Trouncing his critics did little to soften Kaplan's disappointment at the meager, withholding response of his Seminary colleagues, who either acknowledged the book's publication with little more than a polite "congratulations" as they passed its author in the hall or said not a word. If Kaplan had hoped that *Judaism as a Civilization* might establish his scholarly bona fides and place him within the good graces of, and on a par with, his academic colleagues on the faculty, he was sorely mistaken. It did no such thing. Instead, it confirmed what the Seminary's leading lights had suspected all along: Kaplan was not one of them.

Of the many pieces of wisdom Solomon Schechter imparted to Kaplan, the one that Kaplan took most to heart was his admonition to "get into the ring." Much as the Seminary president admired his protégé's leadership of the Teachers Institute and valued his pedagogical and oratorical skills as a teacher of homiletics and midrash, he knew that Kaplan would never be one of the boys until he published a serious work of scholarship.[22] But *Judaism as a Civilization* was not what Schechter had in mind.

On his watch and in the many years that followed, the Seminary's academic economy had little use for anything—or anyone—that smacked of practical rabbinics, or what Schechter dismissed as "sociological Torah." Vilna, Brisk, even Pumbedita lay closer to the institution's heart than New York City, to whose values and inhabitants it gave a chilly reception. The faculty, unable to conceal its disdain for the flatfooted, bumptious American-born students who filled their classrooms, couldn't be bothered to say hello when running into them on the street, in the subway, or even at festive Seminary dinners, treating them as if they were "so many dish towels."[23]

Its animus more systemic than personal, the faculty didn't treat Kaplan as a dish towel, but only just; it could be cruel, unforgiving, snide, and downright hostile toward him. True, everyone, or nearly everyone, went through the motions of collegiality, extending the occasional invitation to drop by of an afternoon, but at these stiff and brittle domestic gatherings, it was the wives, blessed with the social graces their husbands lacked, who filled the silence with small talk and made nice. Sprung from their living rooms, Seminary men made Kaplan feel small, an outsider. When, in 1930, the Seminary complex at 3080 Broadway was finally completed, he wrote of a "novel and thrilling sensation" walking under its newly colonnaded passageway. "I felt for the first time the way a professor at one of the universities must feel, a sense of belonging to an academic institution."[24]

It was a bittersweet and fleeting sensation; most of the time Kaplan felt—and was made to feel—like an interloper. For over fifty years he fought against that feeling, but it never went away. No matter how much Kaplan insisted that he did more than any other member of the faculty to develop the intellectual potential of the student body, or that he occupied a "more important place than my colleagues or Adler would care to admit"; no matter how often he insisted, largely to himself, that the "Seminary refuses to recognize that my work deals with the theological concepts of Judaism," he remained on the outs: "shelved," as he once bitterly put it.[25]

Some might say, and did, telling Kaplan to his face that he brought it on himself by throwing caution to the wind and rashly taking the positions he did. The Seminary's professor of homiletics and midrash, it was alleged, "taught irreligion," which at an institution like his couldn't be more unacceptable, a betrayal of its principles. Others marginalized Kaplan, holding him at arm's length, on intellectual grounds. They dismissed the subjects he taught and the ideas he purveyed as fluff, more strategic than substantive. And still others took their cue from Adler, who had no qualms about making known the low opinion he held of his most troublesome faculty member, whose very presence he found disruptive. When, early in the 1920s, Adler was questioned publicly, insistently, by an Orthodox businessman named S. A. Israel about the impact of Kaplan's "pernicious" views on the Seminary's impressionable students, Adler didn't rush to Kaplan's defense so much as throw him under the bus. "His work," he explained, "is to teach the art of constructing a sermon, not the knowledge of Judaism which goes into the construction of the sermon. If he were professor of Theology, the matter ought be more serious." But since Kaplan was not, there was nothing to worry about, his boss concluded, cruelly tarring him with the brush of inconsequentiality.[26]

Louis Ginzberg, then the Seminary's leading light, also made life difficult. To hear Kaplan tell it, the renowned professor of Talmud never missed an opportunity to put him in his place by making cutting remarks about the American rabbinate or snippily alluding to "culture" and "civilization" as if they were frivolous, meaningless concepts. Worse still, Kaplan believed that Ginzberg was forever gunning for him, determined as early as the 1920s to bring him up on "heresy charges."[27]

These and a host of comparable experiences—one being a social gathering at which the trustees and the faculty gingerly mingled and where everyone but he was publicly acknowledged by name and thanked for their service—stuck hard in his craw, but Kaplan didn't crawl into a corner and surrender. He gave as good as he got, belittling the Seminary's preoccupation with the Talmud, making fun of academic culture, and badmouthing his colleagues. Disciplinary turf battles are the coin of the realm within the academic world, but at JTS only one field mattered: Talmud. Jewish education, history, literature, even the Bible and its commentaries stood in its shadow. A product of intensive Talmud study while growing up, Kaplan had no difficulty making his way through its many folios; even so, he chafed under its hegemony. The Seminary "has become so talmudized that the Bible has come to play a secondary role," he observed as early as 1922, concerned about the damage this might do to the students' foundational knowledge of Judaism as well as to their moral education. No fan of the text, Kaplan believed that its contents, or, more precisely, the sensibility it purportedly induced, was responsible for everything he found most troubling about traditional Ashkenazic Jewish culture: its picayune, nit-picking, argumentative nature; its casual attitude toward ethics; its embrace of sophistry. He even went so far as to blame the Talmud for the "perversion of Jewish character."[28]

Kaplan didn't take too kindly to faculty meetings, either, where pettiness and pettifogging—a favorite term of derision—were in full swing. "How I loathe those Seminary Faculty meetings!" At one point he considered channeling his emotions into a play that would spotlight his colleagues' behavior: who read the *Times* and who stared into space, who fiddled endlessly with his pipe, slouched in his chair, or rushed into the room with his hair askew. Alas, he didn't. Still, there's more than enough drama in Kaplan's recurring journal evocations of what went on behind the scenes to satisfy even the most curious: the feigned indifference to what was on the agenda; the plumes of smoke clouding the room; the faculty member who thought nothing of sauntering casually, an hour late, into every meeting; the inevitable verbal fisticuffs over nothing, all that huffing and puffing.[29]

A disgruntled Kaplan didn't leave it at that; within the confines of his diary, he had a field day expressing his not-so-collegial feelings. Name-calling was his way of demonstrating that he would not be pushed around or bullied by the inhabitants of 3080 Broadway. Likening the lot of them to "worshippers of dead letters," who preferred to "escape from life and its problems" by turning to "history and its puzzles," he merrily quoted an acquaintance who, in a play on Adler's first name—it was Cyrus—called him "Tsuris Adler." Kaplan also singled out Louis Finkelstein, Adler's successor, as the "embodiment of Jekyll and Hyde," and described his encounters with Jacob Hoschander, who taught Bible, as comparable to swallowing castor oil. Reserving his fullest ire for Ginzberg, Kaplan drew on a slew of animal-related zingers, writing that the mere mention of his name in front of the Talmudist was like "waving a red flag in front of a bull," and that Ginzberg "love[d] him as a cat loves a dog." In a third and most memorable dig, he described the man as a "porcupine of an individual," adding "if only he wouldn't stick his needles into my flesh."[30]

Kaplan withstood Ginzberg's quills, but the low estimation in which the Seminary held him took a toll; some people accumulate debts, he accumulated hurts. Eager to be seen as a serious, thoughtful academic, as well as a dedicated communal servant, he sought but never received the Seminary's seal of approval. Outside its wrought iron gates, some people might regard him as a scholar, yet, as Kaplan explained woefully to Stephen Wise in one of their many exchanges, "scholarship has unfortunately been with me nothing more than a suppressed wish." In contrast, when his congregants called him "Dr. Kaplan," he didn't demur, though he was never fully comfortable with the title. Having begun but never completed a doctorate, he felt as if he hadn't come by it honestly. The "Dr." attached to his name, after all, was an honorific—a

D.H.L., a doctor of Hebrew letters—which the Seminary had bestowed on him in 1928, not, Kaplan groused, in recognition of his scholarly chops, but in acknowledgment of his twenty-five years of fealty.[31]

Outwardly, Rabbi Dr. Mordecai M. Kaplan radiated confidence and certainty. He was a man who strides: a colossus. Inwardly, he was hobbled by feet of clay, a consequence, in part, of the academic politics that awakened and fueled his insecurities.

What kept Kaplan rooted to 3080 Broadway were his *talmidim*. "Little as I feel at home in the company of my colleagues, I am in my element among students," he related in 1925. Teaching fulfilled him. "Both my work with them and my relation towards them have afforded me more happiness than any of the other activities in which I am engaged." Those who heard, and perhaps even circulated, stories of Kaplan's fraught relationships might be taken aback by these sentences and doubt their veracity. When I was researching this book, tales of his withering impatience, lashing temper, and glum, frowning countenance were often one of the very first, and most frequent, things mentioned by everyone, particularly his former students. Kaplan himself would be the first to agree with these characterizations, recounting in his diary numerous instances of shouting, sputtering, and storming out of the classroom in a huff, especially during the 1950s.[32]

Note the date. Mean-spirited Professor Kaplan was a product of the postwar period. Increasingly embittered by the state of the world, ground down by the hostile reception within 3080 Broadway and the indifferent reception without, he grew more and more out of step with the needs and interests of his students. Feeling underappreciated and unloved—hardly a recipe for effective and rewarding teaching—Kaplan was unable to reach newer generations of students who struck him as ill-mannered and rude, cocksure and impudent, more interested "in putting me in the wrong" than in the honest exchange of ideas. His frustrations accrued, spilling over into and poisoning what had once been a profound bond between teacher and student.[33]

And yet, in the decades before World War II Kaplan took to the classroom with fervor and delighted in his interactions with those who sat in its uncomfortable wooden chairs, fielding his demanding questions. "The only happy moments," he wrote in 1933, "are those I have while teaching. This year, it is the classes at the Seminary that I find most exhilarating." Kaplan's offerings in homiletics, midrash and, eventually, religious philosophies—no easy A—demanded a great deal of students. He set a high bar and expected a lot, perhaps too much, of his intellectually callow charges, many of whom, he related, "seemed afraid of their own shadow," and "acted as though they had been brought up in some little village in Poland."[34]

Many, but not all: some of Kaplan's students, chafing under his exacting ways, let him know how they felt. Critiquing both the manner of his teaching—he didn't make sufficiently clear what he was up to—and its substance—too much emphasis on values, not enough on the mechanics of sermonizing—their observations wounded him. Kaplan's inclination was to label them "hair-splitting, pettifogging and disputatious," but he took his students' concerns seriously enough to document them at some length. And then he moved on, his pique as fleeting as a passing thunderstorm.[35]

Kaplan was able to keep at it, undeterred and with a full heart, because he banked on two key things about the student body: its members routinely asserted that, despite its limitations, his course on homiletics was the "only one" that enabled them to bring together and synthesize their other studies, and they preferred him to Ginzberg. The administration might lionize the professor of Talmud and derogate the professor of homiletics, but the students turned that arrangement on its head, warming to Kaplan rather than Ginzberg. It was no wonder that "he sees in me a menace to his prestige," Kaplan observed of his archenemy, or that Ginzberg believed Kaplan was deliberately out to sabotage his standing among the students: "Here comes along Kaplan who hasn't any pretensions even to Jewish scholarship and tries to overthrow my authority and influence."[36]

Kaplan liked having the upper hand. He also liked knowing that he had "won the confidence of the student body in general and of the leading spirits among them in particular." Grateful to him for sticking up for them, the "men" were well aware that Kaplan had their back, and they often brought him their complaints about the Seminary, certain he would do something about them. They knew, too, of his interest in their professional development as well as in their personal lives. "I somehow identify myself with the students who are studying and training themselves for a calling which has nothing but heartache, and it is as much to persuade myself as to persuade them of the potential worthwhileness of the rabbinate that I evolve some interesting and plausible syntheses and interpretations," he admitted. For all his empathy, Kaplan was not one of the fellas: going out for a beer was never in the cards. And yet, he did have them over to his home for dinner, a meaningful gesture under any circumstance, all the more when that kind of fraternizing was not done at JTS. Each one of these interactions added to his good name. "In general, the students regard me as their president," Professor Kaplan noted with a mix of relief and pride. Better yet, they see me as an "older brother instead of merely a member of the faculty."[37]

Kaplan also enjoyed interacting with students at the Teachers Institute, commenting in 1923 that when he experienced the blues, which happened often, the "sight of thirty-one young people all of whom are vitally interested in Jewish subject matter sitting before me awaiting eagerly what I have to teach them revived my drooping spirits." Their relationship, though, wasn't a close one; Kaplan didn't spend nearly as much time in the company of prospective Jewish educators as he did with prospective rabbis. A cluster of circumstances precluded that possibility, one of which had to do with the composition of the student body which, by the 1920s, consisted largely of women.[38]

Hold the huzzahs. Lest you think that Kaplan welcomed, or sought out, this development, think again. An artifact of Jewish education's low standing, compounded by Samson Benderly's having reportedly siphoned off the best and the brightest of male students for his own rival enterprise, the demographic profile of the Teachers Institute alarmed Kaplan, giving rise to concern that the institution was well on its way to becoming a "mere girl's seminary." That would not do. "The predominance of the feminine element in the T.I. has prevented me from making the T.I. my chief interest, as it should have been," he admitted in 1928, justifying his low-key presence among them. Until he was able to "come to grips with the tougher human material present in the male," Kaplan kept T.I.'s student body at arm's length.[39]

Hamstrung by gender politics, he was also constrained by the responsibilities he had assumed upon becoming principal and later dean of the institution. ("What a joke!" Kaplan wrote upon being given this new title, all too aware that it changed nothing but the stationery.) With administration, not pedagogy, his remit, he was compelled to limit his teaching to one class, "Jewish Religion," which met once a week for those in their junior year of study, twice a week for those in their final year—hardly enough time to make sense of Judaism's complexities or inspire ritual behavior, much less get to know those arrayed before him. "I confess that every time I come in touch with the students and with their work I feel guilty of negligence and lack of concentration," Kaplan remarked in what would become a familiar refrain.[40]

Instead, his energies were taken up with fundraising, or "schnorring," as he put it; with figuring out what kind of relationship the Teachers Institute ought to have with other Jewish communal educational ventures—to cooperate? ignore? co-opt?—and, most pressingly of all, with protecting his enterprise from being encroached upon by the Seminary's powers that be. Inclined to see T.I. as a "stepchild," and an unnecessarily expensive one at that, a drain on the Seminary's finances, its board and president seemed keener on cutting it loose than on keeping it afloat. Warding off one threat after another, Kaplan repeatedly tussled first with Adler and then with Finkelstein, as well as with Louis Marshall, the board chair, about financial matters that ranged from the cost of supplies to the inadequate salaries of the faculty. Over time, the relationship between the Teachers Institute and the Seminary grew so prickly and unstable that Kaplan got the "jitters" every time he received a letter from Finkelstein (aka "Finky" or "F."), certain the axe was about to fall. The Seminary provost and later its president, he believed, was "out to knife the TI."[41]

While fending off "Finky," Kaplan had also to contend with ideological issues that deepened the distance between the faculty and himself. Though an avid participant in curricular discussions, he left most of the big decisions to his colleagues, many of them avid Hebraists whose interests lay in the East rather than the West, in the Yishuv rather than the New World. The Hebraic orientation they increasingly promoted, often at the expense of other, equally pressing subject areas, such as contemporary American Jewish life, furrowed Kaplan's brow, leading him to lament their "self-withdrawal into a Hebrew ghetto."[42]

Putting a premium on Hebraic language and culture as the school's raison d'être meant that its language of instruction and of public discourse was to be conducted in that tongue. This, too, didn't sit too well with Kaplan. Never fully at home in Hebrew, though it certainly wasn't for want of trying, he found the incessant pressure of having to speak it publicly put him at a disadvantage, prone to fumbling the ball. Linguistic missteps lowered his self-esteem and gave rise to snickering on the part of the more fluent members of the T.I. faculty, who were all too quick to make thinly veiled comments about colleagues whose Hebrew was entirely derived from books. Try as he might, virtually every time he had to deliver remarks or teach class in Hebrew, the language defeated him. Despite efforts to "twist my tongue into shape for a Hebrew speech," the head of the Teachers Institute never quite got the hang of it and, much to his chagrin, would lapse into English, his sneering colleagues at the ready. On those occasions when he did acquit himself well (or well enough), he'd make a point of recording the date in his diary, an indication of how pleased he was with himself for giving Hebrew a go.[43]

When it came to the classroom and to his Seminary experiences, Kaplan often felt wanting. But now and again he surveyed his lot and saw that it was good. After one morning of solid teaching in 1930, he returned home for lunch, working up an appetite by walking from Morningside Heights to his Upper West Side apartment. "This is a fair quid pro quo," he said to himself. "I gave the world three hours of homiletics and the world gave me back a nourishing lunch." Elaborating further on his good fortune, Kaplan put it this way: what a "miracle of exchange that makes it possible for me to get asparagus on toast in exchange for the homiletic interpretation of a few paragraphs of Leviticus Rabba."[44]

Asparagus on toast—just to be clear, that's canned asparagus tips awash in cream sauce—went only so far. Much as Kaplan relished the pleasures of the palate—but always in moderation

Kaplan relished his daily walks, n.d.
The Collection of Hadassah K. Musher, New York.

lest he overtax his sensitive stomach—ideas, the knottier, the better, were his primary source of nourishment. Ideas, he once wrote, "are the only worth-while content of my workaday life." Thinking drew him first to the pulpit, then to teaching, and on to publishing, an activity that, in the wake of the successful publication of *Judaism as a Civilization*, beckoned more and more. Having demonstrated that he had it in him, Kaplan couldn't wait to try his hand at another book or two. It's almost as if *Judaism etc.* set his writerly talents free. Though none of his subsequent publications generated as much heat or staying power as the first, they represented the wide range of his interests and kept him going.[45]

Some books, for example, *Judaism in Transition*, came together with dispatch. Picking up where *Judaism as a Civilization* left off—and in many ways its sequel—this compilation of essays came together shortly after Kaplan finished his first book, and subsequently while he traveled by ship to Palestine in June 1935. A swift two months later, he sent the manuscript to the Macmillan Company. An easier read than its predecessor, more tightly structured, and in its tackling of Communism more sharply attuned to the immediate and pressing issues of the day, the volume didn't require much finessing. It wrote itself: the 2.0 version of *Judaism as a Civilization*. When Macmillan seemed to drag its heels, Kaplan showed the manuscript to Pascal Avram "Pat" Covici of Covici-Friede publishers, who, in the wake of a lively and agreeable lunch, agreed to publish it.[46]

Released in January 1936, *Judaism in Transition* was the subject of a crisp and clever (perhaps a tad too clever) review in the *Times* by Alfred Kazin, then fresh out of City College and just about to embark on his storied career as a literary critic. Kaplan's objective, he explained, was not to "set up a new Wailing Wall," to engage in breast-beating, but to make clear why it was necessary for contemporary Jews to embrace the many facets of their identity. "Dr. Kaplan's book may not bring light into Egypt," Kazin concluded, "but it tries, and very intelligently and passionately, too." Another review, this one by Abram Leon Sachar, then the national director of the B'nai B'rith Hillel Foundation, in the *Jewish Advocate* made an even more effective case, lauding Kaplan's attempt to "salvage, to adapt, to win renewed vitality" for Jewish life. Honest, realistic, and thoughtful, the author eschewed "shoddy wish-thinking" and pious sentimentalities in favor of a decidedly modern and positive approach. What he offered, Sachar concluded, was a "program Judaism, not a pogrom Judaism."[47]

Other titles, like an English translation of *Mesillat Yesharim* (The Path of the Upright), had been in the works for years. As far back as 1915, in what turned out to be their last conversation, Schechter had asked Kaplan to furnish an introduction to and render into English the celebrated eighteenth-century ethical text by Rabbi Moses Hayyim Luzzatto, which he promised to do. More than a decade later, Kaplan was still at it, "chomping at the bit that holds me back from getting anywhere" and wondering what took him so long to do right by its insights into living a good moral life. After finally submitting the manuscript for review in 1928, Kaplan had to wait two years before hearing back from his two outside readers, one of whom made a point of searching out every "possible flaw" in his sentences, while the other had little to contribute apart from querying Kaplan's spelling of the word *mesilat* with one *l* rather than two. Four years later, still "puttering" with the text, concerned that its tone and texture strayed too far from the original, Kaplan doubted whether his scholarly contribution "would ever see the light." It did, in 1936, in a handsome Schiff Classics edition put out by the Jewish Publication Society, enhancing his reputation. "Those who think of Professor Mordecai M. Kaplan as the keen rationalist and provocative champion of Judaism as a civilization will be glad to meet him in this new role of translator and popularizer of the 18th century Jewish mystic and ethicist, Moses Hayyim Luzzatto," declared a reviewer in the Reform-oriented *American Israelite*, applauding Kaplan's effective translation and helpful introduction.[48]

An accident of timing brought together *Mesillat Yesharim* and *Judaism in Transition*, two publications that otherwise appeared to have little in common. Thinking of them as companion pieces lessens the temporal and conceptual differences between them. When linked, they brought to life, and showcased, what Kaplan meant by the amplitude of Jewish civilization.

Necessary and vital, books established Kaplan's bona fides, and classroom teaching called on his pedagogical chops. But neither one held a candle to what he valued most: "spiritual companionship," the fellowship and exchange of ideas. Talk was oxygen. High-minded talk, that is. Kaplan had little use for the "pitter patter" of small talk, which bored him and for which he had no talent. But talk that mattered, that went somewhere and gave rise to exclamations of "Eureka!"—an expression Kaplan delighted in using—was something else again, even if finding its high-minded expression often eluded him. So highly did he cherish the "joy of conversation" that the prospect of going without soured him on summer vacations. Well aware of how important it was for his and his family's well-being to spend July and August out of the city, exposed to the sun and fresh air, he grudgingly went along. "Most of the time, however, I experience all the solitude and isolation of a prison," he wrote of his experiences on the Jersey shore, whose diversions were those of the body, not the brain. "Here I am all alone; not a human being who is interested in or troubled by problems similar to mine."[49]

Geography, though, wasn't the culprit: even at home amid the Big Apple's rich cultural environment the right kind of intellectual stimulation was hard to find and sustain. If ever there was a lonely man of faith, it was Mordecai M. Kaplan. He had friends aplenty, a circle of men who were stalwart and true, among them Israel Chipkin, a noted Jewish educator and the longtime registrar of the Teachers Institute. For years, the two worked side by side, socialized together, and corresponded with one another, Kaplan's letters as close to chatty and down-to-earth as could be. "Man alive!" he wrote on one occasion, so taken with Chipkin's ideas that he encouraged him to publish them within *The Reconstructionist*, writing that should Chipkin oblige him, "I shall do anything you want, even if it involved becoming an optimist." Chipkin responded by saying how much he enjoyed Kaplan's letter with its felicitous mix of "philosophic ponderabilities with charming whimsicality."[50]

Despite these expressions of camaraderie, Kaplan felt bereft. Hardly a year went by without bemoaning his intellectual solitude. His confreres, not as agile in their thinking as he, or insufficiently warm to his schemes, fell short and disappointed him. Here he is, middle-aged, in 1922, commenting on how isolated and alone he felt. “My friends who are identified with Jewish religious activity could not sympathize with my yearning for freedom to express my passionate desire for righteousness and peace,” Kaplan explained. “My radical friends failed to see why I loved Jewish traditions, Jewish history and the Jewish land with a consuming intensity.” Five years later, little had changed. Despite his unceasing efforts to find comrades in arms, “there was no sign of co-worker or disciple.” And five years after that, awash in self-pity, Kaplan wrote of being “doomed to unrelieved loneliness. There is not a person around in this large city with whom I can exchange a word.”[51]

His wife and four daughters were no help. “I am a stranger in the midst of my own family,” Kaplan declared, noting how the members of his household had little truck with, or the patience to follow, his intellectual peregrinations. From time to time, his four girls would push back on one of his pronouncements from on high, but for the most part they stood apart, a stance that both baffled and troubled their father who couldn’t fathom why they wouldn’t want to engage. Sitting down to lunch one Rosh Hashanah, hoping to involve them in a serious discussion of the service or the sermon, Kaplan was disappointed that the conversation around the table extended only as far as the “dress, the headgear, the jewelry” of their fellow female worshippers and stopped short at the pulpit. “What hurts most, of course, is that my own children seldom give any sign of being interested in what I preach,” he wrote in the wake of that dispiriting lunch. “Perhaps they do listen and perhaps occasionally an idea sinks in their mind, but I do not recall their ever passing any remarks that would indicate that what I said from the pulpit was even heard by them.” On a tear, he went on to say that “once or twice” Naomi might allude to something he had said, and that if he made a point of drawing Judith into a conversation, she might raise some good questions. As for Hadassah and Selma, they "never afford me even that grudging pleasure." But why should they? Lost in his own world, it never occurred to him to consider why American teenage girls would, or should, share his preoccupations.[52]

Feeling isolated at home and at work, Kaplan was thrilled when, in 1934, Judith married Ira Eisenstein, then twenty-eight years old and SAJ's newly ensconced second-in-command. A "regular guy" with a keen intellect and a shy disposition, the American-born, Seminary-trained Eisenstein devoted himself unstintingly to Reconstructionism, often clashing with his boss and father-in-law over strategy and content. But for now, Eisenstein gladdened Kaplan's heart. "If I could only forget for a moment the threatening clouds of another war, I would be the happiest human being alive," Kaplan declared after officiating at Judith and Ira's wedding. Not only did their union result in the immediate doubling of the male presence and perspective in the Kaplan household—a most welcome development—it also brought into the family someone who could serve as a partner in conversation and commiseration, the two of them regularly giving voice to a "duet of self-pity" over the limitations of their flock.[53]

In Kaplan's shadow for decades, until he took a pulpit hundreds of miles away, in Chicago, during the second half of the 1950s, Eisenstein didn't have an easy time of it. The man he called both "Father" and "the Chief" demanded much of him, expecting him fully to inhabit the role of dutiful son-in-law and conscientious rabbinical subordinate, blurring the line between the two. Their relationship was "complicated," the word family members diplomatically used to describe it. Eisenstein did them one better in an entry in the diary he intermittently kept during the 1930s and 1940s. Uncomfortably aware of how disapproving Kaplan could be of his performance in the pulpit, constantly criticizing both the contents and the delivery of his sermons, Eisenstein questioned in March 1936 whether the "time has come when business and family will refuse to mix well. The point is that he can't very well ask me to go because I'm married to his daughter."[54]

Sometimes, the shoe was on the other foot and Kaplan was the one under the microscope. While the idea of sharing a vacation house on the Jersey shore with his in-laws (and other assorted family members) sounded like a good idea to Ira when first broached, it turned out to be no summer idyll, the behavior of his in-laws a constant irritant. Instead of taking a break and relaxing, Kaplan worked all the time—"He labors incessantly. He sits and sits and sits, his pen poised"—which bugged Eisenstein no end. (Kaplan, for his part, thought his son-in-law played too much tennis.) Domestic squabbles over ritual observance were frequent, tempers ran short, the children ran wild, and even "Mother's" behavior left something to be desired. "I sometimes wonder how long I shall be able to stand the deification of MK by Lena. Nobody exists for her outside him," Eisenstein tartly observed as his mother-in-law waited hand and foot on her beloved Mordecai. And if that weren't enough to get Eisenstein's goat, her "hurrying" about the house, putting it to rights, "drives me nuts." Intimacy had its limitations. "How little it helps to live under the same roof as the living embodiment in the twentieth century of the *matmid* [a devoted, dedicated student] whom Bialik immortalized," he concluded, referring to the poet's celebrated profile.[55]

Living with a legendary character did have some advantages, though, one of which was the opportunity to work side-by-side on all sorts of creative ventures. When, in the early 1930s, SAJ's leader decided to produce a smart "little magazine," Eisenstein was present at the creation. Together with several of his fellow Seminary alumni whom Kaplan hoped to cultivate as disciples—Milton Steinberg, for one, Henry Rosenthal, for another—he shepherded the project from inception to reality as a biweekly periodical. Called *The Reconstructionist*, the magazine gave a name to a school of thought that had, for years, gone without. Throughout his career, beginning as early as 1904, Kaplan had drawn on different iterations of the word "reconstruction," variously deploying it as a verb, an adjective, and a noun without expressly claiming it for himself. But now, much like putting a name to a face, he made it concrete, official: "reconstructionist" would be the banner under which all of his ideas about identity, community, belief, and ritual would now congregate.[56]

How did Kaplan come by the word in the first place? It's a good question. In one form or another, "reconstruction" had been around at least since the waning days of the Civil War when it referred to the controversial restoration of the Union and the rebuilding of the South. It received a new lease on life in the wake of another war—World War I—when talk of the reconstruction of Europe was in the air and in the news. John Dewey further popularized the word in 1920 with the publication of his influential book *Reconstruction in Philosophy*. Many scholars attribute Kaplan's deployment of "reconstruction" to Dewey, whose teachings he deeply valued, but inasmuch as his first recorded use of the word dates to the early years of the twentieth century, that can't be right. The most one can say is that Dewey's use of the word gave it an intellectual pedigree. Looking elsewhere, then, it's tempting to think that Kaplan's notion of a systemic overhaul took its cue from the post–Civil War campaign to remake the South, but there's no evidence of that. Given the spottiness of his secular education, Kaplan might not even have been aware of Reconstruction's existence. Had he known how very badly that experiment in social engineering turned out, he might have stayed clear of the word.

Instead, he embraced it, insisting that the magazine should be known as *The Reconstructionist* even over the objections of colleagues who thought the title too unwieldy and too apt to be misconstrued. Kaplan liked its tensile strength and the many uses to which it could be put. *The Reconstructionist,* he conceded, was no "ear-alluring catchword," but it effectively conveyed its "mind-compelling call to thought and action."[57]

Seeking to live up to Kaplan's vision, the slender periodical, which typically ran to no more than twenty pages, had two objectives. One was to spread the word and serve as the rallying cry of Reconstructionism, which at the time was more of a sensibility than an organization. Not as stuffy and high flying as the *Menorah Journal* or as fiercely doctrinaire as the *Jewish Forum,* the periodical sought to be as open-ended and inclusive as Jewish civilization itself, demonstrating through its essays and book reviews how this notion was no empty catchphrase but a meaty way of engaging with everything that touched on the modern Jewish experience: "Jewishness as a source of enrichment," its inaugural editorial of January 11, 1935, proclaimed. Art, economics, politics, both domestic and global, religion, social justice, and all things Palestinian and then Israeli was fair game. Maimonides's eight hundredth birthday in 1935 was grist for its mill, as was Henrietta Szold's eightieth five years later, opportunities to acknowledge and grapple with their respective contributions to Jewish intellectual and political life. A hard-hitting piece by Milton Steinberg on "What Religion Is Not" (an exercise in therapy), another by Gerhard [*sic*] Scholem on the academic study of Kabbalah at the Hebrew University, and a playful contribution by Judith Kaplan Eisenstein on "Ten Songs Every Jew Must Know"—a Hasidic *niggun,* perhaps? *Adon Olam*? or the latest in Yiddish swing, courtesy of the Bagelmann Sisters (later known as the Barry Sisters)?—suggest something of the publication's intellectual and tonal range during its formative years.[58]

The second, less explicit but no less exigent, of the magazine's aims was to foster an intellectual environment in which Reconstructionism would flourish, assuring a constant flow of ideas and a steady supply of the right people to wrestle with them. Acting as a ringleader, or "impresario," Kaplan assembled on the page a constellation of thinkers, writers, artists, educators, and rabbis whose exchanges, much like those that once took place in a salon or, better yet, in the hothouse ambiance of a creative collaborative, would be in a continuous state of fermentation. It's not for nothing that he aspired to be the Jewish William Morris, hoping to do for Jewish civilization what the British polymath had done for Victorian England: stimulate, goad, excite, challenge, reenvision.[59]

Unlike Morris's contributions that pleased the eye as much as the mind, Kaplan's creation was not much to look at. Although the paper stock, at least at first, was high grade and textured, the impression one had of the magazine was of words, words, words rendered in a dull, serviceable font, enlivened by an occasional photograph or drawing. Yet it made up in intellectual cachet what it lacked in visual appeal and in a substantial base of subscribers. *The Reconstructionist*, declared the literary critic Charles Angoff, was "tops," deserving of a wide readership, which eluded it. The magazine struggled to find and retain readers. "Every day, I rack my brains—and Miss Mac's—for ideas for the extension of our circulation," Eisenstein noted shortly after the magazine's debut, referring to the SAJ's dedicated secretary, Hannah Machlowitz, who kept things humming and on track. Its subscription base, never large to begin with—SAJ members received a free subscription and other interested parties paid the full freight—grew from one thousand in 1935, its first year of operations, to anywhere between three thousand and five thousand by the mid-1950s. During most of those years it had been "virtually at a standstill," Kaplan recorded unhappily. The magazine's critics, though, were numerous. Some faulted it for being unduly "theological," freighted with lumbering discussions about faith; others took it to task for being excessively political, insisting that it had no business weighing in, say, in defense of Thomas Mooney or roiling the waters in favor of unionization. Stick to Jewish issues, Kaplan was told.[60]

Over time, the magazine did just that, increasingly concentrating on the "fight for Reconstructionism." Narrowing its sights, "graz[ing] in a quiet little pasture," the periodical became more and more concerned with internal matters, its fate paralleling—and perhaps accelerating—that of reconstructionism as it migrated from being a leavening agent into a bona fide movement, and then into a denomination. The more *The Reconstructionist* deepened its institutional profile, the less appeal it had for the general reader, a process hastened by the debut in 1938 of the *Contemporary Jewish Record*, followed in 1945 by that of *Commentary*, two glossier and more financially stable publications sponsored by the American Jewish Committee, each with a far more extensive and authoritative coverage of politics and culture.[61]

For much of *The Reconstructionist*'s run during the interwar years and into the immediate postwar era, Eisenstein did the heavy lifting. Attending to the technical side of things, to proofreading and production, as well as to editorial matters, he put his "whole heart and soul into the magazine." Kaplan, in turn, shouldered the financial and intellectual demands the publication generated. When not going hat in hand to donors for support, putting out fires, prodding his "lackadaisical" editorial board to do better or writing editorials himself, he was constantly on the lookout for people and topics to fill its pages. Soon enough, the magazine's many needs enervated rather than energized him. At the same time, the SAJ's leader grew increasingly weary of his congregational pursuits, every Sabbath the same as the last. "It finds everybody just where they were a week ago, a year ago, a decade ago," he glumly observed, disheartened by the status quo. Feeling as if he were getting nowhere fast, Kaplan privately derided his congregants as a bunch of rapidly aging "deadheads." Since the younger generation found "being a Jew so irksome," hardly anyone under forty attended services. From his perch on the pulpit, the future looked bleak.[62]

Stuck in a rut, Kaplan felt as if he were either "choking for lack of air to breathe" or trapped like a squirrel in a revolving cage. Despite the magazine and the congregation and the teaching and the lecturing and his many publications, Kaplan believed he had gone as far with American Jewry as he could possibly go. Greener pastures beckoned: Palestine, here I come. Perhaps he would be more effective there. Perhaps the time had come for him to put his commitment to the Zionist project to the test, to stop talking about *Eretz Yisrael* and to contribute directly to its well-being. And yet, characteristically, having decided to throw in his lot with his fellow yishuvniks, Kaplan blew hot and cold, hemming and hawing about taking off for the Middle East. "One moment I am all for Palestine, for going there with the view of settling there permanently," he wrote in February 1935. "The next moment, at the thought of the wrench such a change would mean to my way of life and of the possibility of doing something constructively Jewish in this country, I give up the idea of going to Palestine altogether." And then, the moment after that, he was back on board. "As I sat at the meeting of the SAJ Board tonight," Kaplan noted in March 1935, bored silly and irritated by its nitpicky deliberations, "I wished I could take the first boat to Palestine."[63]

Three months later, Kaplan and Lena set sail, hoping to spend the entire year in Jerusalem. By mid-August they were back in the Big Apple, the threat of hostilities between Italy and Ethiopia fueling Kaplan's "panicky" nature and making a hash of their plans. Thanks to a stroke of good fortune—an invitation to teach at the Hebrew University's newly established education department—the Kaplans were able to pick up where they had hurriedly left off and, for two years, between 1937 and 1939, to call Jerusalem their home. Busying himself with academic affairs, preparing a new suite of lectures on the history and principles of education, meeting with colleagues and students, Professor Kaplan fit right in. "I can't tell you what a joy it is to be teaching Jews without being aware all the time that the question they really would like you to answer is 'Why be Jews at all?' " he reported in a letter to his children. "From this standpoint, my work here is not only a change from what I've been doing all these years but a real vacation." The only hitch: he was too much in demand. "One has to spend a great deal of time on such incidentals as meetings and social affairs and teas and dining and being dined and schmoozing in general," Kaplan wrote, worried lest these extracurricular activities cut into his work, which he very much wanted to "count" for something.[64]

Lena had a harder time adjusting. With little Hebrew to speak of and only a few friends to keep her company, she experienced the challenges of daily life in a foreign land, especially the marketing and housekeeping, more acutely than her husband. It's not as if Kaplan sailed through life in Mandate Palestine oblivious to its privations and dangers. When the supply of water to their Talbieh home was cut off, which happened often and for days at a stretch, he pumped several buckets worth from a "reserve supply." When, for security reasons, he was unable to take his daily constitutional along Rehov King George, he made the rounds on his building's roof, quipping there's "nothing like having a roof under your feet."[65] But Lena bore the brunt of it, and in a series of newsy, affectionate letters to her "dearies" back home gave voice to the many dislocations of—and occasional bright spots in—her new routine. An agile writer with a keen eye for the finely grained detail, she wrote of the food ("God bless Heinz") and the faculty wives (they're "not so hot"), the weather ("if the hamsin [heat wave] keeps up much longer, we will melt away to nothingness"), the rituals of sociability ("Shabbat is a very strenuous day here"), and of having to steer clear of the Old City, even during the day: "Some life. . . . I think we have forgotten how to laugh."[66]

To offset her description of these tough moments, Lena made a point of recounting the delights of a leisurely two-hour lunch on an ordinary Thursday; the appeal of a Jewish holiday that lasted for one day rather than two ("What a pleasure not to have two days yomtov. . . . I am urging Papa that if and when we get back to the States he should introduce one day yomtov"); and the unanticipated thrill of Papa doing something he had never done before ("He window shopped with me for about an hour [when in Tel Aviv]. How do you like that?"). She wrote, too, of keenly missing her growing family, of yearning for an ice cream soda at Schraft's, and of the satisfaction in serving tea and cake to the students, a practice that reminded her of home. Besides, she added, "here it is a real mitzvah to give these poor students a good piece of cake . . . and a warm place" in which to enjoy it.[67]

A dutiful wife who would follow her husband anywhere, even to the Fiji Islands "if that's what he wanted," or so her eldest child would have it, Lena made the best of it. "We are very happy together in our comfortable home with plenty to nasch [*sic*] and plenty of tea to drink," she informed her children, reassuring herself as much as them that Papa and she were quite content, thank you. These reassurances became increasingly necessary as the Yishuv plunged into a period of physical upheaval and things went from bad to worse. "Between the Arabs and the Revisionists and the military, we are kept on the jump all the time," Lena explained, nerves fraying and hopes fading amidst a soundscape of explosions and gunfire. "It seems that God is good," she wrote, her amiability giving way to facetiousness. "He lets us experience all kinds of things here from curfew, shooting, bomb throwing, siege of the city, unbearable hamsin and even rioting." And yet, on a number of volatile, threatening occasions when Kaplan was ready to call it quits and pack his bags, Lena made the decision to "stick it out" and stay where they were: "I am all in emotionally."[68]

For Kaplan, one of the dividends of being in Jerusalem were the people who lived either in his neighborhood or its immediate vicinity. With Hugo Bergmann, Ernst Simon, Gershom Scholem, and Martin Buber close by, he found the intellectual companionship he missed back home and eagerly sought out their company. Kaplan was particularly keen on befriending Buber, with whom he felt a real bond—when they bumped into each other on the bus, they talked about God—and made numerous overtures as if an anxious suitor, even entertaining the prospect of their joining hands to develop an interpretive approach to teaching Bible. But before long, Kaplan felt rebuffed, as if their relationship were entirely one-sided, more "I" than "thou." "Silly of me to entertain the thought even for a moment that the two of us could work together," he related in a November 29, 1938, diary entry. "We are worlds apart in our temperaments and ways of thinking. But I was so starved for cooperation that I followed even what I knew in my heart was a will-o'-the-wisp." A few days later, still smarting, Kaplan had more to say about Buber. "He is not what you would call a big man. He lacks a sense of humor and displays little interest in you when you talk to him. He is interested mainly in Buber."[69]

Dispiriting revelations, it turned out, were thick on the ground even though life in *Eretz Yisrael* was anything but dull. "Anyone who speaks of the sleepy orient doesn't know what he is talking about," Kaplan bluntly observed. "New York is absolutely bromidic in comparison." And yet, any expectation that his experiences would be generative as well as lively fell wide of the mark. More sobering than revitalizing, corrosive even, the years he spent in the Holy Land impelled Kaplan to temper his belief in Zionism as the antidote to what ailed the modern Jewish world. "If you are fond of eating your heart out there are plenty of occasions for doing so in this part of the world. They serve it to you here well boiled with plenty of sauce," is how he dispiritedly conveyed its emotional landscape. "You can't take a step without coming up against chauvinism, fanaticism, and apparently insoluble difficulties."[70]

It's not as if the scales suddenly fell from his eyes. A veteran of Zionist politics, familiar with and often bruised by recurrent instances of infighting, Kaplan was under no illusions about the movement's complexities, its stresses and strains. When it came to Zionism, he was no wide-eyed innocent, no babe in the woods. But his sojourn in Jerusalem enabled him to see things and "fully appreciate [them] as I could not before I got here." Constructs that had lived comfortably in his head or on the page—democracy and its relationship to religion, unity amid diversity, cultural vitality, comity with the Arabs—read differently, less agreeably, on the street. Sometimes, Kaplan would be amused, writing to the family about a recently posted sign on Rehov King George that read: "Shortly Will Open Here. Corsets Saloon. Malke Singer. Specialist in figure fundations." At other, more frequent, moments, he didn't care much for what he saw. Any hope that a vibrant Jewish cultural life would emerge organically, as a matter of course, went by the boards. "It is no doubt that one can live here as a Jew without doing anything about it. But all that means is that we have here a modern ghetto where the Jew doesn't feel the challenges to his civilization and his religion. . . . We must give up the notion of spontaneous regeneration in Palestine."

More upsetting by far was the intractable political situation. "Every time I see them my blood boils," Kaplan wrote, referring to the local Arabs who had recently taken to donning the keffiyeh as a symbol of resistance. "It is as if they wore a big sign saying 'Jew, my mission in life is to destroy you . . .' To have that thrust at you in the only place in the world that is really and truly yours is just a little bit too much to endorse with equanimity."[71]

Equanimity was the least of it. "Oh God how I pray to get out of here safe and sound," Lena wrote anxiously to her children as she and Kaplan prepared to return to the States in the summer of 1939. "It is getting too much for me already. Until now I was the strong one but now I too am getting weak. I am all worn out from aggravation." Not wanting her letter to conclude on such a sour note, Kaplan appended a paragraph of his own, explaining that Mother had the "jimjams," using a colloquial expression seldom heard these days. "Both of us have our ups and downs," he went on to say, "but fortunately, when I have my downs, she has her ups and vice versa, so that we have managed to balance each other pretty well."[72]

Outside the precincts of the Kaplan household, balance was hard to find. Zionism seemed more of a chimera, a pipe dream, than ever before, but relinquishing hope in a Jewish homeland and its fructifying potential was not an option. An article of faith—albeit one whose contents zigged and zagged—Zionism had colored Kaplan's perspective for as long as he had been a Jewish communal servant. As early as 1905, when he first came of age, the young rabbi wrote of how he was "more convinced than ever that Ahad Ha'am's conception of nationality plus Arnold's interpretation of Israel's (ancient) genius for righteousness contain that which could form a positive expression of the Jewish spirit." In the years that followed, in the first flush of enthusiasm for the Balfour Declaration, which, in 1917, publicly acknowledged and ratified the Jews' claim to a "National Home" in Palestine, Kaplan spoke of his longing to settle in the land, of how that prospect "has put new life into me. May God grant that my hope be realized and that my lot ultimately be cast among those who help rebuild the ruins of our land."[73]

A decade later, he had second thoughts about "this Zionist business." In the aftermath of the horrific 1929 riots, which laid low hope of a Jewish homeland anytime soon, he wrote "At last I see the light. The Balfour Declaration has been like a foreign body in the system of Jewish revival, causing irritation and liable to set up a dangerous prison." For clarity and peace of mind, he reread Ahad Ha'am to "see to what extent he thought out clearly his program of Palestine as a cultural, and not political center." But neither clarity nor peace of mind was at hand; instead, Kaplan confessed to being "all at sea about the solution of the Jewish problem in general and of the Palestine problem in particular." Ahad Ha'am might have been prescient, incisive, and clear-eyed, but he was no prophet, and right now, his devoted acolyte observed, one has to have "the clairvoyance of a prophet to form an intelligent instead of an impulse judgement at what should be the next step."[74]

In the absence of a prophet, contemporary Jews had lost their way. "A more muddleheaded people there can scarcely be found in all the world. We haven't the power to think out any idea to its consequences and implications," railed Kaplan, sounding very much like a latter-day Jeremiah. "Shouldn't we have insisted from the very start that an instrument like the Balfour Declaration should be definite and lucid? Talk about not looking a gift horse in the mouth. The Declaration isn't even a horse, it is a hypogriffe or a centaur." He went on to rebuke his people for failing to ask the right questions lest the answers stump them: In the absence of a majority, how can we have a national homeland in Palestine? And might it also be possible for the Arabs to have a homeland in Palestine? These and other questions, he concluded bitterly, "were regarded as too intricate and therefore to be avoided. Likewise the question of religion to state, etc. etc."[75]

Asking the right questions became even more of a moral imperative amid the rapidly growing number of displaced European Jews, whose presence transformed Palestine of the 1930s from a fount of renewal into a "land of refuge from destruction." The time has come, Kaplan noted, to "reformulate" Ahad Ha'am and bring his views "in line with present day realities." The "need of revising our conception of Jewish nationalism" was the order of the day. In 1938, Kaplan sent Eisenstein the equivalent of a position paper outlining his latest thoughts. Sharpened by his day-to-day experiences in the Yishuv, they were to be shared with the members of the "Friday night group," an informal monthly gathering of rabbis and Jewish communal professionals sympathetic to and, in some cases, allied with Reconstructionism, which Eisenstein affectionately called a "sort of unofficial plotting and scheming society." In an attempt to reckon with the notion of nationalism at a time when it was in very bad odor, Kaplan twisted himself in knots in an attempt to resolve how and under what circumstances it was a "social concept that fit the case of the Jews" and therefore applicable to Zionism. His ideas as thorny as the reality that shaped them, he distinguished between "de facto nationhood" and "messianic nationhood," locating the Jews in the latter camp. "The indispensability of Palestine is due to our regarding Judaism as a civilization and the Jewish people as aspiring to messianic nationalism and it is not to our being a de facto nation," he declared, muddying the waters rather than parting them.[76]

To a man, everyone rejected what Kaplan had to say, their reaction "most violent." The distinctions you drew "did not appeal to them as either an effective clarification or as good tactics," Eisenstein explained in a detailed letter. It was almost as if you sought to stem the tide of antisemitism "with a word." More pointedly still, your perspective "indicated for them a willingness to surrender the whole progress of Reconstructionism." If word got out, it would "weaken the morale of Zionists in this country, making them believe that all our efforts for Palestine at this time are not only futile but wrong."[77]

And how did Kaplan respond? "I am not surprised at the reaction," he wrote dismissively, "because I am quite sure they have not given sufficient thought to the problem of nationalism."[78]

Years later, he would write movingly of the excitement, the quickening of the pulse, he felt in the wake of the establishment of the State of Israel, daring anyone not to be as thrilled as he—anyone, that is, in whose veins vinegar did not run. But at this earlier point in his history, in the wake of experiencing the Yishuv firsthand during very dark days, doubts about the viability of a Jewish homeland—in any form—chipped away at his foundational beliefs. Its glaring weaknesses exposed, the Zionism Kaplan carried home with him in late June 1939 was more subdued, far less assured, than the one that had brought him to the Holy Land in the first place. Scheduled to give a series of lectures on Jewish nationalism at the University of Chicago's Divinity School shortly after returning stateside, he had a hard time giving voice to his convictions. Lena attributed her husband's difficulties to his current state of mind, writing, "Oh boy is he disgusted with all nationalism." What, then, was to be done under these sobering circumstances? "The best thing to do is to put on those good ole serviceable blinders," Kaplan wrote consolingly to his family. "What else is there to do if you don't want to go cuckoo?"[79]

"Next year in Jerusalem" assumed a different kind of resonance when, back in the States, Kaplan turned his talents to coming up with a new version of the Haggadah, the ritual text of the Passover seder, in which that phrase memorably appears.

Kaplan and his grandson Daniel at a Passover seder, 1948.
Photograph by Ira Eisenstein. Eisenstein Family Album.

Dissatisfied with what he took to be the plodding pace, dull recitatives, and outworn concepts and practices of the traditional narrative, he toyed for years with compiling a more lively and timely alternative. He experimented with the text at his own seder, adding passages that appealed to him and deleting those that didn't.

Kaplan kept his homegrown, mimeographed Haggadah within the bosom of the family—his own as well as his SAJ family—until 1941, when he released it publicly. *The New Haggadah*, he called it, the title making clear its intention to shake things up. Published by Behrman's Jewish Book House under the aegis of the newly established Jewish Reconstructionist Foundation, the bilingual text didn't have much competition. Today celebrants can choose among a staggering array of *haggadot* keyed to a specific interest (the environment, say), or perspective (feminist), or audience (kids), but when *The New Haggadah* made its debut, American Jews had few options. *The Seder Service for Passover Eve in the Home*, compiled by Mrs. Philip Cowen, was one, the *Maxwell House Haggadah*, another; both left the Haggadah's structure, language, and contents undisturbed. The version that Kaplan, in concert with Ira Eisenstein and Eugene Kohn, released looked and read differently. At once an exercise in concision and amplification, it was punctuated by folksy black-and-white drawings from the hand of Leonard Weisgard, a well-known children's book illustrator, and by musical notations that Judith Kaplan Eisenstein assembled, along with instructions on how each melody should be sung: "triumphantly," "softly with longing," or "gaily."

Out with the hard-to-follow and the hard-to-swallow in twentieth-century America and in with a more fast-paced narrative that included a humanizing profile of Moses (who is conspicuously absent from the traditional text) and supplementary readings in English about liberation. Situating *The New Haggadah* in the context of freedom—"Behold this cup of wine. See its warm glow! . . . The call of freedom rings out again"—Kaplan and the others hoped to inspire American

Jews to take its words to heart rather than go through the motions of turning page after page while counting the minutes until dinner would be served. The big idea, its editors explained in their foreword, was to "keep alive in men the love of freedom, and their faith in it" by "transposing [the Haggadah] into a new key—into the key of modern thought, modern experiences and modern idiom."[80]

Gone were the lengthy mathematical computations that multiplied the Ten Plagues ten- and twentyfold. Gone, too, were the Ten Plagues themselves and Jeremiah's famous imprecation, *Shefokh hamatkha al ha-goyim* (Pour out thy wrath on the nations that do not know you), which preceded the age-old ritual of opening the door for Elijah. Dispensing with the handful of words that laid claim to the Jews' election or chosen-ness, a long-held and much cherished belief that Kaplan dismissed as mere "flummery," was another of its "innovations." Otherwise, the familiar elements of the traditional seder service—the drinking of the four cups of wine, the four questions, and the rousing *Dayenu!* (though truncated)—remained intact.[81]

Well aware that it was one thing to talk about change, quite another to effect it, and mindful, too, that issuing his own Haggadah was likely to bring down a storm of protest upon his graying head, one has to wonder what possessed Kaplan at this point in his career—he was sixty years old—to undertake a project that was as controversial as it was ambitious. The short answer: timing. Kaplan had returned to New York determined to lessen his involvement in the SAJ, which increasingly he saw as a "distraction," and to turn it over to Eisenstein. If everything worked out as planned, he would devote his newly empty hours to a slate of literary and liturgical projects more satisfying than time-consuming, tedious congregational and pastoral affairs. Concomitantly, Kaplan felt that Reconstructionism was at a standstill and stood to benefit from a new initiative to revive its flagging fortunes. Current events, in turn, added more than a frisson of timeliness. As the fate of European Jewry hung in the balance, paying lip service to the Haggadah's evocations of slavery and freedom, treating them as historical phenomena rather than current reality, was no longer tenable—or worse still, verged on the blasphemous. Something had to be done to endow those concepts with meaning, to align them with the present rather than consign them to the past.[82]

As it turned out, Kaplan's expectations were not fulfilled. Despite a flurry of meetings in which he made clear his resolve to become "leader emeritus," insisting that in Eisenstein they had a "man after their own heart," the synagogue's leaders were not persuaded. Besides, SAJ's trustees liked having Kaplan at the helm, deriving much *nahas* (pleasure) from his being their rabbi. Standing their ground, they wouldn't "let him go." Not wanting to create a fuss, Kaplan relented. He went on to serve as SAJ's senior clergy for another six years before being relieved of most of his responsibilities except for preaching once a month. Despite his disappointment—and the burden of an extra workload rather than a diminished one—he pressed ahead with revamping the Haggadah. Keeping Reconstructionism going weighed heavily on him. If *Judaism as a Civilization* represented its manifesto, *The New Haggadah* represented its application, a concrete and congenial way to make good on its promise by "shifting the center of gravity of Jewish religion from the synagogue to the home." There was an additional incentive: well aware of his marginal status at JTS and certain it wouldn't improve anytime soon, not with Finkelstein now in charge, Kaplan didn't think he had anything to lose—and everything to gain—by publishing a Haggadah of his own.[83]

Its three thousand copies sold quickly, suggesting he had his finger on the pulse of American Jewry. *The New Haggadah* "made quite a bit of a stir," its editors noted, happily relaying the news that "there was many a Seder this year where no Seder was before." For those American Jews who lacked either the skills or the patience to navigate the traditional text, or felt it didn't speak to them, this new version fulfilled a need, encouraging them to "make another try at having a meaningful, beautiful and intelligible Seder service." Soon enough, though, complaints from dissatisfied customers came over the transom. Some thought the omission of "Pour out thy wrath" was ill-considered and ill-timed in light of the Nazis' assault on the Jews. Others missed dipping their pinky ten times into a glass of wine to symbolize each of the ten plagues. They missed the plagues, too. As one otherwise "quite intelligent woman" told Kaplan, a Haggadah without them was "like a kiss without a hug." He bridled at that comparison—"What a conceit!"—and shrugged it off as a display of sentimentality, close kin to the kind of mushy, unfocused attachment American Jews had to Kol Nidre.[84]

The reaction of Kaplan's students, with whom he shared an unbound copy, could not be so easily dismissed, especially since none (at least none who spoke up) had a "good word" to say. One characterized *The New Haggadah*'s intended audience as "an inter-faith conference designed to show the goyim what a fine people we are." Another accused Kaplan of "slashing" the text, an act tantamount to a "brutal disregard for the sanctity of tradition." Still others thought it would bring on a "flood of Haggadahs," unleashing anarchy and sowing disunion within the Jewish commonweal.[85]

Kaplan received an even greater shellacking from his colleagues who poured out their wrath upon him. He might have thought he was merely "blow[ing] off the dust," but they accused him of taking a sledgehammer to tradition. Although anticipating a storm, Kaplan found himself in the eye of a hurricane of increasing velocity. First, every member of the faculty (most of their own accord, one or two under duress), put their names to a letter, the equivalent of a cease and desist motion, in which they disassociated themselves from "this book," but not before highlighting its shortcomings, citing chapter and verse. They made much of the fact that *The New Haggadah* opened from left to right, like an English-language volume rather than a traditional Jewish one, and that it contained an unacceptable number of mistakes—it mixed up its Rabban Gamaliels and mistranslated *karpas* as "parsley" rather than "celery," among other things—intimating that its author was out of his depth. (Kaplan acknowledged that the incorrect attributions and translations were his; the positioning of the text, though, turned out to be the fault of the binder. Both sets of errors were corrected in subsequent editions.) Building their case against him, the letter's signatories also "record[ed] with amazement" his decision to "expunge all references to the election of Israel," a stance that ran "contrary to the letter and spirit of Jewish tradition" and to the principles on which JTS stood.[86]

Kaplan's colleagues were just warming up, their harsh bill of grievances only the first salvo. A series of unprecedented faculty meetings in which he was called to account—and, presumably, expected to atone—for his waywardness soon followed, one fiercer and more unrelenting than the next. Subjecting him to "third degree torture sessions," or what Eisenstein characterized as an "Inquisition," the JTS faculty continued to point out the error of his ways. They labeled Kaplan's failure to consult with Ginzberg, Marx, and Finkelstein an unpardonable lapse of judgment and questioned his authority, wondering how he dared of his own accord to "lay hands on the liturgy." In their most withering cut of all, Kaplan's erstwhile colleagues claimed that, in doing away with the notion of chosen-ness, he had not only "broken with" tradition but had cut himself off from Judaism and the Jewish people.[87]

Dayenu.

Kaplan held his own, responding with unusual restraint to their litany of accusations by writing a letter to the faculty, whose concluding passage read: "If we want to judaize [*sic*] the home, it is highly essential to bring back to it the Seder service. That can come about only with the aid of a Haggadah that can make of that service a living religious experience." In his diary, Kaplan proudly recounted how he kept his cool and responded politely and effectively to each of the many charges leveled against him even as his gorge, and blood pressure, rose higher and higher. Those who, like Eisenstein, saw him immediately after the second of these denunciatory exercises, thought otherwise. His father-in-law, he wrote, resembled a "beaten person," his sprint of a walk slowed to a crawl, his gaze directed toward the ground.[88]

Over the next few days, Kaplan considered resigning from the Seminary once and for all, going so far as to reach out to Stephen Wise, yet again, to see about securing a faculty position (a "niche," he called it) at JIR. While awaiting his fate, he elaborated fully on his reasons for rejecting the notion of chosen-ness, filling nearly twenty-five pages in his diary—many of them cross-hatched with excisions—with what he should have said but didn't when in the hot seat. A theological thorn in his side, the belief that "we Jews are [as] different from the other nations as light is from darkness" had no place in democratic America, Kaplan declared. After years of soul-searching, he had come to see belief in the chosen people as a "spiritual anachronism," which made sense for American Jewry's forebears but not for their descendants. Distinguishing between being aware of history and being held captive by it, between tradition as a "peg to hang our collective memory" and tradition as a guide to the future, he said this: "We cannot afford to dispense with the remembrance of our ancient thought life, however much we have outgrown it. But when it comes to affirming what we ourselves believe with regard to God's relation to us, we dare not content ourselves with quoting what our ancestors believed. We must express forthrightly what we ourselves believe." In twentieth-century America that meant that chosen-ness as an ideal to live by was "out of place" and had to be "expunged." Its elimination from the liturgy was not a matter of appeasing Judaism's critics who associated chosen-ness with theories of racial superiority, as some of his critics alleged, but of shoring up the Jewish body politic through an "ethically acceptable" and decidedly modern rationale for Jewish collective identity. As for those who feared that without that sense of "moral or spiritual preeminence," Judaism might collapse, Kaplan had no doubt that the "Jewish will to live" would not only endure but prevail.[89]

Just in case, the beleaguered editor of *The New Haggadah* and his confreres took to *The Reconstructionist*, hoping to dispel any and all doubts about their good intentions. "The impression must not be gained, however, that the New Haggadah is offered in any sense as a new dispensation," they wrote. "It is not revelation; it has no authoritative, or even quasi-authoritative status." In plain English: the latest version of the Haggadah was a gift, not an obligation; an opportunity, not a mandate. Taking the long view, Kaplan, Kohn, and Eisenstein also sought to quell the concerns of those who worried that their version would prompt lots of competing narratives. Wasn't it better that "thousands of Jews should celebrate the Pesah, each with a different Haggadah, than that only hundreds observe it—with a uniform Haggadah?"[90]

A good question, right up there with the traditional four *kashes* of the seder. By the time Kaplan was in a position to answer, the ill will that had fired up the Seminary had quieted down. He was not fired, nor did he resign or go over to JIR. Behrman's Jewish Book House, meanwhile, issued a new printing of *The New Haggadah*, which continued to win adherents, though never as many as those who made use of the *Maxwell House Haggadah*. Life went on. Over a decade later, in 1955, Kaplan gave a sermon at SAJ on "The Significance of *The New Haggadah*," in which he talked about the criticism it had first elicited and how it was now "taken for granted." The text's significance, he proudly told his audience, lay in its "rendering the message of Pesah compatible with our modern world outlook and pertinent to the anxieties and hopes which we experience."[91]

Kaplan's success at breathing new life into the Haggadah encouraged him to think he could—and should—do the same for the *siddur*, or prayer book, especially the one for Sabbath morning services. Looking out from the pulpit at the small number of aging, bored, and restless worshippers in his own congregation and well aware that the dispiriting scene before him was duplicated in scores of synagogues throughout the country, he came to the sorry conclusion that the Shabbos morning service was on its last legs. "Services seem doomed. Of course, they will probably hang on for another half century," he predicted, "just as have the Indians and Civil War veterans and horses and hurdy-gurdys, but they are a dying institution." Were SAJ's leader inclined momentarily to doubt his assessment, his congregants confirmed it, filling his ear with complaints about the ways the use of Hebrew "interfered" with the service and suggestions that it should probably be "thrown out." They also made sure to tell him that they found the Torah reading as dry as the desert through which their ancestors had wandered and that services were unduly lengthy, even interminable. The only feature Kaplan's congregants truly liked was his sermons, but at times, they, too, dragged or were hard to follow. Or both. The state of the daily morning minyan was even worse.

So few members were on hand to constitute the requisite quorum of worshippers that SAJ's board resorted to hiring and paying people to say the prayers—a quick fix but not a long-term solution. Is it any wonder, then, that Kaplan likened the state of public worship to a person breathing his last, and that he felt compelled to do something lest it go the way of the sacrificial cult: an unthinkable but increasingly likely prospect.[92]

In his book, prayer was essential. "To say 'I believe in praying' sounds to me as absurd as to say 'I believe in thinking,' " Kaplan declared in the 1930s, underscoring how much he valued devotional practice. The "question whether prayer is effective is only a special form of the question whether thought is effective," he added in the very next sentence, determined to drive home its centrality. Decades later, Kaplan further essentialized the meaning of prayer, allowing how it satisfies our "spiritual hunger as food satisfies physical hunger." His personal practice, though, appeared to belie these fervently worded declarations. Though he attended Sabbath and holiday morning services religiously, Kaplan's private weekday regimen was anything but regimented. During the week, when the donning of tefillin (phylacteries) was a prerequisite of traditional Jewish prayer, he sometimes put them on and sometimes didn't; at other times he donned them, but in lieu of resorting to the traditional liturgy he'd read from the Bible and the commentaries or from an inspiring secular text like the writings of John Dewey. And sometimes he didn't pray at all, tefillin or no tefillin. Inconsistent? So it would seem and, to some, most troubling. But as far as Kaplan was concerned, his behavior made perfect sense. In his estimation, prayer had to be intentional, volitional, and inspiriting; not for him "the deadening routine of reciting the few meager passages which go to make up our official prayerbook." If he had his way and "had anything to do with the prescribing of rules for prayer, [he] would have insisted upon living up to the principle of Rabbi Eliezer," who deemed fixed, or mechanical, prayer unworthy of the name.[93]

What else would Kaplan have insisted upon? A redefinition of what constituted prayer, for starters. To petition, supplicate, plead, negotiate, and bargain with God—even to evoke the Almighty's name in casual conversation, as in saying "Thank God" for a spell of good weather or a fortuitous occurrence—obscured and undermined what he believed to be the true meaning of prayer, much less the true meaning of God. Kaplan distrusted sentimentality, too. *Yizkor*, the three-times-a-year memorial prayer for the dead, epitomized what he thought was all wrong with the traditional worship service. Repetitive, hollow, long on tears and short on substance, it represented the Jews' "national stupidity" in full flower. When it came to prayer, Kaplan had something else in mind: the expression of Judaism's deepest "spiritual values"; the means by which to cultivate a "sense of belonging to the Jewish people, past, present and future." An opportunity for thanksgiving, for acknowledging gratitude for one's blessings, for "experience[ing] the reality of God," prayer also quickened the individual's will to do good in the world, "to make the most of life."[94]

Lovely words, but what did they mean in practice? For prayer to live up to its name, "we must worship in Hebrew," Kaplan declared. "Far more important than a common bloodstream is a common language for making of many one, of families a community, of communities, however scattered in time and place, a nation that is a living organism." Furthermore, to be a "genuine and satisfying experience," prayer ought to be conducted in public. "Worship is before all else communion with that people which helps to make me holy or whole." In that connection, listening attentively to the Torah reading on a Shabbos morning was key, provided, of course, that its wisdom was understood not as the literal word of God but as a "present-day generator of social energy."[95]

And God? Where, oh where, did the Almighty figure in Kaplan's scheme of things? Prominently, indispensably. As Kaplan told a number of his rabbinical students who, in 1943, doubted His existence, "Jewish tradition minus the God belief is like the play of *Hamlet* without Hamlet." Fair enough, except for one critical detail: Kaplan's God was not the God of their forefathers, a heavenly figure who neither slumbered nor slept. His God was the "Power that makes for salvation," the "Power that makes for growth." Immanent rather than active, more of an abstraction than a being, the divine force to which Kaplan addressed his prayers didn't reside in the heavens but on earth; he didn't dwell among the people so much as live within them. God, Kaplan liked to say, was a "process." Over the years, the notion that Kaplan didn't believe in the divine took hold, giving rise to at least two well-known, heavily trafficked, and sly observations. In one, he was reputed to have addressed God as "to whom it may concern." In the other, it was said of Reconstructionism that "there's no God and Kaplan is his prophet." Both remarks pivot on the notion that the Almighty had little, if any, role to play in Kaplan's kingdom. Not so. God was an active presence with which Kaplan continually wrestled, imagined, and sought out. Owing, though, to both the novelty and the wooliness of his formulations, one more vague, opaque, and open to interpretation than the next, it's easy to see how people had the wrong impression.[96]

Once God was in the right place, secured by a proper understanding of what prayer could and couldn't do, saying the sanctioned words at the proper time and in the proper spirit had the capacity, Kaplan believed, to swell the heart. If they didn't, the fault lay not with prayer per se but with the person reciting it. "The Jew who does not thrill with exaltation when he sings the world's most stirring paean, 'Hear, O, Israel, The

Lord is Our God, the Lord is One!' is either ignorant or has the blood of a fish," he once exclaimed. Most Jews were just bored. Writing to her father on the eve of the High Holidays in 1938, Judith gave voice to that sentiment. Just as it's difficult these days to interest people in the opera, unless it's the old warhorses, it's "equally impossible to interest them in worship," she observed. "Those that crave it, crave the old stuff—the good old meaningless orthodox service and will have none of the new, whereas the others don't want any at all. So year after year, week after week, we have to sit through intolerably boring services."[97]

Ever since his earliest days at SAJ, Kaplan sought to stave off the boredom to which Judith alluded and to make the service "as intelligible and significant as possible." To pick up the pace, he kept the recitation of the Mourner's Prayer to a minimum and eliminated the Musaf Amidah (standing prayer). To render the Torah portion of the service smoother, less prone to bungling on the part of well-meaning but linguistically inept congregants who stumbled over the Hebrew, he instituted the practice of having the congregation, especially those members possessed of a strong voice and a decent Hebrew vocabulary, chant the Haftorah en masse: a "happy solution to a somewhat annoying problem." To keep things in sync with what he preached and published about, Kaplan deleted those passages in the *siddur* that referred to the chosen people, substituting more neutral phrasing for the traditional text. To keep things fresh, he added supplementary prayers or meditations in English, some of his own devising, others drawn from poems and readings that touched his soul.[98]

Kaplan also tried very hard to see to it that his sermons were relevant and "interesting," either by commenting on issues of the day or by interpreting biblical texts in light of what poets had to say about the mysteries of life. Both strategies often fell flat. Lena, who had a much better nose than her husband for what would fly and what would crash among SAJ's congregants, repeatedly told him that the pulpit was no place for talk of politics or economics. Were his people so inclined, they could always hear a lecture about such matters at Town Hall; they "didn't have to come to synagogue for it." Kaplan strongly disagreed, insisting that the pulpit was precisely the right place and the rabbi the perfect person to hold forth on those issues, even as he complained in his diary about the "exasperatingly unresponsive crowd" on whom his remarks fell. Frustrated, he was also a bit befuddled when after applying Walt Whitman's poem "Passage to India" to the first chapter in Genesis, confident his talk would be a surefire hit, he was informed by Lena that she, and everyone around her, was unable to grasp most of what he had said. Momentarily discomfited but unbowed, Kaplan tried again and again to win the minds and hearts of his people (and Lena) by trying different tactics, all the while eschewing what he called the handing out of "homiletic lollipops."[99]

Proceeding on an ad hoc basis, SAJ's leader insisted that it was his prerogative to make any and all changes. Consider this: on being called to the Torah on Yom Kippur in 1935, he took the dramatic step of eliminating the traditional words of the blessing that referred to God as having "chosen us [the Jewish people] from among all peoples" and substituting his own words, "who has brought us nigh to His service." Kaplan explained what he was about to say only minutes before he said it. In other instances, he consulted with the board or the members of SAJ's Synagogue and Liturgy Committees about a possible alteration, but he did so more out of courtesy and as a pro forma gesture of goodwill (and smart shul politics) than for their imprimatur. And sometimes, he'd convene a membership meeting to bring his congregants up to date on what lay in store. On a number of occasions Kaplan solicited suggestions from the lay leadership, only to roll his eyes in frustration when the weak-kneed among them wanted to know why they had to stand—and for twelve to fifteen minutes!—during the recitation of the Amidah prayer. Kaplan was also known, in a manner of speaking, to stamp his feet in indignation when a number of the proposals made by the old guard struck him as thinly veiled attempts to "smuggle Orthodoxy" into the proceedings.[100]

Through it all, Shabbos morning services at SAJ remained easily recognizable to most traditional shul-goers. But in the fall of 1942, Kaplan, assisted by Eisenstein, introduced a new liturgy designed to revive the practice of public prayer which, despite all of his innovations, continued to fall into "desuetude." Thinking back only a few years, Kaplan recalled how there was a time "not so long ago, when people took prayer and public worship for granted as they took God for granted." But these days, the "habit of reciting prayers and engaging in religious worship" has been "crowded out" by modern life, causing "man's spiritual values" to attenuate and ultimately disappear. With a "New Order of Service"—its mimeographed pages housed in a looseleaf notebook—and the introduction of a congregational choir for added oomph, Kaplan was determined to bring Sabbath morning services, Jewish spiritual values, and God back into circulation.[101]

With one eye on the clock and the other on his congregants' *sitzfleisch*, he revamped the service from top to bottom. He called it an "experiment," its building blocks those of speed and intelligibility rather than tradition, custom, and familiarity. For years, Kaplan had railed privately and publicly about the enervating effect that repetition had on his worshippers as well as on himself, trying everyone's patience, cooling their capacity to find meaning. At long last, here was an opportunity to do something about it by eliminating those portions of the service, such as the Musaf Amidah, that slowed things to a crawl. In addition, he made a point of deleting another set of traditional references that might, like chosenness, trouble the modern-day worshipper (as they did him), such as the resurrection of the dead and the coming of the Messiah. Reducing the time it took to read the Torah by introducing the triennial cycle, which shortened it considerably, was also high on Kaplan's agenda, but for the time being that innovative measure was placed on hold. Instead, the cantor was encouraged to chant the weekly Torah portion and the Haftorah at "breakneck speed." Tightened and trimmed, the "New Order of Service" was a brisk affair, commencing at the reasonable hour of 10:30 a.m. and running for two hours, much like the Broadway shows that his congregants so avidly relished. Its timetable looked like this:

10:30 a.m.: Services begin
10:30–11: Shaharit (first part of morning service)
11–11:50: Reading of the Torah
11:50–12:15: Sermon
12:15–12:30: Concluding portion[102]

In seeing to it that SAJ's Shabbos morning service was on a fast track, relevant, meaningful, inspiring, and decidedly non-Orthodox—a tall order—Kaplan and Eisenstein had a lot to juggle. It's no surprise they dropped the ball, creating a service that, to many, more closely resembled an intellectual exercise than an emotional experience. Where's the warmth, the "hypnotism," members, including Lena, wanted to know, pointing out that in their efforts to make religious services more comprehensible, the congregation's prayer leaders had gone too far. Kaplan's students added their voice to the chorus, claiming that the people who attended Shabbos morning services needed to feel an emotional connection to Judaism and that emending the language and sensibility of the time-honored prayers, rendering them topical and sensible, was hardly the way to go about it. Several of Kaplan's friends took a similar position, telling him, point blank, that "rationality was the last thing we should consider in worship."[103]

Enter the *Sabbath Prayer Book, with a Supplement Containing Prayers, Readings and Hymns, and with A New Translation.* Published by the Jewish Reconstructionist Foundation in spring 1945, it had been several years in the making, a group effort involving Kaplan, Eisenstein, Eugene Kohn, and Milton Steinberg. Thanks to trial and error as well as careful—and at times contentious—deliberation about what to "repudiate" and what to retain, the 573 (!) pages of this modern-day *siddur,* or what Eisenstein likened to the "script of a play," had it all: ideology, practice, traditional prayers and their modern counterparts, as well as a collection of supplementary readings that comprised more than half of the prayer book's contents. Written in both English and Hebrew, this section was organized according to theme ("Torah and the Good Life"), personal occasions ("Prayer on Behalf of Celebrating a Birthday"), and "other holidays," including the Fourth of July and Thanksgiving. The *Sabbath Prayer Book* was one of a kind. Staking out the Reconstructionist approach to prayer, the hefty text was a lot to hold, both literally and figuratively, and it came into the world freighted with expectations: "Is it too much to hope that when the prayer book finally does appear, it will at least shock our people to attention?" said an expectant Kaplan in January 1945.[104]

Anticipating a certain amount of resistance, he and his coauthors made sure to acknowledge in a thirty-page introduction that theirs wasn't a prayer book for everyone. "We are well aware that great numbers of our people are attached to the traditional prayer book by sentiments of deep and sincere piety and deplore any deviation from the time-honored text." The *Sabbath Prayer Book* was not for them but for those modern-day

Jews who, "unmoved" by prayer, had lost the need to pray or no longer knew how. A restatement, a "new form of Jewish liturgical expression," it was designed to encourage these Jews to identify themselves with and claim as their own the "heritage of habits, traditions, standards and ideals" of the Jewish people, while also furnishing them with the opportunity to solicit "divine help in self-improvement" as well as in overcoming of doubt. A bonanza of options—responsive readings, meditations, time-honored prayers in both English and Hebrew, and headings that functioned as framing devices (the "Thunderstorm Reminiscent of the Giving of the Torah as Pictured in Tradition" preceded Psalm 29; the "Joy of Communal Worship" introduced the recitation of *Mah tovu*, "How fair are your tents, O Jacob/Your tabernacles, O Israel!")—oriented the worshipper, as did a multipage chart at the prayer book's conclusion that aligned the title of a text with its author or translator. A series of capsule summaries of the Reconstructionist position on God, chosen-ness, the Messiah, and the resurrection of the dead and how it differed from that held by Jews of other denominations took up another couple of pages of the introduction. Though it stopped short of providing directions on when to sit or stand, when to pray silently or in audible communion with others, the introduction encouraged worshippers to "create a balanced service, one that observes a due proportion between the new and the familiar, between singing and reading, between silent meditation and oral utterance. Used in that way, the book can help to overcome the tendency to automatism into which communal worship is liable to fall."[105]

So much was riding on the *Sabbath Prayer Book* that its proponents paid no heed to signs that its reception might be bumpier, even nastier, than that of the Haggadah, which was bumpy and nasty enough. When, for instance, the "New Order of Service" was launched nearly three years earlier, it immediately became the "cause célèbre of this season," as Eisenstein noted in his diary. Some of the "old timers" not only grumbled but left the building and made for the Jewish Center. A number of newer members also stopped coming, claiming there was little left for them to pray. Those who stayed had concerns of their own. Why "dissipate your limited energies" on this front when "nobody takes the prayers seriously, anyhow," queried a longtime SAJ member and Kaplan stalwart. Shouldn't he turn his attention to something more important? Another wondered, "Is it good for the Jews?" and wasn't entirely persuaded when told of the increased attendance that ensued ever since the new service had been implemented. A third staunch supporter thought it best if, for the duration of the war, SAJ's leader declare a "moratorium on everything except what is necessary for winning the war." He had a point. Kaplan's timing was off. During a period of prolonged uncertainty, why upset one of the few things that successfully bore the test of time and provided a sense of security?[106]

Kaplan wouldn't hear of it, any of it, and "snapped." These comments, piled one atop another, "were too much for me." Lashing out at his lay leaders, Kaplan "let loose with a good old fashioned temper tantrum," recalled Eisenstein who witnessed the scene. Disheartened and in the dumps, Kaplan resolved to sever his relations with SAJ, and "once I do that, I shall have to follow through and give up Reconstructionism as well. I may do even that. I see nothing but complete failure and frustration ahead." A big showdown was on the horizon, bringing to mind and memory the tussle at the Jewish Center some twenty years earlier, but this time, Eisenstein predicted, "they get out, not we."[107]

Eventually, things simmered down. Hoping this latest flare-up would blow over and that those he had offended would have both short memories and the capacity to forgive and forget, Kaplan apologized, attributed his outburst to frustration, and put it behind him. He would have been better served had he paid closer attention to what the laity was trying to tell him in its admittedly ham-fisted way, for he might have then realized that the consequences of tampering with the *siddur* were many and possibly dire, the stakes quite high. But the principal author and driving force behind the *Sabbath Prayer Book* failed, or chose not, to see the handwriting on the wall, not even after he inquired of Finkelstein whether he should send copies to members of the faculty and was told "he needn't bother."[108]

In the hubbub that greeted its publication, the warning signs grew fainter still. Upon the prayer book's debut in May 1945, SAJ was filled to capacity, its sanctuary abuzz. Some worshippers had come as guests of the *siddur*'s benefactors, Mr. and Mrs. Max Hillson, others in anticipation of a "sumptuous" celebratory lunch, and still others arrived at the appointed hour to see what the fuss was all about or looking to find fault. Whatever their motivation, nearly as many people filled the seats of the SAJ sanctuary that Shabbos morning as on Kol Nidre night, or so Kaplan excitedly noted in his journal. What a triumph![109]

Kaplan's excitement soon curdled. Early in June he learned what lay in store for his prayer book when a congregant, whispering in his ear of gathering storm clouds, informed him that the Agudath Harabbonim, the Union of Orthodox Rabbis, the premier association of traditional, old-school rabbis in America, had publicly announced its intention to denounce a "so-called prayer book issued by atheists and common heretics who call themselves rabbis." Several days later, on the second day of Rosh Hodesh Tammuz 5705, two hundred of its members joined to issue a *herem*, a writ of excommunication, the very first such proclamation in the organization's history to single out an individual, a rare occurrence in the annals of American Jewish history. Vigilant in its defense of what it defined as traditional Judaism, the rabbinic body had had its eye on Kaplan for decades, ever since he first assumed the pulpit at Kehilath Jeshurun, but, with a few minor exceptions, had kept its concerns to itself. This time, though, the errant rabbi had gone too far, warranting drastic measures. Branding the *Sabbath Prayer Book*, or what it preferred to call by its Hebrew title, *Seder Tefilos l'Shabbos*, a "monster," its publication a "scandal," and its author a high-handed and insolent "heretic," the organization declared a "total prohibition and total ban" on the text itself and "banished" Kaplan from the "community of Israel" until he fully repented. To emphasize the error of Kaplan's ways, the Union of Orthodox Rabbis also called forth the "bite of the snake," an ancient rabbinic curse, upon "anyone who holds this siddur in his hand or who looks at it, whether in private or in public."[110]

Stinging in its own right, the age-old proclamation colluded with modern-day spectacle, doubling its impact on the body politic and feeding its appetite for sensation. Everything about the occasion was orchestrated for maximum effect and the widest possible exposure, from being staged in the heart of midtown Manhattan, at the Hotel McAlpin, a huge facility that, ironically enough, had recently been purchased by one of Kaplan's most loyal supporters, to skillful deployment and cultivation of the press, including the *New York Times*, which few, if any, within the orbit of the right-wing Jewish community read. That a member of the Agudath Harabbonim, inflamed by the situation, set fire to the prayer book while his coreligionists looked on, approvingly and complicitly, accentuated the drama of the moment.[111]

Word of the excommunication spread as quickly, generating a slew of articles in both the Yiddish and Anglo-Jewish press, in addition to the *Times*, whose detailed, if slightly baffled, account of the proceedings reportedly "created quite a sensation." While the constituents of the Union of Orthodox Rabbis applauded its action with a hearty *yashir koakh* (well done!), everyone else was alternately dumbfounded and horrified, calling the *herem* a "bizarre act of defiance," "irresponsible," "barbarous," and "repulsive to all right thinking people"—everyone else, that is, with the exception of the pool of paid morning minyan men at SAJ that suddenly dried up; an SAJ secretary, an observant Jewish woman, who felt duty-bound to quit her position; and, most notably, Saul Lieberman, the distinguished Talmudist who had only recently joined the Seminary faculty and honored the ban's provisions by staying as far away as possible from Kaplan, even if it meant absenting himself from significant Seminary events.[112]

Those who anathematized the Union of Orthodox Rabbis' gesture saw it as a power grab, a last-ditch effort on the part of the traditional European rabbinate to assert its authority, thinking that, as one of Kaplan's champions put it, his voice at once indignant and sarcastic, a "good old bonfire may be what is needed." More egregious still was its too-close-for comfort resemblance to the Nazi practice of book burning and its trampling on freedom of worship, responses that had the effect of translating the *herem* from an internal Jewish affair into a thoroughly American one. Still others argued that employing the age-old rite of humiliation, the equivalent of a social boycott, in the United States in 1945, and bringing it back from the limbo to which it had been rightly consigned, made Judaism and its religious leaders look "ridiculous," giving both a black eye.[113]

Uncertain of how to mount the most effective countermeasures but determined to say and do something, anything, in response, a number of Kaplan's peers took to sermonizing. Others, like the members of the Rabbinical Assembly, the official body of the Conservative rabbinate, issued a strongly worded public rebuke, singling out the book burning as a "clear violation of Jewish law . . . a *hillul hashem*," a desecration of God's exalted name. (To some ears, though, its broadside sounded too timid, too mindful of and even deferential to the long-standing animus against Kaplan held by elements of the JTS faculty.) The most aggrieved, especially SAJ's congregants, formed the Jewish Citizens Committee for Freedom of Worship, calling on like-minded people everywhere to make known their dismay and extending an invitation to Albert Einstein, among other luminaries, to join the committee's roster of signatories. Though the renowned scientist declined, explaining that "to take these fools in clerical garb seriously is to show them too much honor," others had no such qualms and rallied round the cause.[114]

Amid the heartfelt petitions and proclamations, Milton Steinberg put it best in a private, two-page letter to his former teacher and coauthor, speaking for himself as well as his wife. "Edith and I are not quite certain we know how to address or what to say to one who is under a ban of Excommunication. Having assumed that such medieval barbarities went out with the fifteenth century we have failed to keep ourselves *au courant* with the etiquette of such situations." All the same, both of them had been "filled with a mixture of amusement and fury . . . amusement at the ineptness and grotesquerie of the gesture, its opéra bouffe, Maurice Schwartz–Yiddish Art Theatre character. And fury that these men should have presumed to pass judgment on you, that the reward they dispense for selfless devotion to freedom and its future should be the hurling of insults and curses." If that wasn't enough to console Kaplan, Steinberg concluded his lengthy letter by pointing out that his father, an Orthodox Jew but "rationally so," was "outraged" by the conduct of his coreligionists. Although he might have "winced" at a couple of passages in the new prayer book, "he loves and reveres the book as a whole"; his "cronies" like it, too.[115]

Despite this and other shows of support that took the form of "unprecedented demand" for and increased sales of the "prayer book that has stirred American Jewry," Kaplan was laid low by the *herem.* It took the wind out of his sails, deflating and even humiliating him. "What a shattering effect this exhibition of moral degeneracy on the part of men who call themselves rabbis has upon me I can hardly express," he wrote in his diary, adding "I find it exceedingly hard to carry on." After four decades of laboring in the vineyards of Jewish life, had it come to this? That his name was now a household word not on account of his good deeds but as the result of "character assassination"? For the very first time in his long rabbinical career, Kaplan stayed clear of Sabbath morning services for reasons other than ill health. He couldn't bring himself to attend.[116]

The excommunicant didn't keep away from the sanctuary or remain on the sidelines for too long. Drawing comfort from the example of Spinoza, whose reputation grew rather than diminished in the wake of his own excommunication in 1656, Kaplan quickly regained his equilibrium. He took up the cudgels against Orthodox Judaism with renewed vigor, his sense of himself and the legitimacy of his mission intact—and strengthened. Putting on a good front, Kaplan gathered his strength and rallied. In language as fierce as that used against him by the Union of Orthodox Rabbis, he publicly condemned the *herem* as the handiwork of an "hysterical lynching mob" and described its participants as "rabbinical gangsters who resort to nazi [*sic*] methods." The issue at hand, Kaplan went on to say, was not whether Reconstructionism was right or wrong; it's whether men should use the "power of a boycott" against those with whom they disagree. "These 'rabbonim' seem to think that freedom of worship is either a joke, or something meant only for the Goyim."[117]

A month later, Kaplan published an even more full-bodied response in "A Challenge to Freedom of Worship: A

Statement," a pamphlet produced by the Jewish Reconstructionist Foundation for the edification of its supporters. An amalgam of exposition and testimony, enunciation and denunciation, the thirty-two-page document also contained a hard-hitting article by Eisenstein that sought to explain what provoked the Agudath Harabbonim's hostility as well as a battery of supportive private letters and public resolutions. Kaplan's feisty contribution constituted the pamphlet's core. Bristling with barely suppressed anger, it began with words that, to some historically minded readers, might have echoed *l'affaire Dreyfus*. "The affair of the *herem*," Kaplan wrote, "is not a pleasant one to discuss. As far as the general public is concerned, it were best to ring down the curtain of silence on the entire shocking episode. But for us Jews it would be a mistake to treat that episode merely as a seven-day sensation." How, then, should they understand it? As a "malignant cancer in the body of Jewish life" that needed to be removed. He went on to define the ban as a dangerous form of coercion, an expression of "force" that had no place in America where freedom of worship held sway. In the Holy Land, though, where the Orthodox rabbinate was "in the saddle," it might have a second lease on life, enabling its representatives to "exercise a stranglehold on the spiritual potentialities of the new settlement." Right-thinking Jews everywhere could not allow that to happen, Kaplan concluded, not if we want to "find a place for ourselves in the future order of mankind, which we hope will be one of universal freedom, justice and peace."[118]

Temporarily flattened, Kaplan rebounded, recasting the black mark on his name as an opportunity rather than a defeat. "All this goes to show how essential it is for our people to be reeducated," he declared, "so that they might be emancipated from those elements in the tradition which has long been outgrown and cultivate those elements which deserve to live." Onward Reconstructionists![119]

But moving forward was not yet in the cards; a second act awaited. In late November, Kaplan was informed by Finkelstein that Ginzberg, Lieberman, and Marx had submitted a lengthy piece to *Hadoar*, the Hebrew weekly, in which they condemned the burning of Kaplan's *siddur* as an "abominable deed" but then went after him tooth and claw. Would he care to respond? Having had his fill of the "tumult," Kaplan declined, much to Finkelstein's relief: the "sooner a quietus is put on the controversy, the better."[120]

The self-styled "tribunal of three" had no such scruples. The article they published in Hebrew early in December, an English translation of which appeared in the *Jewish Exponent*, made the earlier critique of *The New Haggadah* look like the taunts of a playground bully. Taking on Kaplan, the *Sabbath Prayer Book*, and the remarks he had recently made in his pamphlet on religious freedom, they were unsparing and unforgiving, their tone verging on the contemptuous. Ginzberg, Lieberman, and Marx maintained that the position the Agudath Harabbonim had taken vis-à-vis the prayer book was warranted; its only mistake was having gone about it in the wrong way. In lieu of a ban, the organization should have issued a "loud protest" against Dr. Kaplan's "disrespectful" treatment of the "sanctities of our people," its "crude mutilation" of the traditional order of the prayers, and its "ridiculous and stammering Hebrew." Without taking a breath, the three went on to take a series of potshots at the shallowness of Kaplan's Judaic knowledge before deriding his comments about the Chief Rabbinate in Palestine as unfounded. Their parting shot was particularly, needlessly cruel. Years ago, they wrote, "we gave him a hint, and he did not heed it; we pricked him and he did not feel the sting. His latest acts left us no other alternative but to express our views publicly. This is not a time to keep silent and we say to Dr. Kaplan: 'What hast thou to do with Halakha [Jewish law]?' Get thee to Agadah [homiletics]."[121]

No sooner did Kaplan recover from this display of verbal pillorying than he faced another one from an entirely different quarter: the pen of the biblical scholar Theodor Gaster, whose razor-edged critique of the *Sabbath Prayer Book* appeared in the February 1946 issue of *Commentary*. Deliberately sidestepping the *herem*, he analyzed the text on its own terms rather than as a hot-button religious phenomenon. Gaster's take was no less scathing than that of his rabbinical counterparts; given his command of the English language, it was probably worse. By his lights, the prayer book's central concepts did not "hold water . . . by propounding them so rashly, a movement pregnant with so much potential good has all but shipwrecked itself." Unduly doctrinaire, the text, Gaster charged, also suffered from an excess of literalism, displaying an "almost grotesque insensitivity, an unawareness of symbolism, a deafness to poetry." As for the contents of the new prayers that Kaplan and his colleagues had written, the less said the better, though that didn't stop Gaster from coming up with an extraordinarily vivid clutch of sentences: "They bleat where they ought to cry; murmur where they ought to roar; tap on the doors of heaven where they ought to hammer and beat." Nothing Kaplan or Eisenstein might say could measure up.[122]

Under a cloud, subject to a constant barrage of criticism, a less resolute and determined person might have quit the scene, gone quietly into the night. But not Kaplan. He refused to let the *herem* define him, balking at the notion that this would be his legacy. Like the Energizer Bunny, he kept on going, buoyed by the support of his congregants who, to their credit, found humor the most effective form of defense. In "He Made a Little List," an affectionate parody that summed up Kaplan's deeds, or misdeeds, they had the last word. Sung to the tune of Gilbert and Sullivan's patter song "I've Got a Little List," from *The Mikado*, it went like this:

As I pondered Jewish problems in my study, all alone
I made a little list—I made a little list
Of words, ideas, and concepts that our people have
outgrown
And that never would be missed, that never would be
missed!
The *asher bocher banu* that was said before the Torah
(The Chosen-People concept that all modern minds
deplore—ah)
The blood-and-thunder plagues and pests that made the
Seder gory
The double standard *bima* that went back to ages hoary,
The personal Messiah on which the Orthodox insist—
They'd none of them be missed—they'd none of them be
missed.[123]

5

Reconstruction

"MY DAYS DO ANYTHING but creep along. They seem to fly by like the telegraph poles when you sit in a fast moving express. Some days I put in as much as nine or ten hours of work; other days I dawdle away the time" reading and thinking, Kaplan, then sixty-seven, noted in the summer of 1948. At an age when most of his contemporaries had folded their tents, he was busy pitching new ones, his mind as fertile, his spirit as restless, as ever. Exclamations of "Eureka!" speckled his journal as he excitedly hit upon new locutions of which "defrosting" tradition was one, formulated fresh concepts such as "peoplehood," and honed his theory of soterics. Kaplan's enthusiasm for intellectual exchange remained undiminished throughout the postwar years, prompting his supporters on his seventieth birthday to liken him to an "adventurer of ideas," as if he were an aging buccaneer of the intellect. His appetite for ambitious projects also showed few signs of abating, propelling him to establish a

University of Judaism on the West Coast and plan an international gathering in Jerusalem—a modern-day Sanhedrin—to draft a constitution for and "renew [the] covenant" with the Jewish people. "I am by no means run out of ideas. On the contrary, I find myself at the present time of my life in the category of the *ma'ayan hamitgaber*," Kaplan wrote in 1951 in a voice at once complimentary and humble, referring to a passage in *Pirke Avot* (6:1) in which a person devoted to the study of Torah is likened—usually by someone else—to an "everflowing stream" and blessed.[1]

Seeing to it that Reconstructionism remained afloat was another of Kaplan's preoccupations. Making sure *The Reconstructionist* lived up to its potential as the "main instrument" for keeping the movement at the forefront, he beefed up its contents by adding accessible, chatty new features. One was "Random Thoughts," the source, among other things, of the widely circulated quote about the past having a "vote—but not a veto"; another was "Know How to Ask." The latter was the magazine's version of the *bintel brief*, the popular Yiddish advice column in the *Jewish Daily Forward*. It posed questions from readers who wanted to know "how can Reconstructionism appeal to the ordinary person, since it is abstract and intellectual and lacks emotion," and "can you please explain what you mean by the word 'salvation.' " Kaplan answered clearly and, for him, succinctly, cautioning his readers in the first instance that the "fact that Reconstructionism has an intellectual appeal should surely not be held against it. But that does not mean that it is abstract or lacking in emotion." As for his answer to the second query, he put it this way: "Salvation means deliverance from those evils, external and internal, which prevent man from realizing his maximum potentialities. Stated positively, it means the achievement of maximum personality." Kaplan much preferred these kinds of queries (even if he had to write them himself) to the "smart-alecky" ones he often encountered as a guest lecturer when the question he was most frequently asked was to clarify the Reconstructionist position on the eating of shrimp. "Here I was trying to put a bit of soul into their Judaism," he hotly recalled, "and all they could think of was their stomach."[2]

When not harrumphing, Kaplan embarked on a number of book projects, notable, he once quipped, for their "avoirdupois," among them *The Future of the American Jew* (1948), *Judaism without Supernaturalism* (1958), and *The Religion of Ethical Nationhood: Judaism's Contribution to World Peace* (1970). Notable, too, for helping postwar American Jews to "steer clear of the Scylla of denominationalism and the Charybdis of non-commitment," these generously sized texts provided a new generation with the vocabulary and the tools with which to feel at home in the world as Jews. When not writing, the Reconstructionist leader took to the airwaves, the recording studio, and the television station ("I'm told I was wonderful") to sound the drum on behalf of Reconstructionism. He even lent his big birthdays, of which there were many, to the cause. "My birthday hasn't arrived yet and it has already been celebrated thrice and twice more to go, with a different speech each time," a bemused Kaplan wrote Harold Schulweis, his prized disciple, in 1956, on the occasion of his seventy-fifth birthday. "That's going some."[3]

Retirement was out of the question, even if it might have looked as if Kaplan was winding down. In the summer of 1944, he informed the SAJ board yet again of his desire to be relieved of his congregational responsibilities. After "considerable discussion" (read foot-dragging), the board acceded to his request, and early in 1945, SAJ's founder and longtime leader formally stepped down from its pulpit, becoming "leader emeritus." A year later, he relinquished his post as dean of the Teachers Institute, claiming there was "no sense to my pretending to be Dean, since there was nothing left for me to do."

A playful Kaplan at home with Lena in Westport, Connecticut, 1952.
The Collection of Hadassah K. Musher, New York.

In both instances, Kaplan's decision was prompted by waning interest rather than waning powers: he had had enough.[4]

From time to time, especially after Lena and he had purchased a pretty place with a small plot of land in Westport, Connecticut, in 1951—"I love that little house," he exclaimed—Kaplan contemplated "cutting loose" from all of his responsibilities, content to putter around without a to-do list to consult or people to see. What might it be like to "get away from all these problems [of Jewish life], read all the wonderful books on my shelves that are wanting to be read, and listening to some of the many marvelous recordings of music and poetry," he wondered. No sooner did that prospect cross his mind than he'd swiftly rule it out lest he "might discover that I was living in a vacuum. It is fear of such a state of mind that inhibits me from asking Finkelstein to arrange for my retirement,"

Kaplan related, adding a few months later, that the "fear of boredom and loneliness is what keeps me where I am."[5]

Inactivity was not for him, nor was giving in to his aging body. Though his teeth gave him no end of trouble, his legs ached, his stomach churned, and he tired easily, Kaplan paid little mind to these physical ailments or to the increasingly frequent dentist and doctor visits they occasioned except to jot them down in his diary. With so much left to do, he could not allow himself to succumb to any sign of bodily weakness. Redoubling his efforts to promote the "mental and moral healing" of his coreligionists, Kaplan experienced a second wind. His long-held determination to secure a Jewish future was rendered even more pressing by the devastation of European Jewry, which gave him nightmares, and the birth of the State of Israel, whose formal declaration of independence he breathlessly followed down to the wire despite the considerable time lag between Los Angeles, where he was at the time, and Tel Aviv, the site of the declaration. "In fifteen minutes from now, the new Jewish State will officially come into being," read Kaplan's diary entry for "May 14, 1948, 2:45 p.m. corresponding to 11:45 p.m. in E.Y.," Kaplan's abbreviation for *Eretz Yisrael.* Several hours later, he recorded that at 5:30 p.m. "Judith and Ira just phoned telling me that Truman has issued a statement at 6:01 p.m. (N.Y. time) recognizing the Jewish State. It is simply impossible for me to describe how I feel at this moment. Again and again, *barukh sheheheyanu v'kemanu lazman hazeh*," penning this shorthand reference to the traditional celebratory words in Hebrew.[6]

Improved relations with Finkelstein, who, for the moment, seemed to have softened his opposition to Reconstructionism, also played no small part in spurring Kaplan on. Showering him with invitations to events from which he had long been excluded, the Seminary's president asked his former nemesis to draw up "expansionist" plans for what the institution might look like after the war. So pleased was Kaplan by Finkelstein's apparent change of heart, so energized by the chance to think big on behalf of his longtime academic home, that he relaxed his customary suspicions about his superior's motives, choosing not to dwell on whether he had seen the light or was acting opportunistically. Instead, Kaplan accepted—and rose—to the challenge by advocating that the Seminary "convert" from a theological seminary into a full-fledged academic institution where all manner of subjects, from the arts and social service to rabbinics and Jewish education, would be dispensed to a broad constituency by those at the top of their game and their respective disciplines. What Kaplan proposed was nothing less than the Seminary's "metamorphosis," its transformation from a rabbinical school into a university of Judaism, a term he used interchangeably as a talking point, where it worked well enough, and as a proper name, where, too "fancy," it did not. Either way, the designation meant a lot to Kaplan, signaling the project's "novelty of purpose."[7]

A reconstituted JTS would become the central address, the nucleus around which the various elements of the modern Jewish experience would cluster. Working in tandem, the arts and education, theology and Jewish history would stem the ongoing "disintegration" of Jewish life, while also combating the fragmentation brought on by its characteristically duplicative, unwieldy denominationalism. At its core, the University of Judaism would convey what a "de-denominationalizing institution" might look like. Internal factors like these rather than the discriminatory practices of America's leading colleges and universities, then in the news, propelled Kaplan. Not for him a "racial ghetto into which we would be driven in on ourselves by the ill will of the world," a sleight-of-hand reference to Yeshiva University, which had just been established, and Brandeis University, soon to arrive on the scene. What he had in mind was no "mere caricature of Jewishness" but something altogether different: a university of Judaism, not a Jewish university.[8]

Determined, as always, to make his ideas heard, the University of Judaism's biggest fan sought to whip up enthusiasm by lobbying members of the JTS board, holding a press conference, giving lengthy public addresses, and publishing one of them—"A University of Judaism—A Compelling Need," in the form of a pamphlet-cum-brief that set forth the whys and wherefores of his latest scheme. As he wrote in his opening salvo, at a time when one denomination was "alienated from one another," and the synagogue no longer the center of community, relying on religion to unite all Jews was futile. "One might as well try to get the chicken back into the egg." Best, then, to stop "groping and fumbling" and adopt the "civilizational approach" in which those who "belong to the same civilization shall want and welcome one another and not regard one another as rivals and as a thorn in each other's side." How to make that happen? By establishing a new kind of academy at which future generations of leaders would be trained to meet the conditions of Jewish life created by the "fruitful differentiation of Jewish activity." Anticipating the objections of those who thought this proposal far-fetched, even "fantastic," or, more damning still, that JTS was ill-suited to what he had in mind, Kaplan concluded his densely packed text by reassuring his readers that there was "much more to the Seminary than meets the eye . . . [it's] a veritable Niagara of the spirit that could be made to turn the wheels of Jewish life. What it needs is a University of Judaism to convert that knowledge into living energy."[9]

As much an ideological statement as an institutional one, Kaplan's call for an unencumbered institution of advanced Jewish learning, free of labels, furnished him with the opportunity to implement what he called "peoplehood" or "Jewish oneness." Implicit in much of his prewar writings on community, this concept took on more weight, an enlarged presence, in the postwar era, where it figured prominently as one of the ways by which Kaplan reckoned with the Shoah as well as with the emergence of the State of Israel. A central plank of his thinking about unity in an increasingly fragmented, unstable world, peoplehood extended the frame of the Jewish collective, enlarging its parameters beyond that of the congregation, the community, the nation, and the state. Kaplan may have cared little for people in the flesh, especially his coreligionists whose shortcomings he constantly dwelled on, but he fancied them in the abstract: hard to live with, Jewish people were good to think with. By coming up with a new rationale for honoring and sustaining Jewish identity, peoplehood enabled Kaplan in one fell swoop to acknowledge how much had been lost with the destruction of European Jewry, circumvent the glaringly obvious limitations of nationalism, and find a worthy substitute for the affective, mushy, hard-to-pin-down or put-into-words ties that bound the Jewish people to one another. Having anathematized sentiment and prioritized reason, he couldn't very well trumpet the mystical wellsprings of belonging. Enter peoplehood, a conceptual device that covered all the bases.[10]

Despite Kaplan's enthusiasm and Finkelstein's endorsement, the prospect of making over the Seminary into something brand-new generated a lot of noise but little else; it went nowhere fast. Few found the need for a university of Judaism compelling. Others were not convinced that JTS was up to the task, while still others were just as convinced that it shouldn't be put in that position in the first place. And still others, perhaps the most vocal among the naysayers, feared lest Kaplan's heavy hand open the back door to Reconstructionism. Derailed but not defeated, he quickly shifted gears and, with Finkelstein's blessing, tried again, this time putting his ideas to the test in what seemed to both men to be a sunnier and much more congenial environment: the West Coast, where a fierce, intransigent "sectarianism" had yet to take root and the weight of the past did not weigh too heavily—not quite a tabula rasa but close enough. Kaplan "ought to be able to do in Los Angeles what I would not be able to do here," Finkelstein told one of his closest associates, adding "that would be a flank move" against those resistant to change.[11]

Planting the flag of the University of Judaism in the City of Angels, a process that unfolded in fits and starts, added a spring to Kaplan's step. "I have lived more intensely and enjoyably than I have in years," he recalled with relish, singling out the cast of characters he had encountered along the way, from the owner of a chain of West Coast restaurants to Hollywood moguls, among them the producer of the Hopalong Cassidy movies. "I was away from home, met new people, attempted new undertakings with a measure of success, committed no blunders, made no faux pas," he wrote. "I liked what I had to do and proved to myself that I can work with people with whom I don't see eye to eye." Kaplan's days were full, so "busy and dizzy," that he often "lost track of the appointments and meetings which have kept me on the go or on the run," adding whimsically and topically, " 'What made Mordecai run?' "[12]

All that running around took its toll. Laying the groundwork for a university of Judaism was a demanding assignment on its own terms; logistics made it even more taxing. Stuck in a hotel room some three thousand miles from home; living out of a suitcase for long stretches at a time; eating too many starchy, oversalted meals in restaurants, hell on both his stomach and soul (few eateries were kosher); and being driven around town rather than walking its streets, as was his wont, Kaplan didn't have an easy time of it. On occasion, Lena accompanied him, making his transplanted life much more bearable, even pleasurable. When she stayed home, he made do with her frequent letters, which, he told her, were "as sweet and full of goodies just like your cookies when they come out right." In her correspondence, Lena regaled her husband with the latest gossip, while his described what went well and what didn't—like being saddled with a roommate-cum-chaperone in the person of Simon Greenberg.[13]

A high-ranking Seminary official and Finkelstein confidante, Greenberg kept tabs on Kaplan and reined him in lest he go off script by talking more about Reconstructionism than was necessary. But then it wasn't so much Greenberg's presence or his portfolio as much as his piety—he *davened* three times a day and scrupulously observed Shabbat—that "irked" Kaplan, setting him on edge. "Spending the Sabbath in one room with a Tsaddik was a new experience," he devilishly recounted. Greenberg "wouldn't think of eating in the [hotel] restaurant and paying or having the meal sent up to the room and signing for it. Of course, I didn't want to act the Shabbos goy." Consequently, Mrs. Friedgut, the good wife of the Seminary's "man in the field," was prevailed upon. She supplied the two men with hard boiled eggs for breakfast, a roast chicken for lunch, and stewed peaches for both meals. "On the whole," a hungry Kaplan later reflected, "it was to me like half a fast day till the Shabbat was over." Eventually, though, his hunger subsided, as did his unease. He grew accustomed to having Greenberg about, even becoming quite fond of him, and felt remorseful at having complained in the first place. After having recently read of the last days of the Warsaw Ghetto, Kaplan confessed to Lena, "I grew ashamed of bellyaching about any kind of personal inconvenience."[14]

Between winning adherents and "neutralizing" the opposition, Greenberg and Kaplan had their work cut out for them. New York–style denominationalism might have been foreign to Los Angeles, but of boundary making and communal politicking there was plenty. Soon enough, the city's Reform and

Orthodox congregations made known their displeasure at the Conservative movement's territorial ambitions, thwarting its plans by refusing to climb aboard. A substantial Yiddishist population, some of whom were as "well-to-do as the 'Deitscher,'" or German Jews, also drew a line in the sand and balked at cooperating with a religious outfit like JTS. Finkelstein's vague, conditional, and vacillating promises of substantial financial support didn't help matters, generating suspicion and, ultimately, bad feelings when the funds didn't appear to be forthcoming anytime soon. In the end, whatever hopes Kaplan harbored of establishing a nondenominational institution of advanced Jewish learning and doing right by his much-vaunted notion of peoplehood dissolved in the acid of intramural competition. And yet, he persevered, writing in the summer of 1947 of his determination to see things through. "I am too much committed to the idea of the University of Judaism to permit the fact that the institution as planned in LA falls short of what it ought to be to prevent me from taking an active part in translating that idea into reality."[15]

Housed at first in a couple of rented classrooms at Temple Sinai, the University of Judaism opened its doors in 1948, its part-time faculty supplemented by visiting professors from the East Coast and Europe, among them Martin Buber, Abraham Joshua Heschel, and Kaplan, who happily reported that his classes on midrash and philosophies of religion drew a good-sized crowd even when pianist Arthur Rubinstein was in town at the same time and tickets to his concerts a hot commodity. More of an adult education center than a full-fledged, degree-granting university, with varied offerings in arts and crafts, current events, dance, drama, music, group work as well as in Bible, history, Hebrew, and Yiddish that attracted a largely female, and lay, audience, the school billed itself as the "west coast branch" of the Jewish Theological Seminary of America, or, as the *New York Times* informed its readers, the "western unit set up by the Jewish Seminary." In time, the University of Judaism struck out on its own, affiliated with but not run by the Seminary, and took root in Los Angeles. These days, it has a new name: the American Jewish University.[16]

Things were no easier for Kaplan as he struggled throughout the postwar era to put Reconstructionism on a firmer footing, noting gloomily that it took a pound of energy to produce an ounce of results. Painfully aware of Reconstructionism's reputation for being a "cover" for American Jews who preferred to do less than more; frustrated by the longtime members of his own flock who still didn't understand what it was all about—knowledgeable Reconstructionist Jews, Kaplan conceded in 1947, were as "rare as hen's teeth"; given to wondering if his timing was off and Reconstructionism had come too early for the first generation and too late for the second generation of twentieth-century American Jews; and smarting under the tart observation made by Rabbi Joachim Prinz, whom Kaplan assiduously but unsuccessfully cultivated, that Reconstructionism was "too highbrow and lacked Hasidic fire," he wilted. Kaplan did more than wilt when confronted with the more forceful critique of clergy like Milton Steinberg, whose intellectual gifts he valued and whom he had long thought of as an ally as well as an acolyte. He fumed—and for good reason. From the pulpit and the printed page, the celebrated Park Avenue Synagogue rabbi publicly made known the extent of his dissent, distancing himself from Reconstructionism. He admired its flexibility, "intelligence and candor," "non-revelationist non-halakhic ideology of observance," and role as "chief theorizer, prod and rallying point," but not much else. Flagging the movement's "irresolution," "inadequate" conception of God and heavy-handed style of expression—"not light or easy, and certainly not beautiful or incendiary"—Steinberg also had it in for Kaplan, whom he described as "either too much or too little a theologian." Though he acknowledged that no one felt more keenly about the limitations of modern Jewish life or was as determined to correct them as his former teacher, even so, Kaplan, in his estimation, remained "too theoretical for secularists and not theoretical enough for the traditionally or metaphysically minded."[17]

Wounded by Steinberg's observations, and feeling sorry for himself, Kaplan came to believe that he had had about as much impact on American Jewish history as the weather, and that to expect any form of Jewish life to flourish in the New World was "like expecting dates and figs to grow in the arctic." Why do I bother? "Why, then, do I go on?" But go on he did, telling himself that it was the "decent and self-respecting" thing to do. It's not that Kaplan's disappointments were more rhetorical than real, voiced rather than felt, of the moment rather than enduring. They were real, constant, and hurtful enough. But at no point, even in his darkest hour, was he prepared to surrender his long-held beliefs in a reconstructed Judaism and the power of peoplehood. Too much was at stake; besides, his commanding sense of self wouldn't allow it: the "cause of Judaism," Kaplan was wont to say, "is so much part of me." Little wonder, then, that he tacked between despair and determination, between wringing his hands and doing something about it, ultimately resolving that "if I want Reconstructionism to make headway, I must be Mohammed coming to the mountain."[18]

Kaplan took to the road, to Boston and Pittsfield, Harrisburg, Chicago, and St. Louis, among other cities, where he rallied the troops, such as they were; met one-on-one with local rabbis to encourage them to sign on; and counseled the laity, much to its bafflement, on the importance of "organic community." Time and again, this peripatetic personality was certain he had captivated the large crowds that had gathered to hear him speak, only to learn afterwards that fewer than 50 percent had understood him—enough to deplete the enthusiasm of the most gung ho of travelers, which this latter-day Mohammed was not. Travel upset his ego, along with his cherished routine, and consumed too much of his time; its meager returns were incommensurate with his investment of effort and expense. Nor did any great surge in membership or financial support result from his wanderings. The only thing Kaplan had to show for these efforts were stories. Recounted at length and with bemusement around the dinner table and in his journal, they almost made up for the lack of tangible dividends. One can read, for instance, of the time when Kaplan requested of his hosts, affluent Boston Jews, that out of fidelity to the dietary laws he be served fish at Friday night dinner. Eager to oblige and show the colors, the woman of the house proudly served her guest of honor gefilte fish, which wasn't quite what he had in mind. Or take the time Kaplan was walking to shul on Shabbos morning in a city not his own when the incessant tooting of a passing car horn caught his attention, stopping him in his tracks. "Get in," said the driver, rolling down his window. Kaplan declined. The driver persisted. Kaplan explained that he preferred to walk, at which point the driver informed him that his name was Bernard Ginsburg and that he happened to be a relative of Ahad Ha'am. Kaplan got into the car—but asked to be dropped off a block away from his destination.[19]

Grist for his mill, these and other comparable incidents left him with a funny feeling. Ever since its inception, Reconstructionism had waffled on the issue of ritual observance. Ample room was made for "wants"—thirteen of them, to be exact, including "we want the Jewish home to live up to its traditional standards of virtue and piety"—but the traditional dos and don'ts had to fend for themselves. Insistent that Jewish ritual observance be volitional rather than coercive, animated by pleasure and, if need be, by convenience, Kaplan banished discipline and obligation, along with sin, to the outskirts of his religious philosophy. Grace notes rather than commandments, rituals like kashruth or Sabbath observance were lovely—well, more than lovely—but their observance was heralded as a matter of individual inclination, not a collective imperative. When Reconstructionism was new and finding its way, its fluid position on ritual behavior made sense. By the time the shine had worn off, too many American Jews, mistaking latitude for license, believed that Reconstructionism absolved them of doing little more than light candles on Friday night; better yet, it seemed to get them off the hook, guilt-free. All too aware of the situation at the grass roots, where the "main streets of every Jewish community in America bear testimony to the blatant abandonment" of Jewish rituals, Kaplan started to wonder if Reconstructionism had blundered by not making more of them. Perhaps if it had taken a stronger, less equivocal stand or issued a set of standards, its people would have valued Shabbos and kashruth more than they did, or a greater number of American Jews might have enlisted in Reconstructionism's ranks.[20]

Enough second-guessing. After much wrangling behind the scenes and within the pages of *The Reconstructionist*, a pamphlet titled *Toward a Guide for Jewish Ritual Usage* was published in 1942. It took a crack at establishing a definitive position on ritual behavior, though it came with a caution (a warning label?) that the "reader must not expect to be given minute prescriptions on how to conduct his ritual behavior." Designed to be "exploratory" rather than prescriptive, encouraging rather than peremptory, the text set forth the principles that guided the movement's hand—a willingness to modify and reinterpret as well as preserve, maintain, and when warranted, cast aside; the practice of tolerance rather than a rush to judgment; valuing intelligence rather than authority—and contrasted them with the "onesidedness" of the competition. Where Reform,

Orthodox, and Conservative Judaism fell short, each placing a different obstacle or burden in the way of ritual observance, the "elasticity" of the Reconstructionist approach would save the day.[21]

Kaplan could and often did speak lyrically about Jewish rituals, referring to them as Judaism's "sign language." When literary critic and author Charles Angoff informed Kaplan of feeling puzzled and somewhat put off by seeing him fall to his knees during the Aleinu prayer of the Yom Kippur service, the latter sought to assuage the critic's discomfort by explaining that he was "merely using gesture instead of words." " 'You mean, "pantomime"?' Angoff said. 'That's it,' I said. 'The use of pantomime to express ideas and also to evoke those ideas in yourself as well as in others.' " On another occasion, Kaplan attributed his own observance to the "desire to do something each day that is concretely and distinctively Jewish." Little of that language, or motivation, suffused the 1942 appeal to ritual attentiveness. Lumbering rather than inspiring, bogged down by talk of religious authority and "definite disvalues," everything about it, from its title to its text, was either too abstract or too utilitarian. Who could possibly warm to a call for "ritual usage"? Few did, apparently, for six years later, Kaplan tried again by devoting a chapter in his 1948 opus, *The Future of the American Jew*, to furnishing postwar American Jews with a "satisfactory rationale" for making the "most of their Judaism."[22]

Much of the chapter's text centered on the need for and the benefits of a modern-day ritual compendium to enable those American Jews who were neither "dogmatic traditionalists" nor "opinionated secularists" to find "self-fulfillment" as well as a heightened sense of the collective through ritual observance. "A modern guide, unlike the ancient and medieval codes," Kaplan declared, "must be free from the authoritarian, absolutist approach; it must not show an excessive reverence for precedent." Its appeal must reside in a "sympathetic insight into the actual religious wants of living Jews, and be helpful to them in satisfying those wants to the very best of their ability." At no point did he refer directly to the *Shulchan Aruch*, the ritual guidebook that dogged, and darkened, much of his career, but its presence is palpable, much like the negative space on an artist's canvas. His ritual guidebook was everything its predecessor was not. One might even call it the anti–*Shulchan Aruch:* a Jewish ritual compendium that was as unlike the traditional text as could be while still lighting the way. Dispensing with prohibitions in favor of "affirmative adjustment," it inveighed against uniformity, welcomed diversity, and placed the individual rather than God at its core. Characteristically, it stopped short of specifying which rituals called for adherence and which might be given a pass, leaving that decision to those who leafed through its pages.[23]

More like a running argument than an established set of protocols, the Reconstructionist ritual handbook did not settle into a more permanent groove until nearly fifteen years later when, in 1962, *A Guide to Jewish Ritual Usage* was released. An updated, reworked, and expanded version of Kaplan's earlier contributions, it opened with the customary caveats before offering a catalog of suggestions. Neither "infallible," nor "unalterable," this text, as Ira Eisenstein, its editor, affirmed in its preface, was far from the "last word on the subject"; in no way was it to be construed as a "code." Why, then, was its publication necessary? In order to "standardize those ritual usages so that they may symbolize the moral and spiritual values which Jews are expected to cherish." High on the list was keeping the Sabbath, whose observance was designed to "enable man to become more human." Prayer, preferably in public, and if not, at home; family meals; *zemirot* (songs) accompanied by the sounds of the piano or that of recorded music; "creative rest" (as opposed to "physical recess"); reading a Jewish book or periodical; and, of course, the lighting of candles and the saying of *kiddush* were encouraged. Whereas "refraining from the switching on and off of electric lights and the use of the elevator adds nothing to the Sabbath's power to experience life as worthwhile, and, in fact, tends to make the observance of the Sabbath tedious and burdensome." A section on "what to do if the full observance of the Sabbath is impossible" rounded out the proceedings, underscoring the eyes-wide-open, realistic approach characteristic of Reconstructionist Judaism. Much the same could be said of its easygoing treatment of kashruth, "abolishing or relaxing" many of the ritual's traditional strictures and reassuring readers that even a "token observance of *kashrut* would still be possible in abstinence from pig and forbidden sea food." How far could one go before tipping the scales? Decision-making was left to the individual but with a ringing proviso, with which the guidebook came to a close: "He should, however, endeavor to observe as many of the traditional regulations as he can observe without frustrating what to him are more important permanent interests."[24]

Hard to pin down, the relationship of Reconstructionist Judaism to ritual had as much to do with Kaplan's personal uncertainties as it did with the movement's growing pains. He waffled, temporized, and changed his mind from one year to the next and often in between. For someone who championed certitude, Kaplan could be exasperatingly inconsistent, making for confusion and clouding his reputation as a religious authority. Was he guided by flexibility? Circumstance? Convenience? A higher power? Who could tell? Sometimes the founder of Reconstructionism wore a *kipah*, or a "cap," when at the dinner table, the practice an opportunity for "religious color" as well as a "symbol of reverence for the source of life," and sometimes he would not. Sometimes he'd write in his journal on Shabbos without any qualms—a big no-no in traditional religious circles—and at other moments, when caught in the act by one of his children, he'd pretend he was just tidying up his desk. Kaplan also sheepishly confessed in his journal that he "would by no means announce from the housetops" that he used pen and paper on the traditional day of rest—not that there was anything wrong with it. Other examples of Kaplan's malleable approach toward ritual observance abound. Take, for example, Tisha B'av, the solemn day of mourning commemorating the destruction of the First and Second Temples. Sometimes Kaplan fasted the entire day, allowing how he "would think myself a cad if I were to ignore this day's summons to fasting and mourning"; on other days, he'd swear off breakfast only, and on still others, he refrained from fasting altogether. Or consider his stance on driving to shul on Shabbos. The rabbi of SAJ made a point of walking rather than riding in a car even if it meant a trek of several miles, but in the event his resolve—along with his legs—failed him, he had no compunctions about riding the rest of the way. On other occasions, he'd avail himself of transportation right from the get-go. "I don't mind travelling by car on the Sabbath, when not to do so makes the Sabbath a burden and a nuisance," he told Harold Schulweis in a handwritten letter, adding, "I am not sure I would follow through that principle to its logical conclusion, either affirmatively or negatively. That's the Conservative (with a capital C) in me."[25]

Kaplan's fidelity to the dietary laws was of a piece. While on the road in "trefa-land," his pet phrase for America's interior, he subsisted on a diet of sardines and coffee, even though he told his followers that when circumstances warranted, they shouldn't think twice about consuming non-kosher foodstuffs. But in October 1948 when compelled to eat a non-kosher luncheon given by Macmillan, his publishers, he didn't feel so good. "For the first time in my career, I lived up to what I have to say about the dietary practices," Kaplan confessed, noting that "at no time before today did I take advantage of the liberty I extended to my fellow-Jews." He managed to swallow the first course, a cup of beef bouillon, and to consume about half of the main dish whose identity—"some chopped meat preparation"—eluded him, washing it all down with coffee and dessert. "It was an ordeal," Kaplan admitted, "but I went through it unscathed and the better for having had the courage to live up to my conviction on the matter." That may be, but enough of the "old-time religion" lingered for Kaplan to want to "throw in my lot with Jews who have not yet lost the momentum of traditional Jewish life. But where can I find such Jews who would at the same time be willing to give up some of their outworn beliefs and antiquated taboos?" He sought them within Reconstructionism but failed to find their like.[26]

He sought them at home and didn't find them there, either. Much to Kaplan's bitter disappointment, the members of his immediate family were less than rah-rah about Reconstructionism than he would have thought or hoped. Acting more out of deference than conviction, his married daughters and sons-in-law went through the motions, reciting grace after meals and not smoking when Mother and Papa came for a Shabbos visit. But when they were out of range, their now-grown-up children did as they pleased, going so far as to send their offspring to a sleepaway camp where "there is not the slightest recognition of Judaism." Convinced that his children were "Jewish for my sake," Kaplan was still taken aback to discover one summer in 1947, when Lena and he lived down the road from Judith and Ira, how little Jewishness figured in their daily routine. With a few exceptions, "there is nothing in their lives culturally or religiously Jewish from one end of the week to the next," he glumly observed. Given the couple's respective professional involvement with modern-day Judaism, he would have thought the two of them "living exemplars of Reconstructionism," but that was not the case. "They give no evidence of any desire to express themselves Jewishly more than what their professional duties demand of them." Disheartened, Kaplan wondered what would become of the movement if people like Judith and Ira didn't fully commit to it. "If they do not translate Reconstructionism into a throbbing, intensive Jewishness, who will?" He wondered, too, how, in good faith, he could counsel those parents who came to him for advice on how best to transmit Judaism to the next generation when he "cannot even say that I have succeeded with my own children."[27]

At a gathering of American Jews affiliated with Reconstructionism early in the 1950s, one of their number (who remained nameless) asked Kaplan whether there was any "evidence" that the movement had "made an impression" on contemporary American Jews. A very good question not only on the merits but also as a sign of the times: America was then experiencing another of its periodic religious revivals and Conservative Judaism was growing by leaps and bounds. Where, then, was Reconstructionism? Kaplan fudged his answer: "In a sense he is right in demanding such evidence, yet in another sense he is unfair. Suppose somebody were to ask for evidence that the Ten Commandments had affected human life." But Mordecai Menachem was no Moses, nor did the mountain of material he had produced in the course of nearly forty years come close to the moral clarity of the ancient prescriptions. Clarity, in fact, was what Reconstructionism lacked, especially when it came to defining what it was all about and where it fit within the American Jewish scheme of things. "Out here in the open spaces [of the country] the interested laymen are still trying to figure out why it is necessary to inject still another movement, or school of thought, or 'xyz' into Jewish life," Eisenstein, then a rabbi in Chicago, pointed out. "They have a vague notion but that notion must be transformed into burning conviction." Eschewing one overarching definition in favor of a multiplicity of them, Kaplan preferred to think of his contribution to modern Jewish life as a "leaven," a "movement," a "way of speaking," a "school of thought," a "catalyst," an "electric current," a "social strategy," a "method," and a "formula" that consisted of the "three Rs: Reorganization, Revitalization and Replenishment."[28]

Over the years, Kaplan went to great lengths to make even clearer that whatever Reconstructionism was, it was decidedly not a new sect or a fourth Jewish denomination. An "instrument," yes; an "orientation," certainly; a "sense of direction, a sense of values, and a sense of proportion" was as good a working definition as any but on no account a denomination. He wouldn't hear of it, his refusal to embrace an independent identity both a matter of resources and ideology. Nothing if not "impracticable," becoming a fourth denomination entailed the establishment of a rabbinical school and a teachers' training school, and the "energy that would have to go into such an effect would be diverted from the main purpose of getting Jews to rethink their religion, readjust their way of life and reorganize their communal institutions," he explained, as much to himself as to those of his "younger colleagues" who lobbied for it. No good could come of an initiative that sapped the community's financial reserves, erected a new set of boundaries, and "defeated the primary aim of the movement—to bring about an awareness among Jews of whatever they have in common." Far better to think small and to work from within by creating groups of men and women within existing congregations to "rally around the philosophy of Reconstructionism." Without making too many waves, they'd "constitute chapters of a Reconstructionist Fellowship, which should aim to become a Jewish religious order." When, not surprisingly, that idea fell flat, Kaplan concluded that the only way for Reconstructionism to take hold was for it to strengthen its position within Conservative Judaism. "Unless Reconstructionism is given a place in that movement, it is likely to lose out with the average person who cannot be won for an idea unless it is associated with some organizational agency," he acknowledged in the late 1940s, determined as ever to iron out the relationship between the two. Eisenstein, though, strongly resisted and in the years that followed continually urged Kaplan to make a clean break once and for all. Taking that step was a bridge too far for the champion of Jewish unity. "I don't want the Reconstructionist movement to develop into a splinter movement," he'd say, rebuffing his son-in-law and second-in-command. Eisenstein would try again, ratcheting up his calls for a declaration of independence, but his fervent entreaties, far from changing Kaplan's mind, backfired. They left "the Chief," who was never more obdurate than when challenged, more convinced than ever that Reconstructionism had all the answers. "I cannot imagine a more coherent and intrinsically realistic approach to our inner problems as Jews," he ringingly declared.[29]

Kaplan's was a minority opinion. Most everyone else, it seemed, had no difficulty in imagining something or someone else at the helm, someone like Abraham Joshua Heschel, whose persona and perspective ran counter to Kaplan's in every way. A study in contrasts, Heschel was everything Kaplan was not. Where Kaplan ran cold and prioritized reason, Heschel ran hot and emphasized emotion; where Kaplan was given to abstraction, Heschel waxed lyrical; where Kaplan spoke in terms of propositions, Heschel drew on the language of mitzvot. Kaplan was prolix, Heschel aphoristic; Kaplan was resolutely American, Heschel authentically Old World. Where Kaplan alluded obliquely to what became known as the Holocaust, Heschel personified it. Kaplan reconstructed; Heschel recovered.[30]

It's often been bruited about that the Seminary purposefully invited Heschel to join the faculty in 1945 as a counterweight, an "antidote," to Kaplan, but that wasn't the case, at least not at first. Kaplan had a strong hand in securing Heschel's appointment, having vouched for his scholarly credentials. He eagerly anticipated that the new man would inherit his courses and take his advice on how to teach them. Delighting in one another's company, the two initially enjoyed a warm relationship. But it soon grew frosty, especially on Kaplan's part, after finding that Heschel's approach to teaching differed markedly from his own. "He is all I would want him to be both as a teacher and as an inspirational influence for an affirmative Judaism," he wrote, a strong "but" headlining his very next sentence: "But he is not of the type to confront problems and difficulties. As a romantic mystic he shies away from facts and tries to build his own universe of discourse entirely on values." Things continued to spiral downward when, soon thereafter, Kaplan began to feel that "the tide of reaction was running strong" among the students, leaving him feeling beached. Signs of a "mitzvah epidemic," of a "yarmulke and minyan kind of piety" were now everywhere at 3080 Broadway, which disturbed Kaplan no end and for which he laid the blame largely at Heschel's door.[31]

Convinced that what he had to offer "went into one ear and came out of the other," Kaplan also blamed Heschel for eroding his standing among the students, rendering their "addled brains . . . impervious to any corrective thinking," by which he meant his own. When Kaplan asked them to take stock of what they had learned and what they had "unlearned," one student replied that he hadn't unlearned a thing. Another charged Kaplan with having an "axe to grind. You were not trying to find the truth but rather overthrow a point of view." No matter how often the Reconstructionist spiritual leader refined and adjusted his ideas, aligning them with contemporary concerns, an increasing number of aspiring rabbis found his overall approach—and him—old hat, ill-suited to, and out of step with postwar America. They made clear their negative opinion in the best way they knew how: by cutting class. In the brief interval between the conclusion of one session and the start of Kaplan's, the room rapidly emptied of its inhabitants in what he dolefully called a "stampede." Nor did things improve when the students stayed in their seats. Instead of engaging with Kaplan they'd either sit on their hands or act in a hostile manner, repeatedly needling him and interrupting his every sentence. "Oi, the students," he exclaimed, lamenting how they possessed the kind of "immaturity and illiteracy that one would not expect" even among those still in high school. And, in the way of students everywhere, they didn't do the work, which incensed their exasperated teacher most of all. Having assigned *The Future of the American Jew*, his latest book, Kaplan was upset to discover that most of the class hadn't bothered to read it. Angered and hurt by this show of unresponsiveness, he retrieved every single copy, which he had given to one and all as a gift, and in an additional fit of pique he assigned them Nahum Glatzer's account of Franz Rosenzweig's life and thought instead. "Let them stew in the thick soup of Rosenzweig's verbiage," he gloated, his way of saying, *You think I'm difficult. I'll give you difficult.*[32]

Another day, another instance of student malfeasance. "Very few sessions have come off without my being exasperated by the behavior or attitude of the students . . . they make my life miserable," Kaplan repeatedly noted throughout the 1950s. On one such occasion, after being told by the juniors and seniors in his philosophies of religion course that his approach was entirely too "analytic and lacking all emotion and piety," he blew up. "I sputtered and I fumed and I swore," Kaplan recorded in his diary, adding that even though he was well aware that he was "making an ass of myself," he couldn't help himself. When words did not suffice, the JTS professor stormed out of the room, a gesture many frustrated educators, at one point or another in their teaching careers, have undoubtedly contemplated though rarely, if ever, implemented. In the heat of the moment, Kaplan was glad he did. A few hours later, though, he had a change of heart, regretful that he had shown his "inner insecurity."[33]

There was much to be insecure about, as Heschel's fame and his hold on the Jewish body politic grew apace in postwar America, threatening the viability of Reconstructionism and weakening Kaplan's standing. As threats multiplied, so did the latter's animadversions. At a loss to explain Heschel's appeal, he stewed and stewed, spending more and more time thinking about Heschel than Heschel thought about him. The higher Heschel's star ascended, the lower Kaplan sank, giving voice to one nasty comment after another. Outwardly cordial, inwardly, within the safe precincts of his diary, he seethed. Heschel, he noted dismissively, was a "remarkable Jewish replica of Billy Graham . . . quite adept in coining aphorisms which catch the ear, but which are half truths." A "fool" and a "fraud," whose writing was "just a hodge podge of words," his idea of religion a "specious kind of buberized Hasidism," Heschel, he wrote in his diary, was not only "alluringly and dangerously obscurantist" but also on the "warpath against everything I stand for." Kaplan had a point. Without referring to him by name, Heschel had publicly said of his senior colleague that he "attempted to reduce the spiritual to the reasonable, the holy to the social, the unique to the conventional." On other occasions, for example, a 1949 faculty meeting at which Kaplan's draft of the "guiding principles of Conservative Judaism" was on the agenda, Heschel was the "one who had the most to say." Unstinting in his criticism, he belittled as "meaningless" Kaplan's call for a worldwide gathering to devise a new covenant for postwar Jewry. "It simply meant another conference and futile resolutions." Heschel also had little use for his notion of salvation, deeming it a Christian import. Jotting down everything his junior colleague had to say, Kaplan counted the ways in which he took aim, noting that "firstly" Heschel said this, "secondly," he said that, all the way up to "fifthly" and "sixthly." It couldn't have been easy to sit there and take it, but, by his own account that's precisely what Kaplan did. "I tried to display as much savoir faire as I could command," he related after the fact, patting himself on the back for his restraint. A foil as well as a deterrent, Heschel was to Kaplan of the postwar era what Ginzberg had been to Kaplan of prewar America, but with one major difference: Ginzberg had deliberately, maliciously plotted and schemed against him; Heschel, though clearly not shy about publicly airing his disagreements, did not seek his colleague's downfall. Kaplan's tumble came about inadvertently, a consequence of Heschel's teachings rather than due to a frontal assault.[34]

The ongoing standoff between Kaplan and Heschel culminated decades later when, late in 1968, *Newsweek*'s religion editor, Kenneth Woodward, contacted Kaplan, among other Jewish and Christian theologians, inquiring about his views on prayer in modern America. In preparation for a substantive telephone interview, the ever-diligent professor prepared a detailed outline of his thoughts on the subject, invoking meaty concepts such as "spiritual heritage," the distinction between "obligatory prayer" and "private prayer," the relationship between "spirituality" and magic, and how the "conception of prayer [was] a corollary of the conception of God." When the magazine hit the local newsstand a few weeks later, Kaplan was on hand to purchase several copies. While still on the street, he excitedly thumbed through its pages looking for his contribution, only to discover that nothing, not a word, of what he had said, had made its way into print. More "bitterly disappointing" still was that Kaplan himself, much less his ideas, didn't even merit a sentence. Instead, in discussing Jewish views of prayer, the article first reserved several paragraphs for Richard Rubinstein, one of Kaplan's former students who went on to become, in his words, a "theological mortician," and then gave pride of place to Heschel, characterizing him as "perhaps the most knowledgeable theologian on the meaning of prayer" and quoting him as saying, famously, "When I marched with Martin Luther King in Selma, I felt my legs praying."[35]

"What a waste of a dollar," grumbled Kaplan.

In years gone by, when upset by one thing or another, Kaplan turned to Lena for comfort. During the 1950s, she, not he, was in need of succor. Having suffered a series of heart attacks, in declining health, and bedridden for weeks on end, Kaplan's devoted wife of nearly half a century could no longer run the household and manage its finances. Increasingly, many domestic chores fell to her hapless husband who, having relied on Lena to do everything, hadn't a clue about how to balance a checkbook, pay the monthly bills, and supervise the maid; even operating the phonograph machine eluded him. His equilibrium shattered, Kaplan had to make all kinds of decisions, some of which came easily to him, like what to do with their beloved Westport refuge, while others left him scratching his head. It had become clear that their little house at 599 Compo Road had to go; once a source of pleasure, it had become a "burden" ever since Lena took ill and was no longer able to see to its upkeep. Less easily resolved was the nature of her convalescence. On the one hand, Lena's doctors insisted that she be freed of household cares, avoid all forms of "excitement," and rest in bed most of the time; on the other, they cautioned against treating her as an invalid. "In giving that kind of advice," mused Kaplan, "doctors seem to be as logical as theologians."[36]

In winter 1958, Lena's condition worsened, landing her in New York's Beth Israel Hospital, where for a few days her passing seemed imminent. "Each time I would look into my darling's eyes as she lay there in the oxygen tent and she would look into mine I could well imagine the thoughts that were passing through her mind," Kaplan tenderly noted, invoking the specter of death. Weeks later, Lena had sufficiently recovered to be able to return home. Though weak, she was determined to travel to Chicago in May for the bat mitzvah of their granddaughter Ann. Shortly before the big event, Lena collapsed in the bathroom in the middle of the night. The doctors were called, drugs administered, and Lena placed back in an oxygen tent. When she came to in the morning and realized that Chicago was no longer in the cards, she tearfully urged Kaplan to go without her, lest the "very thing she feared, that of disrupting" the festivities, would happen. After an emotional discussion, he reluctantly deferred to his wife's wishes, leaving her in the care of round-the-clock nurses and with Hadassah for company. Early the next morning, she died in her sleep and the "thing I feared came upon me," Kaplan related. "When I left her on Friday morning," he later recalled, "she said to me as she kissed me, 'Darling, don't worry. I slept through the night and I feel much better.' There was something indescribably sad in that kiss as though both of us subconsciously sensed that it was to be the last." He then added, "I am convinced that my darling, realizing that her relapse in no way disrupted the joyous occasion, relaxed in her will to live and no longer resisted the onset of death."[37]

In the months following Lena's funeral and the shivah period of mourning, both of which drew large crowds, Kaplan busied himself with work, filling the pages of his journal with "spelling out the idea of God" and otherwise occupying his time with "trivialities": paying bills, responding to condolence notes, light reading. Keeping thoughts of Lena at bay and to a minimum, at least on the page, he invoked her presence only occasionally—on what would have been their golden anniver-

Theirs was a long and happy marriage, 1956.
The Collection of Hadassah K. Musher, New York.

sary in June, sadly taking note of the date, and on Shavuot when Daniel, one of their grandsons, read from the Torah at holiday services. "I wept," he said, "and could not restrain myself because of the thought of how my darling would have rejoiced had she lived to hear him." From time to time, Kaplan passingly mentioned in his diary how much he missed Lena's kisses, and in letters to Judith over the next couple of months wrote of how he counted the weeks since his beloved's passing and of how, were it not for work, he would have "found it very hard to bear the loneliness which overtakes me in my free moments." And yet, even though the ground of his being had been cut out from under him, Kaplan didn't give himself over completely to grief, acknowledging that he "experienced the sense of bereavement only during the intervals between one activity and the next and at meals." With a handful of projects in the pipeline he made sure those intervals were brief, writing to his daughter of how "Project No. 3" (a letter-writing campaign regarding a world Jewish conference) and "Project No. 4" (putting the finishing touches to "Random Thoughts," a book-length collection of aperçus) helped "keep [him] on an even keel."[38]

His family, in turn, made sure he got through the day, "doing everything they can to make life easy" for him. Constantly on hand, they visited with Kaplan of an evening, organized his affairs, sorted out and settled the unanticipatedly large hospital bills, and secured a live-in housekeeper named Hanna "without an 'h.' " Kaplan didn't care for her, informing his daughters that "she is an elderly, fat, spectacled German-Jewish sourpuss who moves from room to room in goose-step fashion." He stayed out of Hanna's way, his teenaged grandson David assisting him by rigging up an electric bell in his study so that he could summon her when need be and avoid conversation. When, inevitably, tensions flared and the housekeeper threatened to quit, Selma smoothed things over between them, prompting Kaplan mischievously to comment that everything has been "straightened out in Apartment 4A and so *shalom al Yisrael.*"[39]

Concerned about his well-being, Selma and her sisters entertained a proposal floated in June by Marcus Rottenberg, a longtime friend, faithful supporter, and a recent widower himself, that their father move in with him. Kaplan approved of the *shidduch* and "unhesitatingly welcomed the idea." The two men enjoyed one another's company, had only themselves to look after, and given the spaciousness of Rottenberg's apartment at 101 Central Park West, one of the most prestigious buildings on the Upper West Side, they wouldn't get in each other's way. That Kaplan would be within shouting range of two of his daughters and their families—Selma lived in the same building as Rottenberg, and Hadassah was only a block away—added to the attractiveness of the proposition. After their two families convened to talk things over, it was decided to go ahead but to hold off on the move until after the summer. Only Eisenstein gave voice to what was on everyone's mind: What if Rottenberg, then only sixty-four and considerably younger than Kaplan, decided to remarry? Then what?[40]

Surprising no one, that's exactly what happened: Rottenberg was quick to remarry. But then, surprising himself and everybody in his orbit, Kaplan did, too, falling hard for Rivkah Rieger, an Israeli artist whom he had first met decades earlier in Jerusalem when working together with her late husband, Eliezer Rieger, on the Yishuv's educational policy. While in the States visiting her daughters, Rivkah Rieger had accepted an invitation from the women of SAJ to exhibit her paintings at a "Round-the-World Fair" in early March 1959. While in town, she attended one of Kaplan's public lectures. At this point in the narrative, which he vividly detailed in his journal, their respective accounts of "how we met" diverge. He says: Rivkah approached his daughter Hadassah to ascertain if he'd be amenable to having her paint his portrait. She says: Hadassah and Selma asked her if she might like to paint a picture of their father. No matter. Sometime in April, Rivkah, along with an easel, a painter's palette, and an assortment of brushes, turned up at 415 Central Park West. Several sessions ensued and in the course of one, even before Rivkah set up her equipment, Kaplan turned to her and said, "May I ask you a personal question?" "Yes," she replied. At which point, Kaplan's journal continues allusively, the "going was smooth. I could not expect her to give me an affirmative answer at once, but the rest of the time was not spent on the painting."[41]

A whirlwind romance, Mordecai and Rivkah's courtship wasn't without its upsets. He was head over heels, she lukewarm.

Rivkah Rieger Kaplan, ca. 1959.
The Collection of Navah de Shalit, Jerusalem.

Besotted by Rivkah's appearance, "personal charm, keen intelligence, deep insight and above all her fine sense of ethical and spiritual values," Kaplan made up his mind: bring on the huppah. On May 3, 1959, he confided in his diary: "A year ago on this day my darling wife was no more. On this same day, I have good reason to believe I have won the hand of an extraordinary woman who walked into my life only several weeks ago." Not so fast, said she. Beguiled by his gentlemanliness, elegance, and good looks ("he hasn't aged a bit"); by his intelligence, standing in the Jewish world, and commitment to Israel; as well as by his obvious affection for her, Rivkah was equally aware of the many obstacles that stood in their way. The age difference between them was a real sticking point: he was seventy-eight, she eighteen years younger. What kind of future would be theirs to enjoy? Geographical considerations had also to be taken into account. Much as Rivkah enjoyed New York, Jerusalem was her home. Where, then, would they live? And what of the many cultural differences each brought to this union? Having enjoyed a secular life as an adult, would she have to "accommodate herself to his routine," go to shul, keep strictly kosher? Most of all, after five years of widowhood, Rivkah relished her personal freedom, the opportunity to do what she wanted when she wanted. Was she prepared to give that up, to be tied to someone else's needs and demands, especially when that someone was a man in his seventies known to be on the truculent side of the ledger? Rivkah's qualms and "calculations," her pulling back from the brink of saying "yes, yes, yes," kept her suitor in a state of suspense: Would she, or wouldn't she, agree to be his wife? Kaplan's poignant account of what went on between them reads as if written by a moony teenager rather than a seasoned old man.[42]

THE SETTING: A taxi cab.
MMK: Do you love me?
RR: It's growing.[43]

We'll never know what Kaplan said to win her over (or wear her down), but Rivkah eventually assented to his proposal. They were married on June 21, 1959, in Selma's apartment, surrounded by members of both families, the atmosphere one of "simplicity, beauty . . . and the kind of happiness which is so rare in human life," Kaplan recalled. And then, his having been "redeemed from loneliness . . . enabled once again to live a full life," the couple took off for Camp Modin in Canaan, Maine, where Kaplan held court happily while Rivkah, nothing if not a good sport, counted the days until she could be quit of summer camp, hopefully forever; meanwhile, she painted. An "ideal situation for both of us," her new husband wrote enthusiastically to Eisenstein early in July. "We can work at philosophy and art both separately and together." The couple then left for Jerusalem, setting in motion a dynamic that lasted for many years. Rivkah would spend the entire summer in the Holy Land, writing letters, in Hebrew, to Mordecai of "love and longing," as well as of places visited and people seen, while Kaplan would spend part of his stateside, usually at camp, and then join her for the balance of the summer or sometimes not at all. Even when in the same place at the same time, the couple marked out separate territory: "Rivkah in her way and I in my way" was how Kaplan once defined their relationship. He detailed that arrangement while describing a holiday in Haifa, noting that "Rivkah got what she wanted out of the trip—nine sea baths—and I got what I wanted—about 7500 words on what I am working on."[44]

The couple's lives in Israel centered around 3 Ibn Ezra, a compact stone house in the heart of Rehavia. Rivkah's longtime home, it was filled with her things and paintings, which covered the walls from top to bottom. In this new environment, Kaplan tried, and largely succeeded, to keep up his customary routine, eating three solid meals a day, secluding himself in his upstairs study, writing away, and dutifully reading *Haaretz*, not so much for its coverage of the news as for its Hebrew vocabulary; he was determined to augment his own. He also maintained his ambulatory habits, taking at least one and optimally two daily walks, one early in the morning and another at dusk. At those moments when the streets were empty of passersby, this peripatetic Jerusalem resident enjoyed a "wonderful time with myself." But not for long. Rivkah, who called the shots, made sure their life was a sociable one. We spend "on the average of twelve hours a week with guests—mostly Rivkah's," Kaplan observed. One can almost hear him gnashing his teeth. The absence of a shul to call his own was another new, and trying, aspect of his reconstructed life in Jerusalem. He had nowhere to go. A Reconstructionist house of prayer, still in its early days, had not yet jelled, its progress impeded, in part, by the government. Owing to a ruling that no non-Orthodox religious literature might enter the country, a shipment of Reconstructionist *siddurim* (prayer books) sat in Customs. What a "scandalous situation," Kaplan fumed. "Can you imagine such barbarism on the part of the Rabbinate here? The entire country is being overrun by the followers of Hasidic rabbis who sit in Brooklyn and dictate to them what not to do." Outraged, he contemplated bringing suit but on the advice of counsel held his fire, at once fearful lest a Kulturkampf erupt and mindful that the "time for such a struggle is not ripe." That decision left him to his own devices early on a Shabbat or a holiday morning, without a shul, taking a walk in one direction as shul-goers headed in another. Just to be sure he wouldn't be misidentified as a nonbeliever, Kaplan donned a jacket, adding to his discomfort. "Normally, I should have been at services at a synagogue, but there is little that is normal in Jerusalem," he noted.[45]

After close to six months away, Kaplan was relieved to be home at 415 Central Park West, back amid his own family, books, desk, and SAJ. "Here I am at home," he declared. "In Jerusalem I was a tourist. To be at home there I'd have to be an Israeli Jew. Here I'm an American Jew. Too bad one can't be an adjectiveless Jew everywhere in the world."[46]

Life in the State of Israel confirmed what Kaplan had been thinking for years: Zionism was in need of reconstruction. No sooner had its objective been realized, and *medinat Yisrael* (the State of Israel) established, than he began to think about what lay ahead. Without missing a beat, he came up with a "kind of Zionism which makes Jewish peoplehood rather than Israel statehood its all-embracing aim." Calling his version "spiritual Zionism" or, more provocatively, a "new Zionism" and, later, "Greater Zionism," Kaplan sought to save the movement from itself by expanding its parameters. Advocating that it go beyond politics or philanthropy, that Israel be seen as much more than an "emergency affair" or a "refugee movement which has given rise to an Arab refugee problem," he put forward the notion of a new and improved Zionism as a vehicle for the regeneration of the entire Jewish people, "giving it a new lease on life." And not a moment too soon. Were steps not taken in the very near future to stretch the meaning of Zionism, to place the "salvaging of the Jewish people and the regeneration of its spirit" at its center, Kaplan warned that it might well be on its "way out." Opportunities to make of "*Eretz Yisrael* the alpha and omega of Jewish existence" would slip away, the gap between Israeli and Diaspora Jews would widen, and the State of Israel edge closer and closer to becoming little more than "some new Levantine civilization." Or worse. "Unless something drastic be done," he predicted, "disillusionment over the Sabbatai Zevi fiasco will be eclipsed by the disillusion following the Israeli fiasco (God forbid!)." With "Jewish Peoplehood" (Kaplan's preferred spelling) at its core, and elements drawn from *Judaism as a Civilization* as ballast, Kaplan's reenvisioned Zionism—peoplehood with added bounce—just might save the day. "The old Zionism was meant to have the Jewish People rebuild Zionism. A New Zionism is now needed to have Zion rebuild the Jewish People."[47]

Intended to energize Jews everywhere, the "new Zionism" energized Kaplan most of all. What "Jewish civilization" had been to his interwar years and "peoplehood" to the immediate postwar era, this platform was to the 1950s and early 1960s: an intellectual axis, a rallying cry, a "mission." He spent many hours holding meetings; attending conferences and conventions; talking up the "new Zionism" on the lecture circuit; issuing a "manifesto" that ran to more than eight typewritten pages; publishing detailed articles in *The Reconstructionist;* figuring out and finessing institutional alliances to move things along; and, characteristically, writing a book, or as he preferred to call it, a "tract." Invoking Leon Pinsker and Theodor Herzl before him, Kaplan took to words to create a stir and inspire action; he called his new work *A New Zionism*, its unassuming title at odds with its impassioned contents.[48]

First published in 1955 and, after having sold out its initial run of two thousand copies, reprinted in an expanded version four years later, the text called Israel to account. In page after page—nearly two hundred of them—it pointed out the limitations of the new state. Israel's failure to develop "Jewish consciousness," especially one imbued with a religious sensibility, and to put its faith instead in a "completely secularized" form of identity made as little sense as "two plus two equals five," Kaplan declared. Equally troubling was how little effort it made to promote a voluntaristic kind of religion that would "renounce all ambition to engage in power politics." And hovering over everything, clouding Israel's future, was the absence of a "solution for the Arab refugee problem which is at present the greatest threat that hangs over the State of Israel." When *A New Zionism* first appeared, readers were taken aback by its bleakness; nowadays what startles is its prescience.[49]

Its diagnosis astute, its emphasis on peoplehood compelling, the strategy deployed by the "new Zionism" left a lot to be desired, its details shadowy, vague, and overly ambitious. At its heart was a series of interlocking initiatives that Kaplan loftily called the "covenant proposal," whose first order of business was to convene a transnational conference, a "world assembly, a modern Sanhedrin, not of the Napoleonic type but a body representative of the entire House of Israel," to set things in motion. That step would be followed by the formation of a permanent institution to implement the "new Zionism"—a role the Hebrew University, perhaps, might fill—as well as the issuing of a brand-new covenant, a Basel Program for the twentieth century, to which Jews everywhere would pledge their fealty to Zionism much as they had at the first Zionist Congress in 1897. A "ritual of unity" staged at "maturity," much like an "initiation into a fraternal order," would mark and celebrate that commitment. More pie-in-the-sky than realistic, the "covenant proposal" was Kaplan at his most imaginative, especially when he suggested to Finkelstein, whose support he sought, that the Seminary's leading light play Nordau to his Herzl.[50]

The manner in which this latter-day Herzl went about implementing the "new Zionism" was no less inventive. While refining its tenets, he had reluctantly come to the conclusion that his long-held "anti-organizational stance" was no longer in Reconstructionism's best interests and that the "time was ripe" for the movement to "assert itself as an organized force." The growing power of the competition left him little choice lest Reconstructionism be "swamped" by Heschel's influence over the Seminary's "powerful machinery of indoctrination" or "squelched by the growingly aggressive tactics of both Conservative and Reform organizations and institutions." Acting, then, in "self-defense," Kaplan agreed to "go along" with those within Reconstructionism's ranks who for years had been clamoring for the formation of an association of like-minded congregations. Voilà: the Reconstructionist Fellowship of Congregations. It came into the world in 1954, its mandate to standardize liturgy and ritual practice, promote the cause, have a voice. But not on Kaplan's watch. Calling the moment a "providential" one, he hit on the idea of having this new body stay clear of traditional pursuits and to position itself as a Zionist party or faction instead: the liberal progressive answer to Orthodoxy's Mizrachi. Good for Zionism and good for Reconstructionism, too, this proposition, Kaplan enthusiastically explained to anyone willing to listen and to some who, like Eisenstein had no choice, was bound to be "electrifying," as exciting a development as the Jewish Center had been decades before. An effective way to strengthen the cause of Zionism by bringing into the fold "liberal religionists" alongside "orthodox religionists and atheistic secularists," this step would also enhance Reconstructionism by expanding its base of supporters. And, as an added bonus, it would resolve the "dilemma" in which the spiritual movement found itself: an ideology in search of an infrastructure. Having a hand in Zionist affairs would enable Reconstructionism to have the capacity, the reach, of a denomination without being one; at the same time, it sidestepped the prospect of being "stigmatized as a divisive movement."[51]

The "new Zionism" had few takers; advocates for Reconstructionism's role in its future were sparser still. Out of respect, perhaps, for Kaplan's longtime involvement in Zionist affairs, the Zionist Organization of America gave his proposal a hearing, hinting at the possibility of incorporating some of its elements in a revised platform; the World Zionist Organization, its global counterpart, also went through the motions of entertaining the proposition. But neither one ventured much beyond the talking stage. Hobbled by ideological rivalry, how could they? Secularist Zionists were already uncomfortable sitting at the same table with the religiously minded, who returned the favor, and institutionalists didn't want to share their power with upstart constituents who might dilute it. Frustrated, Kaplan turned to the Seminary and the United Synagogue, hoping to gain their support in "carrying the new Zionism." Wary of being dominated by the old guard, and at the same time a bit wobbly in its institutional commitment to the cause, the Conservative movement did not exert itself. Disappointed at first, Kaplan later claimed to have been pleased when Finkelstein "threw back that project into my lap," as it freed him to go all out in promoting the idea within his own ranks, selling Eisenstein on the proposition that "we should organize the Reconstructionist congregations principally around the idea of the New Zionism." Here, too, he encountered considerable resistance. Eisenstein and others within the Reconstructionist leadership feared this strategy would "divert us from the main issues in American life, which are primary," whereas Israeli affairs were not. Eisenstein's overall lack of enthusiasm, coupled with his doubts about the efficacy of peoplehood as one of Reconstructionism's central planks, had a cooling effect. Over the course of their relationship, Kaplan had grown accustomed to having his son-in-law pooh-pooh many of his ideas—it came with the territory, the inevitably fraught relationship between a father-in-law and son-in-law in the same business—but this dismissal bothered him. "No amount of arguing on my part," he related, "swayed Ira from his refusal to go along with me." Kaplan was starry-eyed about its potential—"intangible and elusive as is peoplehood, its power and influence are incalculable," he enthused—but his younger colleague insisted that it was "too abstract in purpose for the average person to grasp." A Zionist-inflected peoplehood, Eisenstein believed, would never draw American Jews to Reconstructionism. For the time being, his view carried the day. The movement went in one direction, Zionism another.[52]

The upshot of so much wheeling and dealing, the "hurdling" of one obstacle after another, was that Zionism was "at a standstill," and a "Lesser," not a "Greater," version here to stay, Kaplan reflected as he contemplated defeat. Unable to overcome the "obdurate resistance" of so many vested interests, his efforts, he conceded, were "doomed to frustration."

And yet, he continued, doggedly, to beat the drum for a Zionism whose coordinates were spiritual rather than territorial, to insist on the importance of Israel creating a "civilization at least as Jewish as American civilization today is Christian," and to hold on tight to his cherished affirmation of Jewish Peoplehood. A decade later, Kaplan was still at it, adding to his repertoire a constitution to "concretize the very idea of Jewish Peoplehood," which he hoped to draft with the assistance of the Decalogue Society of Lawyers, the country's oldest Jewish bar association. And then, inspired by morning flag-raising exercises he experienced at Cejwin Camps in summer 1965, he came up with a Jewish Pledge of Allegiance. Modeled after America's iconic text, it read: "We pledge our spiritual allegiance to the Jewish People and to its Torah. One people, under God, indivisible and dedicated to the cause of universal righteousness and peace." No sooner had he formulated that text than he formulated another, calling this iteration an "affirmation" rather than a pledge. It read: "I affirm my spiritual loyalty to the Jewish people and its Torah, a people one and indivisible, and under God, dedicated to the cause of universal righteousness and peace. Hear, O Israel, the Eternal is our God, the Eternal is One—and in Hebrew, *sh'ma Yisrael.*"[53]

Kaplan's "new Zionism" had no effect on the State of Israel, and probably none at all on young American Jewish campers either, but its impact on Reconstructionism was profound and enduring, if unintended. As a consequence of promoting the notion that the movement might best be served were it to become a Zionist faction—an organization, that is—Kaplan could no longer bat away and dismiss other people's arguments in favor of Reconstructionism concretizing itself. His adamantine stance having softened, he heeded more attentively than ever before to calls coming from both the top and the grass roots for the movement to assume a different form. Willy-nilly, Kaplan came to see that some kind of "agency is indispensable to the movement . . . that the average layman cannot be expected to grasp a new philosophy, whether of life or a movement, by means of any abstract presentation. He requires some embodiment of that philosophy in a symbol or institution." With its own liturgy, publishing house, magazine, and a network of synagogues that flew the Reconstructionist flag, didn't the movement already have the perquisites of a denomination? Why not become one in name as well as in function: why not make it official? Another striking argument in favor of autonomy, which Eisenstein personally advanced, made the case that unless Reconstructionism, so heavily identified with Kaplan, drew a line between itself and Conservative Judaism, it might run the risk of "evaporating" once he was no more. Reconstructionist's founder didn't need much persuading on that score. Well aware, especially as he aged, of the evanescence of both people and of once-formidable institutions, one example being Dewey's Progressive Education Association, which shut its doors in 1955, he wondered "how soon will that happen to Reconstructionism?" If a rock-solid institution like Dewey's could crumble, how much more so the rickety house that Kaplan had spent most of his life building? Waiting around to find out was not much of an option.[54]

The first order of business—the necessary preamble to Reconstructionism's embrace of denominationalism—was for Kaplan to resign from the Seminary and sever his ties with the Conservative movement. "Before long it turned out that I was to blame for inhibiting [Reconstructionism] from becoming an out and out fourth movement or denomination," he sourly recalled in 1963 upon hearing firsthand what its members had to say. (He had heard much the same thing years earlier from Eisenstein but paid it little mind.) Though not convinced that the fault was entirely his, Kaplan accepted his culpability and resolved publicly to do something about it. Having recently completed fifty years of teaching, a milestone his students greeted with a standing ovation, the longtime professor was in a position to make a graceful final exit when the occasion warranted, as it would three years later. "Finis," Kaplan wrote in his journal, bringing to a staccato finish a relationship that was as complex as it was lengthy. Dating to before his bar mitzvah and extending through his eighty-second birthday, its longevity masked a lifetime of unresolved conflict: a stew of aggrievement and ambivalence. Characterizing the Seminary's leaders as "all in a tangle because they want to hunt with the hounds and run with the foxes," he was just as quick to acknowledge that when away from the Seminary environment "I am like a fish out of water, even though I don't much relish the muddiness of that water." More bluntly, as late as 1958 Kaplan wrote of how "verily, the Seminary is my cross," only to muddy the waters of his own accord by admitting that "it was not easy for me to overcome the momentum of 70 years of association." No wonder he didn't go anywhere, even when presented with the opportunity. Trapped, Kaplan stayed on at 3080 Broadway, seeming to prefer martyrdom to bettering his lot until the Seminary "atmosphere," he wrote to a friend, "has become too suffocating. I couldn't take it anymore." At the breaking point, he submitted his resignation. A rationalization, perhaps, but one that enabled him to make good on that "finis." (To some of his colleagues, Kaplan attributed his resignation to more benign forces, claiming he wanted to devote the years he had left to advancing Reconstructionism.)[55]

Great excitement, both within and without Reconstructionist circles, greeted the news. Some of Kaplan's supporters wept with excitement, the intensity of their response surprising him. "Is it that they expect me to usher in a new era in Jewish life by devoting all my energies to Reconstructionism? Is it that Judaism means so much to them that the merest chance that it might receive a lift from Reconstructionism makes them exult?" Whatever their reasons, Kaplan was determined to "work even harder than I have for Reconstructionism." These were not words Seminary people wanted to hear. Some, like Finkelstein, who feared a stronger Reconstructionism would come at the expense of a weaker Conservative Judaism, wasted no time in calling the decision a "calamity." He hastened over to the Kaplan apartment to see if he might persuade his longtime colleague to change his mind. Stepping down from teaching after so many years in the classroom was understandable, the Seminary president-turned-chancellor told the Kaplans over lunch, but walking away from an institution to which you've devoted your life? That would never do. Later, when the Kaplans relocated to Jerusalem for the summer, Finkelstein visited them in their Rehavia home to "talk business," hoping that perhaps a change of scene would make Kaplan see things more clearly. It didn't. Digging in his heels, Kaplan wrote to Judith and Ira that Finkelstein was headed his way for a "final bout. He will make a final attempt. It will be a K.O. for him." Having made and stood by his decision, Kaplan's pugnacious side in full flower, he was unbudgeable. "Nothing now stands in the way of having my retirement from the Seminary properly interpreted as prompted by my intention to start a new movement in Jewish life, instead of merely developing a new school of thought in Judaism." Could his declaration of intent be any clearer?[56]

Maybe not. But his vision of what this newly emancipated Reconstructionism would look like on the ground remained up in the air—and stayed there—for a number of years. Kaplan didn't rush headlong into denominational mode. Still not convinced that the formation of a rabbinical school "of our own" was the answer, he stalled or, to put it more charitably, tried on different approaches: How about a "peaceful invasion of the existing training schools by seeing to it that on their faculties there be some one who could present the case for

Reconstructionism"? Or a Reconstructionist Research Institute for Contemporary Judaism, perhaps something on the order of the Rand Institute, the newly established postwar think tank devoted to research and development? Kaplan even brought back into circulation an idea he had touted at the start of his career—reimagining Torah study, not worship, as the primary function of the synagogue—but it met up with as much success the second time around as it had a half century earlier. None of his suggestions, in fact, went far enough to address the needs of Reconstructionists in search of more than a "way of speaking." Much as Kaplan tried to reinvent the wheel, there was no forward motion without it. Putting on a good face and lending his good name, he resigned himself to change and went along with the collective decision to launch a rabbinical school to which, as a sign of good faith, he promised five thousand books from his library.[57]

The planning process went from the visionary stage to a let's-get-things-done phase by early in January 1968, thanks to a substantial infusion of more than $100,000 in contributions ($1 million in today's currency). Even so, little fell automatically into place: more funds had to be raised, curricula developed, faculty rustled up, institutional alliances forged, official recognition from the credentialing authorities sought and won, a building secured, and a name settled on. Would "institute" do? How about "academy"? Or "college"? Any of these options would work, save for calling the facility the "Kaplan XYZ." Its potential namesake wouldn't hear of it. And why was that? "Whenever I walk in Jerusalem on streets named after Maimonides and Nachmanides, I would wonder how many of the men, women and children associate anything of consequence with those names." He didn't want "Kaplan" to suffer the same fate. Ego, of course, had a lot to do with his decision—Rambam, Ramban, and wait for it—Kaplan?!—but so, too, did doubt. He was not entirely one with the project. "Although I accepted that version of Rec. [*sic*] after Ira had insisted upon it," Kaplan confessed in his journal in 1967, referring to the decision to become a denomination, "I have never been too happy about it." He'd much prefer to think of Reconstructionism as a broad-based "Jewish historical ethnic movement," analogous to Zionism, stretching the comparison between the two. "As little as one would regard Zionism as a denomination, so little should we think of an 'evolving religious civilization' as a denomination." But no one was listening. Reconstructionism had moved on. A year later, the Reconstructionist Rabbinical College opened its doors in Philadelphia with suitable fanfare, marking the debut of American Jewry's "youngest" denomination, over fifty years in the making.[58]

Kaplan was at loose ends, adrift from what had anchored him for most of his life. In search of a focus, of something meaningful to do, he spent a substantial amount of time on the West Coast. Despite having cut his ties to JTS, he maintained his involvement with the University of Judaism, nurturing its commitment to Reconstructionism. Kaplan would teach for a semester; lecture around town and as far up the coast as Portland, Oregon; spur on the creation of the Jewish Reconstructionist Society of California; and lead a busy social life along with Rivkah who, with access to a studio, spent her time painting. Though constantly on the go, and at times even run ragged, Kaplan found his Los Angeles existence a satisfying one. One year, he even extended his stay for a few more weeks when invited to do so by some of the locals. "I am tempted to listen to them," he explained to Judith and Ira, as he weighed the pros and cons of staying on or returning home, "because in contrast with N.Y., where I am merely being accepted but not needed, out here I am needed. Like everybody else I need to be needed."[59]

Israel also beckoned. Once he no longer had to answer to an academic calendar, Kaplan was able to spend longer periods of time in Jerusalem where he taught the occasional class, delivered public lectures, busied himself writing papers on the (no longer) "new Zionism," and participated in conferences that he knew in advance would go nowhere and resolve nothing despite their high stakes and top-drawer speakers. Anticipating his children would question why he bothered to spin his wheels, Kaplan had a ready response: "My answer is vanity. I could well live without it, but to be in Jerusalem and to be left out from such important goings on would irk me." It wasn't just that Kaplan needed to be in the game. To keep boredom, his biggest bugaboo, at bay, he had to keep busy or, as Rivkah liked to put it, "active." His energy might flag, his body ache, and his spirits droop, but if he had a speaking engagement or a project in the offing—"brain work," he called it—life was good. "It meant health and high spirit reigning in our home," Rivkah noted with relief. Having an audience yielded similar dividends. Having been in the public eye for much of his life, Kaplan didn't take well to receding into the background. Sensitive to his needs, Rivkah saw to it that her husband didn't want for company and encouraged a steady stream of visitors—congregants, colleagues, and rabbinical students in Jerusalem for the year—to make their way to 3 Ibn Ezra, transforming their home address into as much of a pilgrimage site as the Kotel (the Western Wall), replete with its own set of rituals. After a few moments of desultory, awkward conversation during which the students were expected to fill the air with their anxious chatter, Kaplan, listening politely, would ask a few questions—nothing too demanding, mind. Rivkah then served tea and cookies or *mitz* (juice), which, once consumed, would signal that the audience with the great man had come to a ceremonial close. They then went on their way, eager to recount to their roommates and decades later to historians like me what it was like to encounter Mordecai Kaplan at home in Jerusalem.[60]

But this was entertainment, not intellectual stimulation. What the longtime teacher really needed were *talmidim*, not guests, and they were in short supply. Once again, Rivkah came to his rescue. In the wake of what could only have been one lament too many, she inveigled her grandson, Hanan, then a schoolboy, into studying with Kaplan once or twice a week during the school year. Predictably, this arrangement didn't last too long—the generational, cultural, and linguistic divide between them was too big to be bridged—but before the bottom fell out, a ninety-year-old American professor of Religious Philosophies A and B could be found of a Jerusalem afternoon initiating a ten-year-old, soccer-loving Israeli boy in the mysteries of *Judaism as a Civilization*.[61]

With time on his hands and few obligations to meet, Kaplan became more fanciful than ever. In the past he had no shortage of far-fetched ideas but someone, usually Eisenstein and Lena, or something, usually JTS or SAJ, counseled restraint or put on the brakes. In 1954, for example, while in the throes of excitement about the "new Zionism," Kaplan added another string to his bow by suggesting that Israel apply for admission to the Union as its newest state, believing it to be the only way the young country's precarious military situation could be stabilized. "Please don't think I'm nuts," he wrote to Eisenstein with whom he privately shared this "worthwhile solution." In response, his son-in-law diplomatically brought up the equally far-fetched nineteenth-century scheme of Mordecai Manuel Noah to resettle the Jews on an island in upstate New York, intimating—but nicely—that, yes, it did seem as if Kaplan had taken leave of his senses. There have been "all sorts of ideas for resolving the political and military problem, but this is one for somebody like Mordecai Noah. . . . Who else is likely to be in favor of it?" And that was the end of that. But now, with Eisenstein thousands of miles away,

Lena in the grave, and no institutional fetters on his freedom, Kaplan went his own way. It wasn't just that he pushed the peoplehood concept too often and too far. People have enough trouble understanding the concept of God as Process without your "confus[ing] further those who don't understand and alienat[ing] those who do," Eisenstein chided. To no avail. He found even more worrisome Kaplan's banging on about a constitution for the Jewish people, a daft idea under the best of circumstances, how much more so when the State of Israel didn't have one. "This is the sort of thing, which created in a vacuum, will be in a class with the various utopias which people have written about in years gone by," he cautioned, worried lest its promotion tarnish his father-in-law's reputation.[62]

All these miscalculations, though, paled in comparison with Kaplan's decision in 1972 to support Alan Miller, SAJ's embattled rabbi, in a long-simmering dispute with the congregation. No sooner had the British clergyman been hired a decade earlier than doubts surfaced, and then multiplied, as to whether he was "foursquare" with Reconstructionism. His abrasive, dismissive manner, often openly disdainful of SAJ's history, didn't help matters, alienating longtime congregants. By the mid-sixties, Kaplan routinely heard from former SAJ constituents that the situation had gone from "bad to worse." And now, on the eve of the congregation's fiftieth anniversary celebration, the SAJ, he was told, was being "torn apart, worse than ever." Amid "widespread disaffection," formerly stalwart members had resigned, finances were in a parlous state, while the man in the pulpit ranted, berated, insulted, and offended those in the pews, poisoning the atmosphere. A nasty split was imminent. "What a mess! And what a tragedy!" Eisenstein lamented. Strongly urged by him and every other member of the family to stay above the fray—better yet, to stay put in Israel and not even think about attending the fiftieth anniversary celebration—Kaplan agreed at first, only to zigzag and disregard their collective advice. He came to town for the festivities, which the pro-Miller faction construed as an endorsement, a vote of confidence, the anti-Miller faction a resounding slap in the face. Or worse. For Eisenstein, Kaplan's volte-face was a double whammy of a betrayal, at once familial and institutional, or, as he told his father-in-law to his face, "You did, in fact, abandon me in favor of him—and that is what hurt." The founder and longtime leader of SAJ didn't see things that way. He viewed his decision to participate in the semi-centennial celebration as a gesture of support for the institution, not the man, and as a way to avoid a "repeat performance" of what, ironically enough, had given rise to the SAJ a half century earlier: a split in the ranks. But Eisenstein, the extended Kaplan clan, and the anti-Millerites believed he had taken a side—and the wrong one at that. They interpreted Kaplan's presence to mean that it was "more important to woo Miller" than to stay neutral and that, rather than make waves, he chose to disbelieve the highly negative things he had heard from his own family about the man who now occupied SAJ's pulpit.[63]

In no time at all the situation escalated. Shul politics became personal, opening up a gully-sized rift between Kaplan and Eisenstein, who threatened not only to expel the SAJ from the Reconstructionist family of congregations but also to wash his hands of the entire movement. This business, Eisenstein confided in his diary, "closed a door in my mind . . . it was for me the end of my association with the movement which I served all my life, and in which MMK has been a deterrent and an obstacle from the start." Decades' worth of slights and grievances, of being second-guessed and disregarded, cascaded from Eisenstein's pen, starting with his standing in the movement. Several years earlier, Kaplan had designated Eisenstein the "founder" of Reconstructionism and himself its "ideologist." Though he intended the designation as a compliment, a salute to the younger man's key role in rendering Reconstructionism a full-fledged denomination, its recipient saw it as an "empty honor," a form of derogation that consigned him to a much lesser and decidedly inferior status: Kaplan the idea man, Eisenstein his water carrier. In this instance, as in many others, for which he cited chapter and verse, Eisenstein had kept mum, acting out of *derekh eretz* and for the good of the movement. But no more. "You have always assumed that whatever you said, or did, or wrote *was* Reconstructionism. Well, some of us don't agree—and you may have to endure what Freud endured from his disciples, dissent and sometimes even disagreement, publicly." While he was at it, Eisenstein also took several potshots at Kaplan's style of leadership, maintaining that while his ideas were cogent, their "implementation has never been clear, either in your own mind, or, consequently, in those of your followers." When it comes to action, he continued, "you seem to have no basis for what you propose."[64]

As these remarks rained down upon him, Kaplan, undaunted, responded vigorously in an exchange of letters, telling Eisenstein how "shocked" he was to hear of his discomfort with his title, to which, in all the years of their working closely together, he "never, never gave the slight indication." Privately, Kaplan dismissed the complaint as "petty nonsense," but that didn't stop him from also charging Eisenstein with deliberately misinterpreting his intentions by thinking that "all that I expected of you was to obey orders." And then suddenly in the very next paragraph, Kaplan's tone became downright inflammatory. "I gave birth to the S.A.J. amid the cruelest labor pains," he wrote with mounting indignation, his choice of imagery, much less its import, designed to wound, even shock. "By expelling it from the Reconstructionist Federation or Fellowship you would be murdering my spiritual child," he railed, adding that this would be an "act far more brutal than that of those who excommunicated me from the Jewish People." Reading these words decades later is a searing experience; one can only dimly imagine their effect on Eisenstein. To his credit, he stood his ground even when Kaplan subsequently pleaded with him not to make good on his threats, beseeching him "please do it for my sake, if you don't want the sun of my life to set amid a sky darkened by stormy clouds." Defiant and sensitive in equal measure, Eisenstein responded by informing Kaplan that he could not "in all conscience compromise because my teacher and father-in-law wants the sun of his life to set in a cloudless sky." That far he wouldn't go. On the other hand, he was sympathetic to Kaplan's call for reconciliation. "Sh'lom bayit [*sic*] is what you want—and I don't blame you for that. If I were 91, I would love a little peace, too."[65]

Peace—a satisfying resolution to this contretemps—was in short supply. Relations between Eisenstein and Kaplan remained chilly for quite some time. In a futile attempt to ensure that the fiftieth anniversary convocation in October would go off without a hitch, Kaplan asked Eisenstein in advance of the festivities to agree to present a united front when addressing the gathering. He declined, eager for "people to realize that we do not agree with one another on our Reconstructionist view of Judaism." Equally wide of the mark and puzzling, or so it seemed to the anti-Miller faction, were Kaplan's efforts to finesse the situation at SAJ by devising a plan in which Miller would "continue to serve the S.A.J. without a sense of insecurity." Even after acknowledging that Miller was a "problem rabbi"; even after being exposed to and witnessing firsthand the ways in which he made light of, and subverted, some of the congregation's long-standing practices and ideals—restoring the traditional Kol Nidre, for one; maintaining from the pulpit that Richard Rubinstein's theology was as valid as Reconstructionism, for another—Kaplan put the best possible light on the situation in the hope of salvaging it. Invoking the principle of religious pluralism, he "instructed" the congregation's powers that be that he, its founding rabbi and guiding light, recognized Miller's "right" to preach a theology other than Reconstructionism—but with the proviso that "his version also leads to the primacy of Jewish peoplehood, God as Power that makes for salvation, and the observance of the Sabbath and Kashruth." And with that in place (though with no mechanism to monitor or enforce it), his conscience intact that he had done all he could to keep the peace at SAJ, Kaplan returned to Jerusalem. Fast forward: eventually, the icy relationship between Eisenstein and Kaplan thawed; things between them went back, at least on the surface, to their pre-imbroglio status. Though a number of disgruntled members had left SAJ to form the Manhattan Havurah, the congregation remained intact until 1985 when yet another breakaway, the West End Synagogue, was formed. Miller remained at SAJ for an additional seven years, occupying its pulpit for a total of three decades, longer than either Kaplan or Eisenstein; the SAJ remained in the fold; Eisenstein continued to be at the helm of the Reconstructionist Rabbinical College until retiring in 1970; and Kaplan continued to be Kaplan, acknowledging only a few years later that he was far more indebted to Eisenstein than he "is to me."[66]

The raw, messy business of shul politics, let alone the volatility of family quarrels, rarely leaves a paper trail. But Kaplan's journal was at the ready. Throughout the 1970s, he continued the practice of writing in it as much for peace of mind as for posterity. It was the only place where his sense of self remained intact; in its pages Rabbi Dr. Mordecai M. Kaplan was no wispy ghost of the past but a person, fully present and accounted for. Over time, his handwriting grew spidery, the space between entries larger, and their contents more spare, closer in tone to the brisk notations in his day calendar than to the baroque musings that had long filled his journals. Still, he had things to say, and judging from the number of times "Eureka!" rang out, the commensurate enthusiasm with which to say them. Well into his mid-nineties, Kaplan continued to grapple with the meaning of God and the role of salvation, yet he also tackled new themes, such as the fragility of world peace and the difference between religion and patriotism, which, as he put it, had become as clear to him as the difference between the right and the wrong side of a Turkish carpet. Religion, he jotted down, "leads to universal happiness, ethical nationalism and world peace. Patriotism leads to dictatorship, unethical nationhood and international war." Sometimes, though not nearly as frequently as in the past, Kaplan also took note of the human condition. Attending a seder at the Tel Aviv home of Rivkah's brother, Joshua, and his wife, he brought along a dozen copies of *The New Haggadah* as a gift, only to find them unopened and unappreciated. "Joshua monopolized the show by leading the Seder and reading from the traditional hagadah in a singsong wail of a Galician Hasid," with his head uncovered, no less. "It was to me a most boring experience," Kaplan declared peevishly, put out by not being given his due.[67]

Letter writing also kept Kaplan in touch with ideas, words, and, most especially, the family. After he and Rivkah settled permanently in Jerusalem in 1975, a weekly exchange of letters became increasingly necessary to his well-being. Even though an overseas phone line was by then an option, it remained expensive and too rushed a medium for effective communication. Kaplan preferred the aerogram, making use of every inch of its pliable flat surface and multiple flaps to bring his close relatives in the States up-to-date on how he and Rivkah passed the time, transforming the thin sheet of blue, sea green, coral, or beige paper into an exercise in ingenuity, a piece of origami. Recipients had first to unfold its flaps and then turn them every which way to follow his sentences as they meandered up, down, and sideways across the page. In his letters he recounted how much or how little progress he had made on his various book projects, of the frosty reception he had received from kibbutzniks when he made the rounds giving lectures—"not Moses, but Karl Marx is their prophet," he observed by way of explanation—and of the latest ideas that had just occurred to him. He might be an "old codger," Kaplan, soon to turn ninety-four, wrote Judith, but he still got "so much fun out of theology." To make his case, he went on to share with her his latest thinking about Maimonides's understanding of the sacrificial cult, bringing Durkheim, Spinoza, and Kant into the mix. "I hope that what I have just written won't prove to you that I am in my dotage. In any event, I can see further than both Spinoza and Kant for the simple reason that I stand, so to speak, on their shoulders." He then quickly added: "I better stop at this point, or you will get to think that I must be somewhat screwy."[68]

Somewhere—it's hard to pinpoint exactly when but 1978 seems about right—the aging process took hold of this mightiest of intellects and most formidable of personalities. As he ascended into his mid- and then late nineties, both Kaplan's correspondence and his journal entries bore witness to the relentless accumulation of indignities that come with old age, the gradual but steady process of disengagement and the recentering of the self to the exclusion of just about everything and everyone else. It's all there, visible on the page. Little by little, what had been a crowded canvas of words dwindled to an empty slate inhabited by a lone paragraph or two, their tone querulous and pinched. Complaint took the place of contemplation: the difficulties of getting about with a walker, which Jerusalem's hilly streets made especially challenging; the enervating presence of maladies that made his life a "misery," transforming the body over which he had once exerted such tight control into an instrument of defiance; of hopes fading, "render[ing] impossible" that he would "live at least 100 years." Never the most easygoing or patient of men, Kaplan became so frustrated by his physical limitations that he lashed out and often at Rivkah, taking her to task for "constant nagging" and for venturing opinions about his work when he hadn't elicited any; occasional disagreements degenerated into frequent squabbling. And yet, he recognized that her ministrations kept him going. "My physical condition is such as to wish I were dead," he wrote plaintively in November 1978. "My darling Rivkah keeps me alive." Intimations of mortality, allusions to death, like this one increasingly shadowed the journal, leading one to expect a grand summation, a valedictory statement, a farewell in its pages. The only thing that came close—perhaps close enough—was this: "It goes without saying that I expect all my own books to be studied." Next sentence: "Schechter always said 'Read Me!' " And that was that. The journal, like life itself, petered out, one blank page after another.[69]

Mindful of the preciousness of time, Kaplan's family brought up his one hundredth birthday as it approached. Plans were afoot to do it up in grand style, to orchestrate a worldwide celebration, or so Eisenstein informed his ailing father-in-law, encouraging him to keep the faith as well as his stamina. "For this purpose (among others), it is important for you to be well and strong. . . . Hazak [be strong]!" Playing up Kaplan's birthday had ample precedent; one might even call it a tradition. In years gone by, much had been made of his sixtieth, seventieth, seventy-fifth, eightieth, eight-fifth, ninetieth, and ninety-fifth. These celebrations usually took the form of interminable fund-raising dinners with too many speeches that drew as many as 1,300 dressed-up and soon-to-be-bored people to New York's fabled Waldorf-Astoria or the Pierre. More imaginative by

Rivkah sustained Kaplan as he aged, n.d.
The Collection of Navah de Shalit, Jerusalem.

far was "Mordecai Kaplan Sabbath," another birthday-turned-eleemosynary moment, though a more elaborate one than most. Five hundred congregations from coast to coast, with an assist from a specially designed "kit" prepared by the Jewish Reconstructionist Foundation, sang his praises on the occasion of his eighty-fifth birthday, integrating his writings into that Shabbat morning's prayer service. A decade later, in 1976, Kaplan's ninety-fifth was another multipronged affair, the first element of which was Judith, Ira, and Naomi's visit to Jerusalem. Their mere presence, Kaplan recalled, was "enough to make me ignore my chronic rheumatism." Rivkah, in turn, arranged for an "at home celebration," which he particularly enjoyed as it placed no burden on him other than having to put on a tie and shake hands with the guests; no speeches required. The celebrant saved that for the third and concluding phase of the festivities, a luncheon at the Knesset orchestrated by the Jewish

Reconstructionist Foundation, at which he delivered a peroration on the significance of Reconstructionism, culminating in a call for a "reconstitutional convention in Jerusalem." The purpose of such a gathering, Kaplan told his guests, was to "reassert our historic right to the Land of Israel," to call on the State of Israel to grant all of its citizens the "democratic rights of life, liberty and the pursuit of happiness," and to organize the Jews of the Diaspora into "organic kehillot" in which every Jew would be registered and taxed—not exactly the usual bill of fare at a birthday party.[70]

As for his one hundredth birthday, by the time it rolled around, Rivkah and he were back in the States, the move necessitated by his advanced age, declining health, and the manifold challenges of caring for the two of them. Kaplan and Rivkah took up residence in the Hebrew Home for the Aged in Riverdale, New York. Despite the agreeableness of their surroundings—Rivkah had a "wonderful room with an exceptional view of the Hudson River," she told her granddaughter Navah, while Kaplan lived in another part of the facility where all of his medical needs were met—neither one wanted to be there. Rivkah much preferred to be on her own, in her own home, and to come up with a "different arrangement, if I manage to carry it out. Simply living together with him." Kaplan just wanted to return to Jerusalem. But that was not to be. He celebrated his centennial in June 1981 and lived out the rest of his days at the Hebrew Home for the Aged. At a modest champagne reception in honor of his birthday, toasts were made and telegrams from civic officials read, to which Kaplan responded. In one hand he held a sheet of paper on which he had prepared some closing remarks, in the other, a copy of *The Purpose and Meaning of Jewish Existence*, whose title beautifully suited the occasion. After dispensing with his thank-yous, Kaplan opened the book to the dedication page and read aloud its pithy inscription—"To Rivkah"—at which point everyone rose to their feet and applauded. "Isn't that a lovely way to include me?" she related. The presentation of a "centennial salute" in the form of a scroll was another highlight. Signed by two hundred of Kaplan's rabbinic colleagues, it extolled the accomplishments of this "rabbi, teacher and leader of generations, founder of Reconstructionism, shaper of twentieth-century Judaism, prophet of our own age," reading much like a eulogy. That would come soon enough—hundreds of them—when Kaplan died two years later, at 102, having exceeded his goal of living to 100. Not long after, Rivkah returned to Jerusalem where she died in 1986, at the age of eighty-seven.[71]

Never one for what he wittily called a "self-celebration," finding it overindulgent, Kaplan allowed himself only a soupçon of enjoyment at being laureled in so grand and public a manner. "I could almost feel myself being sublimated into a legend or a myth," he remarked as tributes poured in at an earlier birthday bash, concluding "There is nothing so dizzying as being put on a high pedestal." And with that, he closed the book; what more could be said? Perhaps had he lingered a little while longer on the relationship between a pedestal and the sensation of being dizzy, Mordecai M. Kaplan might have come to see that it was his gift for balancing on a tightrope that made him a legend and a myth in the first place.[72]

6

Portrait Gallery

For someone who didn't care much for portraits, Mordecai Kaplan appears in a strikingly large number of them. The Jewish Theological Seminary holds two oil paintings of him, the handiwork of Fred Bretten and Lionel Reiss, as does the American Jewish University, one by Max Band and another by Rivkah Rieger. The Reconstructionist Rabbinical College in Philadelphia is home to a pencil sketch by Joseph Tepper, perhaps a preparatory study for an oil painting he subsequently made of Kaplan, as well as a pen and ink drawing by Rieger. A third work by her hand, an oil painted in Jerusalem, was donated by members of her family to Kehillat Mevakshei Derech, the Reconstructionist synagogue that Kaplan attended late in life while living in the holy city. It would be lovely to think of each one as the equivalent of a plaque signaling "Mordecai Kaplan was here," but in only one instance—that of the Jerusalem portrait—is his fierce countenance on

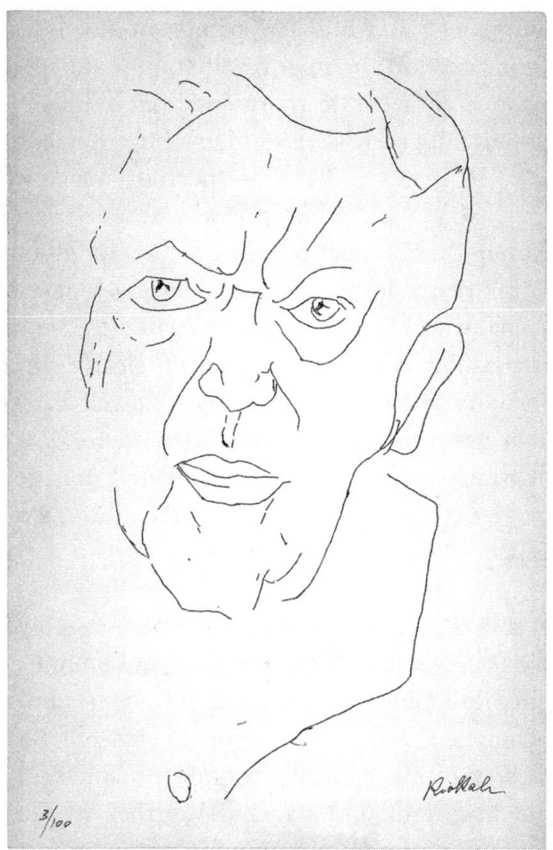

Portrait of Mordecai Kaplan by Rivkah Rieger, ca. 1960s.
The Reconstructionist Archives, Philadelphia.

display; the rest have been consigned to a storeroom or, in the case of the Tepper oil, gone missing.[1]

It's probably just as well. No matter the medium or if its subject faced the viewer, pensively gazed off into space, was captured in a suit and tie, wearing a light blue sweater that matched his eyes, or more abstractly rendered as a series of lines, Kaplan never saw the point. He disliked having to sit for hours on end while the painter wielded his or her brush, nor did he find the final result commensurate with the effort, let alone an accurate representation. With one or two exceptions—usually of Rivkah's doing—he rarely cottoned to his likeness. To his eye, the Reiss portrait was "awful," the Band didn't look at all like him nor was "it much as a work of art," and though the Tepper caught the "wistful gloom" of his mien, it didn't really do him justice, an assessment with which his wife Lena, who proposed it be relegated to the basement rather than exhibited in the living room, clearly agreed. The Kaplan portraits share a common origin as well as a common fate. Kaplan never commissioned any of them. The institutions with which he had long been affiliated did the honors, calling for a portrait as a gesture of recognition, a visual acknowledgment of deeds well done: a hip, hip, hooray in oil or pencil.[2]

Often told that his was a sad Jewish face, possibly the saddest people had ever seen; an angry face; and on one occasion, even a demonic-looking one, Kaplan did not see any of those qualities when he gazed in the mirror. Then again, he was surprised when he came upon photographs of himself, his features scrunched tight and scowly. Was that what he really looked like? "No wonder young people take me for a bear when they first meet me." The disconnect between what we think we look like and how we actually present is a common human trait, to be sure, but in Kaplan's case, the gap between how he saw himself and how others saw him ran deep, affecting his sense of accomplishment as well as his presentational self. To the outside world, Mordecai M. Kaplan appeared a human juggernaut, an Olympian figure who strode across the modern Jewish landscape, reconstituting everything in sight: fearless, resolute, bold, demanding. Kaplan viewed himself differently, as a "veritable Don Quixote": a faltering, tentative, ineffectual soul, a "knight of the long face, always grumpy, always in a bad humor." His many breast-beatings, of which this was arguably the most striking, may seem like momentary bids for reassurance or fleeting instances of self-pity. But the conviction that he was destined to tilt at windmills was perennial rather than episodic. Time and again, Kaplan spoke of "struggling with the angel of darkness and despair," and of the futility of his efforts at keeping Judaism alive: "What a Sisyphus affair!" He also wrote that "being disillusioned is so much a part of my way of life that I am beginning not to mind it," the last part of that admission hard to believe.[3]

The particular set of challenges Kaplan set for himself accounted for his disillusionment; the nature of the American Jewish rabbinate exacerbated it, creating a double whammy of a predicament. "It may be that we rabbis take ourselves too seriously," he cautioned shortly before *Judaism as a Civilization* was released, perhaps thinking of himself. "We experience bitter disappointment because we misconceive our calling and dream of achieving things way beyond our reach. We have talked it into ourselves that we are the successors of the Prophets and therefore believe that we are a failure unless we devote all our energies to the cause of social justice. . . . But ours is an entirely different calling. We are not world reformers or improvers. As rabbis our function is to keep alive the culture or civilization of the Jewish people." Awareness, though, was one thing, acceptance quite another. The tension between the two made for a lot of unhappy men in the pulpit, Mordecai Kaplan chief among them. Just ask his wife. Lena, who knew her spouse better than he knew himself, attributed his lugubrious emotional state to his career as a rabbi and communal servant. After being married to him for more than twenty years, she floated the possibility that had she known how out of sorts he would be, day in and day out, she probably wouldn't have wed him in the first place nor would she want any of her daughters to marry a man of the cloth.[4]

How much happier Kaplan might have been had he known the extent to which his contributions suffuse contemporary Jewish life. Detached from their denominational moorings, floating free, they eventually caught on. After lying fallow for decades, his conception of Judaism and of Jewishness belatedly spoke to and captivated a new generation of American Jews: the current one. These days, when they talk about the bonds that unite; celebrate a bat mitzvah; expect their neighborhood synagogue to offer much more than religious services and an afternoon Hebrew school; pick and choose among Jewish rituals and attribute their choices to personal need; hold Israel dear and also firmly to account by pushing for a democratic and pluralist society; define themselves proudly as post-denominational Jews; and even flounder in search of a Jewish identity that is neither racial nor religious but something much more vague though no less powerful, contemporary American Jews are echoing Kaplan. Chances are they're hardly aware of the connection, so deeply have his once-radical ideas become normative and, in ways he never would have imagined, even prescriptive, especially in liberal circles. But that's now.

Back then, when Kaplan was riding high, caught in the spotlight of American Jewish life, his ideas didn't take off as he had envisioned they would. Reconstructionism "has had something of an impact on Jewish life in terms of self-concern and social concern," he admitted to Harold Schulweis in 1970, "but virtually none whatever in terms of action. By action I refer to social engineering," to affecting behavior. Despite being the only thoroughly American expression of Judaism, Reconstructionism didn't take hold. It's not that Kaplan didn't have what to offer American Jews at the grass roots or that Reconstructionism was much more effective as a diagnosis than a cure. It had plenty to offer. Some of its features, like Kaplan's constant wrestling with the meaning of God, were hard to follow; he himself often got lost in pursuit of the divine. But redefining religious belief, locating it in the here and now rather than in the supernatural? Associating faith more with belonging than with believing? Heralding traditional Jewish rituals as enjoyable rather than enjoined? Taking the sting out of religion, relegating sin and guilt to the sidelines? Defining Jewish identity as "dynamic"? Celebrating the Jewish people? Attractive, sensible, undemanding positions, all. Why, then, did they not take root or, more to the point, why did they not fully take root as articles of Reconstructionist Judaism?[5]

Any number of explanations come to mind, the simplest of which has to do with generational change. What one generation finds fresh and exciting, the next invariably finds tired and dull; enthusiasm wanes, ennui sets in. Reconstructionism, as Kaplan knew all too well, was no exception. Those who formed the SAJ felt a "sense of responsibility for keeping Judaism alive," but the cohort that followed "knew even less about Judaism and felt less of a responsibility for its conservation and enhancement," he observed in 1963, forty years after having established the movement's first beachhead, regretting its lack of progress. By then, the dampening effects of declension were joined and perhaps even jolted by an additional factor that no one saw coming. In the wake of the Shoah and the rise of the State of Israel, once regnant assumptions about identity, faith, and community no longer held true among postwar generations of American Jews. Where decades before, the New World had taken center stage, the Old banished to the margins; where, thanks to Kaplan, the interwar cohort of young rabbinical students at JTS had "discovered American Jewry," emancipating New York from its dependence on Tzernowitz and Jerusalem; and when, back in the day, the "curative balm of reason" was heralded tout court and high-flying philosophical propositions were more seductive than sentiment, a new postwar order began to emerge that turned its back on these elements.[6]

At once a memorialization and a reclamation, postwar American Jewish life increasingly esteemed what Kaplan had not: East European Jewish history and its traditions. Clustering under the banner of what he called Orthodoxy, the rituals, languages, and sensibility of the Old World had given American Jews a past but at too heavy a price: that of "intellectual, and to a large extent, spiritual suppression." When Kaplan made that pronouncement, at a 1917 meeting of a group of young American Jews in search of a community to call their own, it seemed to be the right call. But the alternative he proposed turned out to be evanescent rather than enduring; it would wear thin instead of gathering steam. The sea change that engulfed the modern Jewish community a half century later rendered his once cutting-edge ideas all but obsolete. Increasingly, growing numbers of young American Jews hungered for connection with *yidishkayt* in all of its varied manifestations, from *davening* to speaking Yiddish. "With the rise of Hippiedom, it became fashionable to attack Reconstructionism as having become outdated," Kaplan acknowledged in 1972. Even so, he clung to the belief that he himself, if not the movement he had created, was up to the challenge. "The truth is that despite my being a 'patriarch' by virtue of age, my mind happens to be of the kind that improves with age and when it comes to coping with the age of Hippiedom I manage to think as well as those half my age."[7]

If only. No matter how much Kaplan tweaked and tinkered, adjusted and reformulated, no amount of rewording or recalibration could change Reconstructionism's stripes. Most effective as a declaration, a pronunciamento, even a clarion call, it stopped short of providing a template by which a broad swath of postwar American Jews might live their lives as Jews. It lacked an essential ingredient: warmth. It's this factor, even more than generational change, that put the brakes on Reconstructionism's appeal. From the get-go, large numbers of

American Jews had charged Reconstructionism with championing the head at the expense of the heart. Supplanting affect with abstraction, the movement was said to be "too coldly rational . . . its conception of Judaism cerebral, and its program neatly academic. Reconstructionism is a philosophy of Judaism which leaves untouched and removed the Jewish heart and the Jewish will to live." After hearing Kaplan speak, lay members of the audience often approached him to ask why *The Reconstructionist* couldn't publish articles that "people can understand," or they'd tell him that what he had just talked about "sounded like Greek to them . . . his entire approach too abstract." At a Shabbos weekend seminar held in 1955 in what was then the resort town of Lakewood, New Jersey, a much-anticipated event sponsored by Joachim Prinz's B'nai Abraham Congregation of Newark, Kaplan repeatedly heard that "Reconstructionism had nothing to offer the average Jew who is not an intellectual."[8]

Even intellectuals had difficulty. Consider this head-scratching exchange between Kaplan and Jacob Agus, a former student who went on to become a leading figure in Conservative Judaism. Agus took his teacher to task for defining God as a phenomenon, arguing that "we can't pray to a what." In response, Kaplan retorted that a "person is also a what," adding, none too helpfully, that "what matters is the kind and order of whatness." Is it any wonder that Theodor Gaster, no slouch when it came to matters recondite, found Kaplan's ideas to be confined to a "strait jacket of literal rationalism" and "so vague and woolly, in fact, that they really mean very little at all." Rising to even greater rhetorical heights, Gaster compared Reconstructionists to a "band of butterfly-catchers rushing to and fro across the green pastures of faith, trapping each loveliest specimen in their nets, diligently transforming it and trimming it for exhibition without for a moment realizing that by that very process they are robbing it of its life."[9]

Those within the highest reaches of the Reconstructionist movement had heard it all before, though not as elegantly; from time to time they themselves had voiced a similar critique. Well aware of how much their coreligionists at the grass roots valued gesture and affect—feeling Jewish—and frustrated by how little headway they were making among them, they didn't hesitate to tell Kaplan when they thought he had gone too far, his language "too academic and abstract." Writing in his diary, his tone curiously distant, if emphatic, Eisenstein put it this way: "Dr. Kaplan is all wrong. In stressing theology the less said the better. Maybe actions are louder than words." As late as 1971, Eisenstein reported to "the Chief" that the rabbinical students at the Reconstructionist Rabbinical College expressed a "craving for heightened emotional expression. They do not necessarily reject the intellectual aspects of religion and Judaism in particular, but they feel that these are in a sense argumentative. . . . It's as if they operate on two levels—the classroom should be the place where they learn; the synagogue and its equivalent the place where they are inspired."[10]

Kaplan took this in but did little, if anything, to ameliorate the situation; by then, it was probably too late anyway. He could not have anticipated what the future held, but he certainly could have done more to balance head and heart. He chose not to, relishing his reputation as a "logic-chopping theologian," abstraction his Achilles' heel. Placing too much of a premium on reason, Kaplan either overestimated its appeal among American Jews or their capacity for rationality and wouldn't hear of lowering the movement's intellectual decibel level. Attempts to make its ideals more accessible, he charged, would only compromise its integrity by "cater[ing] to the salesmanship mentality," of which he wanted no part. Besides, how was it possible to "avoid dealing with principles when setting forth the meaning of Reconstructionism?" It couldn't be done, he insisted, comparing it to Communism. The latter "expects its adherents to master abstractions compared with which those of Reconstructionism sound like a kindergarten story. But the difference is that Communists are in earnest. This is why they don't have to be spoon-fed," when "so far there are hardly two or three zealous Reconstructionists. Our most active workers ... have not even made the grade of 'fellow travelers.' "[11]

When he first started out, Kaplan was responsive to the need for a balanced approach, welcoming a good chuckle when cultivating one's spiritual development. "Much good and no harm can come from laughter," he declared as early as 1906, adding "I am quite sure Cervantes has done more good to the world than Thomas Aquinas." Two decades later, he lamented the absence of a playful spirit at the Jewish get-togethers he attended, noting how "disheartened" he was by the "inability of our people to enjoy themselves as Jews." When our people are unable to "play as Jews ... I cannot see how there can be any Jewish life." And just a few years after that, in 1929, Kaplan took things even further: "If Jewish life is to have particularity, it must be a thing of the senses. It must be tangible, visible, audible. ... It must be redeemed from mere abstractness," making room for a "maximum of folkways, folk habits and folk arts," for pleasure and conviviality. But as Reconstructionism spread its wings, moving away from its original focus and becoming more and more of an ideology, it lost in spiritedness what it gained in intellectual coherence. Lightheartedness leached out of Reconstructionism, theorizing took its place: a maximum of discourse, a minimum of everything else. In his more reflexive moments, Kaplan would concede that "Jewish thinking and Jewish living" had to walk hand in hand and that without a "social environment" to foster the two, his efforts were pointless, "like trying to heat the street." Reconstructionism's founder was equally aware of his own shortcomings, of the drawbacks of his living in a "universe of words." He allowed that "if I had possessed the power of song and poetry, or at least of wit, I might have succeeded in winning men's hearts for God and Israel. Men can't be reached through their minds." But that's precisely where Kaplan set his sights and concentrated his efforts; words are what he bequeathed. Tidal waves of words. A raft of books, articles too numerous to count, thousands of sermons and lectures—and talk, lots of talk. Perhaps too much of it, as Eisenstein remarked in his diary: "He does talk a lot—his actual achievements are few, except in writings."[12]

A substantial number of American Jews read what Kaplan wrote and many, many more listened to what he had to say, but their interest went only so far. It's possible, of course, that their own limitations, fueled by the structural constraints of group identity in America, held Reconstructionism in check even more than the movement's limitations or Kaplan's deficiencies. Today, difference announces itself in many forms; at the time Reconstructionism came into its own, the only acceptable form of, and rationale for, difference found shelter under the umbrella of religion, crowding out peoplehood and civilization. It's also possible that the generations Kaplan addressed were content with their lot, getting out of Jewish identity exactly what their members wanted, unwilling to be pushed or challenged, much less reconstructed. Milton Steinberg intimated as much. Having hoped that Reconstructionists would "rouse a revolution, kindle a fire," only to discover that "we have not started and are unlikely ever to start a general conflagration," he wondered whether the "deficiency is in us," whether American Jewry was "no longer flammable."[13]

Kaplan would have none of it. Giving up on his beliefs in the regenerative power of Reconstructionism, or on American Jewry, was never an option. No matter how often he was called on to explain what it was all about—*Time* magazine pegged it

Kaplan worked well into his nineties, n.d.
The Collection of Hadassah K. Musher, New York.

at a "hundred thousand" times—he kept at it. Was he frustrated, stymied, disheartened, and aggrieved? Yes, yes, and yes again, but Kaplan was also steadfast, ever true to his belief in the viability of Reconstructionism and the potential of the Jewish People. As Emil Fackenheim wrote of him in a 1974 tribute,

Kaplan was "undaunted" and "indomitable." Years earlier, when Eisenstein was about ready to leave both the rabbinate and American Jews far behind, he sought Kaplan's counsel. His nerves frayed, his patience shot, his disappointment in full flower, what should he do? Though Kaplan knew firsthand what Eisenstein was experiencing, he told him not to give up. Is it "useless to work with people? May be [*sic*] it is. But the reason we work with people is that life compels us to not merely for economic reasons, but because we can't help ourselves, and those we work for need us, otherwise they wouldn't have us."[14]

There you have it. All the books, articles, sermons, lectures, classes, correspondence, and journal entries boiled down to a simple, winning formula: we + them = us.

Eureka!

RECONSTRUCTING A LIFE

A Note on Primary Sources

Given the length of his days and the range of his motions, reconstructing Mordecai Kaplan's life was hardly a walk in the park. Thanks, though, to the archival material within reach, it came close enough: more sprint than amble. An abundance of letters made Kaplan's voice vivid and real. Caches of correspondence to and from his immediate family as well as from academic and communal colleagues are housed in the Reconstructionist Archives at the Reconstructionist Rabbinical College (RRC) in Philadelphia, as are the invaluable Judith Kaplan Eisenstein and Ira Eisenstein papers. Material from the desk of Jacob Billikopf, Louis Marshall, Harold Schulweis, and Stephen S. Wise, among other American Jewish luminaries, are readily accessible at the American Jewish Archives in Cincinnati, as are the Milton Steinberg papers at the American Jewish Historical Society in New York. Gilding the lily, Navah de Shalit, Rivkah Rieger's granddaughter, made available a number of surviving private letters, as did Tamar Chipkin Orvell, the daughter of Kaplan's longtime friend and ally Israel Chipkin. An unusual assortment of papers at the Society for Advancement of Judaism (SAJ) in New York City topped things off. Its holdings encompassed mimeographed versions of synagogue bulletins, skits, and songbooks; stenographic accounts of board of trustee minutes, and handsomely printed pamphlets and brochures. When I had the good fortune to train my sights on this miscellany, it was housed in cardboard packing boxes and stored throughout the West 86th Street building. By the time you read this, their contents will have been transferred to the Library of the Jewish Theological Seminary, where they are now known as the Society for the Advancement of Judaism (SAJ) (New York, NY) Collection.

Pocket-sized notepads and reams of index cards, calendars, sermons, files, memorabilia, and drafts of manuscripts call the Reconstructionist Archives their home. This array of materials spans a hefty chunk of time, but it's spotty, with multiple gaps between one folder and the next. Why were some things preserved while others of comparable or greater significance were not? It's hard to say. Happenstance? Spatial constraints? Evasion? Even so, there was more than enough material to keep me busy for several years.

The key to the kingdom was Kaplan's handwritten, ledger-sized journal or diary. Most people keep clothes, shoes, belts, and handbags in their closet. Kaplan kept his journal, dozens of volumes worth, neatly housed on floor-to-ceiling shelves. From time to time, he'd take colleagues and students into his sanctum sanctorum and, throwing open the doors to the closet, reveal his journal in all its accumulated glory. "I believe—and I don't think I am wrong— . . . the mere quantity of words in it is bound to produce an effect similar to that of a large mountain." But then, characteristically, Kaplan experienced remorse, as if he had engaged in behavior unbecoming a man of his stature. These days, he needn't worry: the closet is a digital one. Thanks to JTS, where the original journals reside, twenty-five volumes running from 1913 through 1972 are accessible online. The twenty-sixth and twenty-seventh volumes from 1973 through April 1976 and the balance of 1976 through 1981, respectively, live at RRC, as do the earliest volumes of Kaplan's musings, from 1904 through 1906, and 1907.[1]

Spanning a lifetime, Kaplan's journals contain bulletins from the beginnings of the modern Jewish experience in the twentieth century, and the outline of much of what became celebrated publications, lectures, and sermons. They're written in English, though now and again, eager to both test and hone his linguistic skills, Kaplan expressed himself in Hebrew. Contemplative and, at times, remorseful, the journals are also rich in witty, razor-sharp observations, sociological snapshots of the people with whom Kaplan tangoed or observed in passing. With a gimlet eye, a sharp tongue, and a raised eyebrow, he took note of how American Jews of the interwar years named their daughters Gwendolyn and Hyacinth rather than Sarah and Rachel, and characterized upwardly mobile American Jewish men as nudniks, their wives as featherbrained creatures, and the average synagogue president a Jewish version of a Tammany Hall politician. His rabbinical colleagues didn't fare much better. Kaplan thought those who lived in his own backyard put on airs, much like their puffed-up Upper West Side congregants, and the clergy he encountered on his periodic out-of-town trips struck him as a dull bunch. On one occasion, while visiting Harrisburg, Pennsylvania, Kaplan was taken aback by the host rabbi's taciturn nature, an unusual quality in a man of the cloth, whose position mandated that he be out and about among the people. "He had nothing to say and when he did say something, I wished he hadn't," Kaplan remarked. "His speaking was much worse than his silence." More lamentable still in Kaplan's book were those who took strong exception to his views and opposed them publicly: Obstructionists, he called them, a play on Reconstructionists.[2]

An exercise in interiority, the journals usually reflect Kaplan's thoughts as they occurred to him; sometimes, a chance encounter in the present triggered reminiscences of the past. Otherwise, very much in the moment, each entry bore a date and sometimes a time, an indication that Kaplan was aware of the world outside of the journal's ruled pages. The world further intruded in the form of references to Billy Sunday; the trial of the Scottsboro Boys; the end of World War I and World War II; FDR's death, which "stunned" him; the atomic bomb; and the Kennedy assassination, which prompted a "Woe unto us!" Kaplan took quite seriously the responsibility for making entries and was hard on himself when, having let the momentum slacken, he missed too many days in a row. Not that he didn't complain about finding diary keeping a chore, an extra claim on his time. He did, often. Nor was he above poking fun at his diaristic diligence and the strong sense of self that prompted it, pasting into the journal's pages a cartoon he clipped from the August 14, 1932, issue of the *Saturday Review of Literature.* It depicted an oversized wife and her undersized husband entering a stationery store whereupon the wife peremptorily says to the proprietor, "A diary for my husband, please. He's a regular Samuel Pepys."[3]

Like the celebrated late seventeenth-century diarist, Kaplan wrote not only about himself but for himself. Mordecai Kaplan was at once subject and audience. From time to time, he looked over his shoulder, referring expectantly to the possibility that a "future historian might chance" upon his journal. At other moments, he had the general reader rather than Clio in mind, intimating that his musings might make for a good read. A detailed account of "all the mental tortures I went through before and after the talk I gave last night should, it seems to me, be more interesting than my theory about God," he wrote. Otherwise, journal entries were for his eyes and his benefit only: a demonstration "that I have lived." Kaplan meant that quite literally. Charles Liebman relates that when interviewing him for his influential 1970 *American Jewish Year Book* account of Reconstructionism, Kaplan would "refer to the journal to refresh his memory, or corroborate a point. At such times he would ask me to read aloud from it, and we would then discuss the passage in question."[4]

More than an exercise in documentation, the journal served as a blackboard on which Kaplan wrestled with the thorniest moral equations of the day or generated his own. "I've used the journal to think with," he remarked, emphasizing its role as an interlocutor, a sounding board, an "intelligent friend." Its function was therapeutic, too. "What I shall say now will surely sound silly, but what's this journal for if not to serve as a kind of 'father-confessor,' " he noted revealingly, sounding anything but silly. The equivalent of a confessional or a therapist's couch, his journal freed him to vent and, now and again, to wallow: writing in the diary, he said, was an "act of self-revelation" as well as a barometer of his moods. As the years advanced, Kaplan cast it more and more as a memoir. On the cusp of turning eighty, in 1960, he observed that "the older I get, the more I realize that the future ahead of me is getting even shorter and the more eager I become to conserve whatever I remember of the past."[5]

For all of their amplitude and the many uses to which they were put, Kaplan's journals do not cover everything. Readers who expect to find skeletons in his closet will be disappointed, as will those looking for dishy observations about his family. There are some, usually references to their hurtful indifference to Kaplan's intellectual or communal struggles, but they are not plentiful. References to family milestones—births, bar and bat mitzvahs, weddings, and travails—illness and death—dot the text, but they're more perfunctory, even dutiful, than charged. Aware of how seldom he brought his family into the journal's pages and that when he did his accounts resembled a "character certificate," Kaplan questioned his motivations. "Is it because I take them for granted as part of the normal course of domestic life or because I find it difficult to keep up the proper balance between appearing sentimental and appearing cold?" Whatever the reason, he couldn't help himself: "I somehow can't unlimber." The only two exceptions—and striking ones at that, blistering with emotion—had to do with Lena's final illness and demise, which flattened him, and his subsequent courtship of and union with Rivkah Rieger, which buoyed him. Otherwise, he stayed clear of family entanglements.[6]

Sitting at his desk, his pen at the ready, Kaplan performed the ritual of journal writing usually at day's close—and never on a Saturday. Well, not at first. For decades, he hewed to the traditional interdiction against writing on Shabbos and Jewish holidays, which defined the act as work (*melakha*). But then, paralleling his own change of heart and increasingly relaxed ritual practice, Kaplan would scribble away on a Friday night or a Saturday morning, though a frisson of compunction accompanied him each time he did. It was only once Kaplan reached his twilight years and was finally at peace with who he was and what he could or could not do that he saw things differently. Drawing in 1973 on the traditional Hebrew word for a ritually approved, Sabbath-sanctioned pleasure, he pronounced writing in his journal on Shabbos an *oneg*.[7]

Reading Kaplan's journals, eavesdropping on his thoughts and inching my way closer to him, was an *oneg* for me, too—every day of the week.

NOTES

Introduction

1. Mordecai M. Kaplan diary, May 24, 1926; May 10, 1934; April 9, 1932; November 25, 1906. Twenty-five of Kaplan's diaries, from 1913 through 1972, are housed at the Jewish Theological Seminary (JTS) and are accessible online at https://makor.primo.exlibrisgroup.com/discovery/collectionDiscovery?vid=01JTS_INST:01JTS&collectionId=81549909900007706&lang=en&sortItemsBy=title. They are cited here as "Kaplan diary." The earliest volumes of the diaries, from 1904 through 1906, and 1907, and also two volumes covering the years from 1973 through 1981 are at the Reconstructionist Archives at the Reconstructionist Rabbinical College, Philadelphia, and are cited here as "Kaplan diary, RRC Archives."

2. The quotes in this and the next paragraph are drawn from Mordecai M. Kaplan, *The Future of the American Jew* (New York: Macmillan, 1948), p. 13; Mordecai Kaplan to Harold Schulweis, July 19, 1954, Mordecai M. Kaplan Correspondence, SC-6102, American Jewish Archives (hereafter AJA); Kaplan diary, August 8, 1932; August 16, 1929; July 23, 1947.

3. Kaplan diary, October 31, 1972; Jon Butler, *God in Gotham: The Miracle of Religion in Modern Manhattan* (Cambridge, MA: Harvard University Press, 2020), p. 183; Kaplan diary, May 10, 1933.

4. This paragraph and the one that follows draw on Kaplan diary, March 26, 1951; March 16, 1926; November 30, 1926; November 3, 1930; January 16, 1914; August 9, 1951; December 29, 1955; November 30, 1951; December 31, 1958; March 24, 1958.

5. Kaplan diary, July 23, 1951; July 10, 1959; June 21, 1955. Given Kaplan's declarations of indebtedness to Dewey, the paucity of references in his journal to the philosopher is both striking and curious. Mordecai Kaplan to Judith Eisenstein, March 14, 1974, Correspondence of Judith K. Eisenstein with Mordecai M. Kaplan (hereafter cited as "Judith K. Eisenstein correspondence"), RG1_RS01, box 26, subfolder 2, Reconstructionist Rabbinical College Archives (hereafter "RRC Archives").

6. Mordecai Kaplan to Ira Eisenstein, September 2, 1938, Correspondence of Ira Eisenstein with Mordecai M. Kaplan (hereafter cited as "Ira Eisenstein correspondence"), RG1_RS01, box 7, RRC Archives; Kaplan diary, September 15, 1949.

7. This and the succeeding paragraph draw on Kaplan diary, December 1, 1971; November 12, 1930; September 16, 1955; August 28, 1954.

8. Kaplan diary, March 28, 1948; October 5, 1951. "I always try to get [my friends] to excuse me," Kaplan told one of them, Emanuel Gamoran, after turning down an invitation to officiate at his nuptials to Mamie Goldsmith in 1922. When Gamoran refused to take no for an answer, Kaplan yielded, allowing how he didn't want to ruin their friendship by "taking my chances with you." A number of years later, when asked to officiate at the funeral of Israel Unterberg, a longtime supporter of his as well as a major contributor to the Seminary, Kaplan's anxiety level rose so high he was tempted to "devise possible ways of being out of the country at the time." He didn't and stayed the course. See Mordecai Kaplan to Emanuel Gamoran, November 17, 1922, reproduced in Mamie Gamoran, "A Family History," unpub. ms., 1985,

p. 87. I'd like to thank Naomi Gamoran, the Gamorans' great-granddaughter, for bringing this memoir to my attention, and her grandfather, Hillel Gamoran, for permission to quote from it; Kaplan diary, May 2, 1934.

9. Mordecai Kaplan to Judith Eisenstein, July 24, 1968, Judith K. Eisenstein correspondence, RG1_RS01, box 26, folder 2, RRC Archives.

10. Kaplan diary, July 3, 1929.

11. Ira Eisenstein journal, September 7, 1941, Ira Eisenstein and Judith Kaplan Eisenstein Journals, RG 2, subfolder 3, RRC Archives (hereafter cited as "Eisenstein journal").

12. Kaplan diary, July 17, 1945.

Chapter 1. The Sermon

1. Kaplan diary, October 25, 1914; "Letter to the Editor: Mr. Eisenstein's Criticism," *American Hebrew* (hereafter *AH*), December 30, 1904; Kaplan diary, February 8, 1959; Mordecai M. Kaplan to Moses Davis, November 16, 1903, and April 3, 1904, Kehilath Jeshurun Archives, Congregation Kehilath Jeshurun, New York.

2. Mordecai M. Kaplan to Moses Davis, April 3, 1904, Kehilath Jeshurun Archives.

3. Aaron Rothkoff, "The American Sojourns of Ridbaz: Religious Problems within the Immigrant Community," *Proceedings of the American Jewish Historical Society*, 57, no. 4 (June 1968), pp. 561–62; "Reverence and Modesty," *AH*, September 30, 1904.

4. Kaplan diary, January 17, 1929. The text of Kaplan's letter can be found in Mel Scult, *Judaism Faces the Twentieth Century: A Biography of Mordecai M. Kaplan* (Detroit: Wayne State University Press, 1993), p. 73.

5. Kaplan diary, February 2, 1917.

6. "Letter to the Editor: Mr. Eisenstein's Criticism," *AH*, December 30, 1904; "Reverence and Modesty," *AH*, September 30, 1904; Phineas Israeli, "The Orthodox Rabbi of American Training," *AH*, January 6, 1905; "Reverence and Modesty." See also, "Communication: The Slutzka Rav," *AH*, October 7, 1904.

7. J. D. Eisenstein, "Letter to the Editor: A Condition, Not a Theory," *AH*, December 9, 1904.

8. "Letter to the Editor: Mr. Eisenstein's Criticism."

9. Kaplan diary, August 1, 1905; April 29, 1917. The first reference can be found in Kaplan's earliest set of diaries which he called "Communings of the Spirit," RRC Archives; the second in the diaries housed at JTS and available online.

10. "Arnold Bogumil Ehrlich: Greatest of Living M'forshim," *Hebrew Standard*, February 7, 1908; Kaplan diary, June 13, 1958; Israel Friedlander, "A Great Bible Scholar," *The Nation*, January 10, 1920, p. 41.

11. "Joseph L. Sossnitz, Philosopher, Dead," *New York Times* (hereafter *NYT*), March 3, 1910; Kaplan diary, October 16, 1948; "The Sossnitz Celebration," *AH*, December 6, 1907; Mordecai M. Kaplan, "The Influences That Have Shaped My Life," *The Reconstructionist* 8, no. 10 (June 26, 1942): 27–36; Kaplan diary, February 7, 1959.

12. Kaplan diary, December 12, 1906; November 25, 1906, RRC Archives.

13. Kaplan diary, September 23, 1934; "Letter to the Editor: Mr. Eisenstein's Criticism."

14. Kaplan diary, May 8, 1906; "Pulpit Topics," *AH*, December 20, December 25, 1907.

15. S. N. Behrman, "Daughter of the Ramaz," *The Worcester Account* (New York, 1946), p. 105.

16. Kaplan diary, December 31, 1906; December 2, 1906, RRC Archives.

17. Kaplan diary, May 23, 1907; May 7, 1905; December 31, 1906, RRC Archives.

18. Kaplan diary, December 8, 1904. For additional references to Kaplan's use of the term, see Kaplan diary, November 23, 1906, and "Judaism Reconstructed," in Kaplan diary, November 24, 1907. Kaplan diary, March 22, 1905; November 24, 1907, all in RRC Archives.

19. Kaplan diary, May 23, 1907; January 30, 1907, RRC Archives.

20. Kaplan diary, August 23, 1905; August 1, 1905, RRC Archives.

21. Kaplan diary, August 1, 1905; March 17, 1907; January 3, 1907; November 25, 1906, RRC Archives.

22. Kaplan diary, December 2, 1906; August 23, 1905, RRC Archives.

23. Kaplan diary, August 23, 1905; December 27, 1906, RRC Archives.

24. See, for example, "Betrothal," *AH*, February 28, 1908; *Hebrew Standard*, March 20, 1908.

25. "Affidavit for License to Marry," May 19, 1908; "Certificate and Record of Marriage," June 2, 1908, Historical Vital Records Collection, New York City Municipal Archives. I thank my steadfast colleague and longtime friend Kenneth Cobb, assistant commissioner, New York City Department of Records and Information Services, for sharing these documents with me; Kaplan diary, February 7, 1959; Scult, *Judaism Faces*, p. 97.

26. Over the course of researching and writing this book, I had the pleasure of talking about Mordecai and Lena Kaplan with their grandchildren, Ann Eisenstein, Miriam Eisenstein, Dr. Daniel Musher, and Dr. David Musher and his wife, Ruth. They generously—and lovingly—shared their memories of their grandparents, sharpening my sense of their personalities.

27. Kaplan diary, October 8, 1928.

28. Lyrics to "I Love to Lean on Lena," 1933, "Sheet Music" box, SAJ Archives. Once housed at SAJ, the congregation's archives can now be found at JTS, where they are in the process of being re-catalogued.

29. "Lena Kaplan—This Is Your Life. Presented to You by the Israel Group of Hadassah," May 10, 1954, p. 19. Dr. David Musher was kind enough to bring the text of this detailed and warmhearted presentation to my attention.

30. Kaplan diary, October 4, 1918.

31. Kaplan diary, January 30, 1942; April 21, 1918.

32. Kaplan diary, September 11, 1933; April 1, 1917.

33. Kaplan diary, May 3, 1943; May 24, 1926.

34. Kaplan diary, January 30, 1942.

35. Kaplan diary, August 29, 1917; January 15, 1928.

36. Kaplan diary, January 27, 1918.

37. Kaplan diary, August 1, 1905, RRC Archives.

38. Kaplan diary, February 7, 8, 1959. This entry afforded him the opportunity to reminisce at some length about his encounter with Schechter fifty years earlier. In an entry the very next day, Kaplan added the choice detail that it was largely due to Henrietta Szold's having put in a good word on his behalf that Schechter approached him in the first place. For a more contemporaneous reference, see Solomon Schechter to Cyrus Adler, June 29, 1909, Solomon Schechter Family Collection, ARC 101, series 9, box 38, Schechter Chronological Correspondence, folder 38/8 (6 of 12), 1909, JTS Library.

39. Kaplan diary, February 7, 1959.

Chapter 2. The Blueprint

1. Kaplan diary, April 10, 1915; August 29, 1917.

2. Mordecai M. Kaplan, "What Judaism Is Not," *Menorah Journal* 1, no. 4 (October 1915): 214.

3. Kaplan diary, September 16, 1908; Kaplan, "What Judaism Is Not," p. 215.

4. Kaplan diary, April 12, 1917. See also Meeting Minutes, April 3, 1917, "Early Kaplan," box 1, folder 13, RRC Archives, and Mordecai M. Kaplan, "What Is Judaism?," *Menorah Journal* 1, no. 5 (December 1915): 318; Kaplan diary, April 16, 1918.

5. Kaplan diary, August 17, 1916.

6. The quotes in the following paragraphs are drawn from Kaplan, "What Judaism Is Not," pp. 208–216, and "What Is Judaism?," pp. 309–318.

7. Kaplan diary, April 10, 1915; undated SAJ Minutes, ca. 1922, p. 12, SAJ Archives.

8. "The Real Estate Field," *NYT*, October 10, 1912; "Fifteen Story Apartment House Ready," *NYT*, May 6, 1928; "The Reconstruction of West End Avenue," *Real Estate Record and Builders*

Guide 89 (June 22, 1912): 1359; Kaplan diary, September 17, 1918; *Jewish Center Day: Dedication Exercises and Festivities*, March 24, 1918, p. 8, in the possession of the author.

9. "Promotional Booklet for the Jewish Center," reprinted in undated SAJ Minutes, ca. 1922, p. 12, SAJ Archives.

10. Kaplan diary, October 25, 1914; September 4, 1915.

11. Kaplan diary, August 29, August 31, 1917.

12. Kaplan diary, February 22, 1917.

13. Kaplan diary, June 18, 1916; November 11, 1917; March 2, 1918.

14. Kaplan diary, April 17, 1915.

15. Kaplan diary, June 18, 1916.

16. Kaplan diary, November 9, 1917.

17. Kaplan diary, June 18, 1916.

18. Kaplan diary, July 26, August 14, 1916.

19. Kaplan diary, March 2, 1918.

20. Kaplan diary, March 2, 1918.

21. Kaplan diary, April 6, 1918.

22. See, for example, Louis Marshall to Mordecai Kaplan, May 16, 1921, in which the Seminary leader chided him for failing to consult with the Seminary administration before making these kinds of financial arrangements. Louis Marshall Papers, MS 369, box 1591, folder 3, American Jewish Archives, Cincinnati, Ohio.

23. Kaplan diary, July 22, 1918.

24. Kaplan diary, July 22, 1918.

25. "Program," *Jewish Center Day*, pp. 24–30.

26. Mordecai Kaplan, "The Place of the Jewish Center in American Life," *Jewish Center Day*, pp. 17, 18.

27. Kaplan diary, July 28, 1919; Transcript, "Get-Together Gathering at the Jewish Center, February 9, 1921," p. 2. I'd like to thank my colleague Professor Zev Eleff for generously sharing this revelatory document with me.

28. Kaplan diary, August 14, 1918.

29. Kaplan diary, May 6, 1921. This is one of many gimlet-eyed comments Kaplan made throughout his tenure at the Jewish Center. Kaplan diary, December 26, 1918; October 31, 1918; August 14, 1918; December 26, 1918.

30. Kaplan diary, May 7, 1918; July 22, 1918.

31. Kaplan diary, December 26, 1918.

32. Kaplan diary, July 28, 1919; July 27, 1920.

33. Kaplan diary, May 12, 1921.

34. Kaplan diary, May 12, 1921.

35. What follows is drawn from Mordecai M. Kaplan, "A Program for the Reconstruction of Judaism," *Menorah Journal* 6, no. 4 (August 1920): 185–196, and Mordecai M. Kaplan, "The Society of the Jewish Renascence," *The Maccabaean* 34, no. 4 (November 1921): 110–113.

36. Kaplan diary, December 29, 1918.

37. See also *The Society of the Jewish Renascence: Its History and Aims*, n.d., in folder marked "Re: The Society of the Jewish Renascence, 1920," Early Kaplan Early Reconstructionist Society of Jewish Renascence, 1919–1921, RG1_RS19, RRC Archives. See also, Minutes of the Morning Session, July 7, 1920, and Minutes of the Morning Session, July 8, 1920, RG1_RS19, RRC Archives.

38. Jacob Heller, "And the Heretic Spoke Saying . . . ," *Hebrew Standard*, January 21, 1921, p. 13. See also, "Official and Personal Heresy," *Hebrew Standard*, January 7, 1921, p. 8.

39. What follows is drawn from "The Third Anniversary of the Jewish Forum," *Jewish Forum* 4, no. 1 (January 1921): 647; "Reconstructing Judaism?," *Jewish Forum* 4, no. 1 (January 1921): 645–646; Bernard Drachman, "An Examination of Prof. Mordecai M. Kaplan's Views of Judaism," *Jewish Forum* 4, no. 2 (February 1921): 724–731.

40. "Reconstructing Judaism?," p. 646; "Get-Together Gathering," p. 3; Kaplan diary, May 27, 1921.

41. "Reconstructing Judaism?," p. 646; Jacob Kohn to Herman Rubenovitz, February 9, 1921, reprinted in Rabbi Herman Rubenovitz and Mignon L. Rubenovitz, *The Waking Heart* (Cambridge, MA: Nathaniel Dame, 1967), p. 147.

42. Kaplan diary, May 27, 1921; May 9, 1921; May 17, 1921. The text of this maternal advice appears in "My dearies!," n.d., RG1_RS01, box 26, subfolder 13, RRC Archives.

43. "Get-Together Gathering," p. 21.

44. "Get-Together Gathering," title page and pp. 2, 4, 3.

45. "Get-Together Gathering," pp. 2, 5, 9.

46. "Get-Together Gathering," pp. 7, 9, 13.

47. Numerous references to the audience's response are strewn throughout the stenographic account of the proceedings; "Get-Together Gathering," pp. 25, 26, 27.

48. Kaplan diary, May 14, 1921; undated SAJ Minutes, ca. 1922, pp. 1, 2, SAJ Archives.

49. See, for example, Kaplan diary, September 21, 1921; undated SAJ Minutes, ca. 1922, pp. 18, 19; Kaplan diary, May 9, 1921; undated SAJ Minutes, ca. 1922, p. 19, SAJ Archives.

50. Undated SAJ Minutes, ca. 1922, p. 19. This document also contains several references to Magnes's arbitration efforts. See, for example, J. L. Magnes to H. L. Simmons, December 21, 1921; J. L. Magnes to Reuben Sadowsky, December 22, 1921; J. L. Magnes to H. L. Simmons, December 25, 1921, in undated SAJ Minutes, ca. 1922, pp. 5–9.

51. Mordecai M. Kaplan to William Fischman, January 16, 1922, and William Fischman to Mordecai M. Kaplan, January 19, 1922, Mordecai M. Kaplan Correspondence, RG1_RS01, box 10, RRC Archives.

52. Kaplan diary, August 24, 1916; September 21, 1921.

53. Kaplan diary, April 25, 1921.

Chapter 3. Musical Chairs

1. Minutes of the Seating Committee, May 25, 1925, SAJ Minutes, SAJ Archives. The committee was sometimes called by this name, and at other moments it was known as the Seats Committee or the Committee on Seats.

2. Undated SAJ Minutes, ca. 1922, p. 20, SAJ Archives.

3. Kaplan diary, March 15, 1926.

4. These references are drawn from undated SAJ Minutes, ca. 1922, pp. 16–18.

5. Undated SAJ Minutes, ca. 1922, pp. 18–19.

6. Undated SAJ Minutes, ca. 1922, p. 21.

7. Kaplan diary, May 22, 1922; undated SAJ Minutes, ca. 1922, pp. 21, 22.

8. Undated SAJ Minutes, ca. 1922, p. 21; Minutes, Members' Meeting, January 24, 1922, SAJ Archives.

9. Kaplan diary, May 29, 1923; Minutes, Members' Meeting, January 24, 1922.

10. Minutes of the Morning Session, Society of Jewish Renascence, July 8, 1920, Early Kaplan Early Reconstructionist Society of Jewish Renascence, RG1_RS19, RRC Archives.

11. Kaplan diary, May 24, 1958.

12. Undated SAJ Minutes, ca. 1922, p. 20.

13. In a very early speech to the membership, Kaplan likened SAJ's brand of Judaism to an "old ship," which was "still good" if only its "barnacles" would be moved. He had originally written, and subsequently crossed out, the word "carbuncles," which, had he said it aloud, would have made quite a splash. Minutes, Members' Meeting, January 31, 1922, SAJ Archives.

14. Ruth Glazer, "Holiday Cook," *Commentary*, March 1956, p. 294; "The Nation's Business," April 1933, www.vintagepaperads.com, accessed July 29, 2023.

15. "Remarks at the SAJ Annual Meeting, May 11, 1924," in folder marked "SAJ-Annual Meeting Remarks of Mordecai M. Kaplan," in box marked "SAJ Liturgy/Revised Haggadah and SAJ Other," RG 1_RS20, RRC Archives.

16. Kaplan diary, April 27, 1922; March 28, 1922; September 29, 1926; "Remarks at the SAJ Annual Meeting, May 11, 1924."

17. SAJ Minutes, February 5, 1922, SAJ Archives.

18. Over fifty years later, in response to questions from her father about her bat mitzvah, which she was unable to answer, Judith had this to say: "I'd like to be more helpful about my own Bat Mitzvah. . . . The fact that I don't remember what I read is due to the fact that you decided what it was to be the Friday evening before the occasion—I read it through for you once or twice—you corrected my diction and that was all. There was no extended period of preparation such as later generations went through! Sorry, papa. But that's the best I can do." See Judith Eisenstein to Mor-

decai Kaplan, April 14, 1975, Judith K. Eisenstein correspondence, RG1_RS01, box 26, subfolder 2, RRC Archives.

19. Judith Eisenstein to Mordecai Kaplan, April 14, 1975.

20. The promised details never materialized.

21. "Our Activities," *The S.A.J.*, March 11, 1923, p. 5, folder "SAJ Program and Menu—First Anniversary, 1923," in box marked "SAJ Anniversary Celebrations," RRC Archives; SAJ board minutes, May 3, 1922, SAJ Archives.

22. Kaplan diary, May 31, 1933.

23. Kaplan diary, April 27, 1922.

24. Kaplan diary, April 27, 1922; "Remarks at the SAJ Annual Meeting, May 11, 1924."

25. Mordecai M. Kaplan, "Moshe Nathanson—A Personal Tribute," *SAJ Yearbook Dedicated to Cantor Moshe Nathanson on the Occasion of the Thirty-fifth Anniversary of His Affiliation with the Society for the Advancement of Judaism*, June 2, 1959, p. 3, folder marked "Nathanson Photos; 1959 Yearbook," in box marked "Music at the SAJ," SAJ Archives; Kaplan diary, May 29, 1923.

26. Kaplan diary, April 22, 1927; October 3, 1922.

27. Kaplan diary, October 5, October 18, 1925.

28. SAJ Minutes, May 29, 1922, SAJ Archives.

29. Kaplan diary, September 22, 1922.

30. See, for example, Kaplan diary, August 31, 1922.

31. Transcription (in English) of a letter written in Yiddish by Anna Kaplan to her son, Mordecai, n.d., Mordecai M. Kaplan Correspondence, RG1_RS01, box 14, subfolder marked "Israel and Anna Kaplan," RRC Archives. Either in response to that communication or independently of it, Kaplan penned a rather heated letter in November 1927, indicating that his mind was made up, for one thing, and for another, no longer could anyone, not even his mother, tell him what to do or what to think. "I am no more bothered by the Rambam [Maimonides] than I am by the Slutzker Rav," the forty-six-year-old rabbi told her, dismissing her concerns for his reputation and well-being. She never saw it. "At the last moment I weakened and did not send the letter," Kaplan wrote at the top of its first page. Still, its contents go to his state of mind

after receiving one too many complaints about his stance vis-à-vis Kol Nidre and experiencing too much parental oversight. See Mordecai Kaplan to "My Dear Folks," November 11, 1927, Mordecai M. Kaplan Correspondence, RG1_RS01, box 14, subfolder marked "Israel and Anna Kaplan," RRC Archives.

32. Kaplan diary, November 7, 1930; September 30, 1927; October 4, 1930.

33. Kaplan diary, October 19, 1927; September 29, 1930.

34. Kaplan diary, September 29,1930.

35. The Kol Nidre exchange between Kaplan and Eisenstein, including multiple copies of Eisenstein's October 5, 1930, letter, can be found in RG 1, box 28, subfolders 2 and 3, OIS Oversize, RRC Archives.

36. Kaplan to Eisenstein, October 12, 1930, RRC Archives.

37. Kaplan diary, November 7, 1930.

38. Kaplan diary, October 2, 1922.

39. Kaplan diary, October 3, 1922, April 27, 1922, October 3, 1922; October 8, 1922.

40. SAJ Minutes, January 29, 1922; Minutes, Members' Meeting, January 31, 1922.

41. Kaplan diary, May 22, 1922.

42. Kaplan diary, August 22, July 10, 1922.

43. Kaplan diary, April 27, 1922.

44. Kaplan diary, July 27, 1920.

45. Kaplan diary, May 17, May 27, 1921.

46. Kaplan diary, April 27, 1922.

47. Kaplan diary, May 1, 1922.

48. Kaplan diary, May 1, May 5, 1922.

49. Stephen S. Wise to Solomon Goldman, n.d. [1922], box 22, folder 11, MS-19, Jewish Institute of Religion Records, American Jewish Archives, Cincinnati, Ohio (hereafter AJA); Kaplan diary, May 22, 1922.

50. Mordecai Kaplan to Lena Kaplan, June 29, 1923, Mordecai M. Kaplan Correspondence, RG1_RS01, box 14, subfolder marked "Lena R. Kaplan," RRC Archives; Kaplan diary, July 16, 1923; Stephen S. Wise, *Challenging Years: The Autobiography of Ste-*

phen Wise (New York: G. P. Putnam's Sons, 1949), chapter 8, "A Rabbinical Seminary Is Born," pp. 129–142, especially p. 129.

51. Kaplan diary, June 27, 1923; July 16, 1923; Mordecai Kaplan to Stephen Wise, July 1, 1923, box 22, folder 11, MS-19, Jewish Institute of Religion Records, AJA.

52. Stephen Wise to Mordecai Kaplan, July 26, 1923, box 22, folder 11, MS-19, Jewish Institute of Religion Records, AJA.

53. Mordecai Kaplan to Stephen Wise, August 29, 1923, box 22, folder 11, MS-19, Jewish Institute of Religion Records, AJA; Kaplan diary, September 20, 1923.

54. Kaplan diary, September 20, September 23, 1923; February 18, 1926.

55. Kaplan diary, September 23, 1923.

56. Kaplan diary, November 29, December 16, December 4, 1924.

57. Kaplan diary, November 29, 1924.

58. See, for example, Building Committee Report, SAJ Minutes, January 26, 1925; SAJ Minutes, February 2, February 9, March 22, April 6, 1925, SAJ Archives.

59. See, for example, letter from G. Richard Davis to Israel Unterberg, February 3, 1925, in SAJ Minutes, February 2, 1925; Building Committee Report, April 6, 1925, SAJ Minutes.

60. Kaplan diary, April 1, 1925; "Now My Joy Is Complete," *S.A.J. Review* 4, no. 30 (April 14, 1925): 2–7; Mordecai Kaplan to Lena Kaplan, April 3, 1925. This is one of a batch of letters Kaplan wrote his wife while in Palestine, which Professor Mel Scult graciously shared with me (hereafter cited as "Lena letters").

61. Lena letters, April 20, April 22, and April 12, 1925.

62. Lena letters, April 3, April 22, 1925; Lena Kaplan to Mordecai Kaplan, March 27, 1925, Letters to Mordecai Kaplan, in box marked "Mordecai Kaplan: Photographs, Essays, Etc.," SAJ Archives; Lena letters, May 10, 1925.

63. Kaplan diary, September 24, 30, October 15, 1925.

64. *S.A.J. Review*, September 18, 1925, p.3.

65. Kaplan diary, March 22, March 16, 1926.

66. Kaplan diary, September 12, March 10, 1926.

67. Conversation with Edward Schachner, April 15, 2021; email exchange with Anthony Robins, August 21, 2023.

68. Temima Nimtzowitz, "Mural Decorations in Synagogues," *The Reconstructionist* 1, no. 10 (May 17, 1935): 6–12, especially pp. 10–12. Much of the magazine that week was given over to a discussion of Jewish art and its relevance to modern-day Jewish life. See also, Mordecai M. Kaplan, "The Place of the Jewish Center in American Jewish Life," *Jewish Center Day: Dedication Exercises and Festivities, March 24, 1918*, p. 11.

69. Eisenstein journal, May 20, 1935, RG 2, subfolder 3, RRC Archives; Kaplan diary, May 20, 1935. See also Deborah Waxman and Joyce Galpern Norden, "The Challenge of Implementing Reconstructionism: Art, Ideology and the SAJ Sanctuary Mural," *American Jewish History* 5, no. 3 (September 2009): 195–224.

70. Kaplan diary, September 30, 1925; November 29, 1924.

71. Kaplan diary, October 4, 1924; October 22, 1927; December 16, 1924, November 28, 1927.

72. Kaplan diary, December 29, 1924.

73. Kaplan diary, October 4, February 10, December 16, December 29, 1924.

74. Kaplan diary, December 23, 1926.

75. Kaplan diary, January 12, 1927.

76. Kaplan diary, January 19, 1927. A copy of the actual letter can also be found in box 22, folder 11, MS-19, Jewish Institute of Religion Records, AJA.

77. Cyrus Adler to Mordecai Kaplan, January 26, 1927, box 22, folder 11, MS-19, Jewish Institute of Religion Records, AJA.

78. Kaplan diary, February 10, 1927; "We, the Undersigned, to Cyrus Adler, February 17, 1927," box 22, folder 11, MS-19, Jewish Institute of Religion Records, AJA; Teachers Institute Faculty to Mordecai Kaplan, January 23, 1927, box 22, folder 11, MS-19, Jewish Institute of Religion Records, AJA; Kaplan diary, February 23, 1927, June 17, 1927.

79. Kaplan diary, January 12, 1927; Extract of the Minutes of the Faculty Meeting, January 12, 1927, box 22, folder 11, MS-19, Jewish Institute of Religion Records, AJA.

80. Stephen Wise to Judge Mack, February 24, 1927; Mordecai Kaplan to Judge Mack, March 9, 1927, box 22, folder 11, MS-19, Jewish Institute of Religion Records, AJA.

81. "Extract of Letter from Judge Mack to Dr. Wise Re: Dr. M. M. Kaplan," March 11, 1927; Wise to Mack, February 24, 1927; Wise to Louis I. Newman, February 25, 1927; Wise to Mack, February 24, 1927, box 22, folder 11, MS-19, Jewish Institute of Religion Records, AJA.

82. Kaplan diary, November 5, 1927; December 14, 1924.

Chapter 4. Fighting Words

1. Kaplan diary, December 7, 1904, RRC Archives; Kaplan diary, March 18, April 3, 1935. See also Mordecai M. Kaplan, "How Maimonides Reconstructed Judaism," *The Reconstructionist* 1, no. 5 (April 1935): 7–15; Kaplan diary, March 17, 1929.

2. Kaplan diary, March 17, 1929.

3. Mordecai M. Kaplan, *Judaism as a Civilization* (New York: Macmillan, 1935), p. 118.

4. Mordecai M. Kaplan, "Toward a Reconstruction of Judaism," *Menorah Journal* 12, no. 2 (April 1927): 114, 120, 122, 116, 123, 126.

5. Kaplan diary, September 25, 1929; June 25, 1929; January 10, 1930.

6. Kaplan diary, November 7, 1929; March 17, 1933; January 10, 1930.

7. Kaplan diary, January 1, 1929; May 24, 1926.

8. "$10,000 for Essay on Jews," *NYT*, October 7, 1929, p. 28; "Julius Rosenwald Offers $10,000 Prize for Essay on Jews," *Chicago Daily Tribune*, October 7, 1929, p. 39; "Prize Essay Contest Is Announced," *American Israelite*, October 11, 1929, p. 1.

9. Kaplan diary, October 6, 1929; December 11, 1930; May 8, 1930: October 10, 1930; December 11, 1930; July 14, 1931.

10. "Prize Essay Contest Is Announced."

11. Kaplan diary, May 31, 1933.

12. Kaplan diary, February 20, 1933; January 28, 1933; February 20, 1933; February 5, 1933; June 10, 1933; February 5, 1933; February 28, 1933.

13. Kaplan diary, February 5, 1933.

14. Kaplan diary, March 16, 1933.

15. What follows is drawn from Unprocessed Rosenwald Essay Contest Collection, American Jewish Archives. See, especially, Minutes of a Meeting of the Judges of the Julius Rosenwald Essay Contest and Members of the Executive Committee, n.d.; Samson Benderly to Mordecai M. Kaplan, September 11, 1933; Samson Benderly to Eugene Kohn, September 14, 1933; Samson Benderly to Lee Levinger, September 14, 1933; Samson Benderly to Elisa Friedman, December 8, 1933; Abba Hillel Silver to Samson Benderly, December 22, 1933; Samson Benderly to Abba Hillel Silver, January 3, 1934. I'd like to thank archivist Jae Heisler for making this material available to me.

16. Kaplan diary, November 15, 1934.

17. Throughout 1934 and 1935 (and sometimes beyond), Kaplan jotted down other people's remarks about his book in his journal. This paragraph draws on those comments as well as on the following: Jacob Weinstein, "Two Studies of Judaism as a Civilization," *New York Times Book Review*, July 21, 1935, p. 14; Beryl Harold Levy, "Jewish Social Planning," *The Nation*, July 8, 1934, p. 82; Rabbi Victor E. Reichert, "From the Rocking Chair," *American Israelite*, January 24, 1935, p. 4; "Asserts Judaism Remains Religion," *NYT*, June 2, 1935, p. 22; Kaplan diary, June 17, 1934; Rabbi Aaron Rosmarin, Ph.D., "Whither the Jewish Theological Seminary?," *Jewish Forum*, September 1934, pp. 239–246, especially pp. 242, 243, 245; Reichert, "From the Rocking Chair"; Kaplan diary, June 11, 1935. See also, Kaplan diary, July 10, November 12, 1934.

18. Eisenstein journal, May 29, 1935, RG 2, subfolder 3, RRC Archives; "Two Studies of Judaism as a Civilization." See, for example, Kaplan diary, September 23, September 17, October 9, 1934.

19. Eisenstein, however, did not keep silent, noting in his diary that "Yesterday's Times finally carried a review . . . and coupled it with Levinthal's terrible tripe." He went on to say that we shall never know if suspicions that "Adler had tipped off the Times people to lay off MMK's book" were unfounded, but they

"certainly did linger long enough." Eisenstein journal, July 22, 1935, RG 2, subfolder 3, RRC Archives.

20. Kaplan diary, September 7, 1934.

21. Kaplan diary, May 15, 1935.

22. Kaplan diary, September 15, 1915.

23. Kaplan diary, March 12, 1917; Solomon Schechter to Cyrus Adler, November 6, 1912, Solomon Schechter Family Collection, ARC 101, series 9, box 38, Schechter Chronological Correspondence, folder 38/9, 1912, JTS Library. See also Solomon Schechter to Cyrus Adler, September 22, 1913, in which he laments that the "Seminary is just now too much in the sociological current and I despair to get the necessary means for scholarship." Solomon Schechter Family Collection, folder 38/10, 1913.

24. Kaplan diary, October 12, 1930.

25. Kaplan diary, September 1, 1933; January 5, 1925; December 25, 1923.

26. Kaplan diary, September 23, 1923; "A Plea for Justice," *The Light of Israel*, July 27, 1923, p. 3.

27. Kaplan diary, March 30, 1923. In that year, the celebratory promotional pamphlet that Kaplan produced in honor of SAJ's first anniversary, touting its accomplishments and highlighting its offerings, drew "unfavorable criticism" from the Seminary faculty, especially from Ginzberg. He objected to what he took to be its downplaying of religion or theology. "That was enough to condemn it," Kaplan recalled.

28. Kaplan diary, October 18, 1922; June 16, 1923.

29. Kaplan diary, November 17, 1931.

30. Kaplan diary, May 3, 1929; December 26, 1923; August 17, 1958; November 24, 1926; September 29, 1926; May 24, 1926; July 7, 1927; September 12, 1926.

31. Mordecai Kaplan to Stephen S. Wise, November 21, 1922, MS-19, box 22, folder 11, Jewish Institute of Religion Records, AJA.

32. Kaplan diary, October 15, 1925; April 1, 1918.

33. Kaplan diary, December 15, 1941.

34. Kaplan diary, January 28, 1933; October 6, 1925.

35. Kaplan diary, November 12, 1934.

36. Kaplan diary, February 20, 1933; July 7, 1927; July 6, 1926.

37. Kaplan diary, February 21, 1917; January 28, 1933; April 1, 1918.

38. Kaplan diary, September 27, 1923.

39. Kaplan diary, October 8, 1928.

40. Kaplan diary, October 20, 1930; July 5, 1926; April 9, 1918; September 17, 1924.

41. Kaplan diary, June 18, 1916; June 3, 1934; April 13, 1941; June 5, 1940.

42. Kaplan diary, October 29, 1934.

43. Kaplan diary, October 9, 1934; September 17, 1924; September 20, 1935.

44. Kaplan diary, November 12, 1930.

45. Kaplan diary, April 12, 1958.

46. Kaplan diary, November 14, 1935.

47. Alfred Kazin, "Judaism in Transition," *New York Times Book Review*, June 21, 1936, p. BR26; Abram Leon Sachar, "What to Live For," *Jewish Advocate*, January 1, 1937, p. 2.

48. Kaplan diary, November 20, 1915; June 11, 1928; November 3, 1930; September 4, 1934; August 10, 1934; Rabbi Victor E. Reichert, "From the Rocking Chair," *American Israelite*, February 25, 1937.

49. Kaplan diary, December 14, 1939; October 25, 1914; June 30, 1916; September 13, 1916.

50. Mordecai M. Kaplan to Israel Chipkin, December 20, 1953; Israel Chipkin to Mordecai M. Kaplan, January 13, 1954, Tamar Chipkin Orvell personal collection. I'm grateful to Ms. Chipkin Orvell for kindly sharing these documents with me.

51. Kaplan diary, May 10, 1922; November 28, 1927; July 30, 1932.

52. Kaplan diary, July 30, 1932; October 6, 1929.

53. Ira Eisenstein, *Reconstructing Judaism: An Autobiography* (New York: Reconstructionist Press, 1986), pp. 75, 118; Kaplan diary, June 1, 1934; September 13, 1932.

54. Eisenstein journal, March 11, 1936, RG 2, subfolder 3, RRC Archives.

55. Eisenstein journal, August 11, 1941; August 17, 1941; August 11, 1941, RG 2, subfolder 4, RRC Archives.

56. Kaplan debuted the term in an editorial titled "Why 'Reconstructionist?' " which appeared in the January 20, 1928, issue of the *S.A.J. Review*, but at the time it had little traction outside of his congregation. He subsequently reprinted the piece in the very first issue of *The Reconstructionist* 1, no. 1 (January 11, 1935): 2, hoping for a bigger and more receptive audience.

57. Mordecai M. Kaplan, "Milton Steinberg's Contribution to Reconstructionism," *The Reconstructionist* 16, no. 7 (May 19, 1950): 10; Kaplan diary, June 29, 1940.

58. "The Reconstructionist Position," *The Reconstructionist* 1, no. 1 (January 11, 1935): 3–5, especially p. 3.

59. Kaplan diary, March 17, 1929.

60. Kaplan diary, October 15, 1955; Eisenstein journal, March 1, 1935, RG 2, subfolder 3, RRC Archives; Kaplan diary, September 21, 1955; January 1, 1946; January 3, 1940.

61. Kaplan diary, August 30, 1940; October 15, 1955; April 3, 1942.

62. Kaplan diary, March 16, 1940; March 23, 1935; April 14–15, 1928; January 20, 1935.

63. Kaplan diary, March 23, 1935; September 13, 1932; February 28, 1935; March 4, 1935.

64. Eisenstein journal, July 31, 1935, RG 2, subfolder 3, RRC Archives. During their two-year stay in Jerusalem, the Kaplans wrote often to their children. Much of Kaplan's correspondence (hereafter cited as "Kaplan letters") can be found in RG1_RS01, All Subfolders, box 27, subfolder 2; additional letters can be found in RG1_RS01, All Subfolders, box 26, subfolder 1, RRC Archives. Lena's correspondence (hereafter cited as "Lena correspondence") can also be found in RG1_RS01, box 27, subfolders 10-55, RRC Archives. See, for example, Kaplan's letters of November 5, 1937, and October 25, 1937.

65. Kaplan diary, November 12, 1938; March 28, 1939.

66. Lena Kaplan carved out a different day of the week for writing to each of her four daughters: Sundays were Judith's day; Tuesdays Hadassah's, and so on. See Lena correspondence, January 25, 1938, and September 11, 1938.

67. Lena correspondence, September 30, 1937; January 16, 1939; January 16, 1938.

68. Undated letter from Judith Eisenstein to Gayil, RG1_RS01, box 27, subfolder 6; Lena correspondence, February 9, 1938; February 5, 1938; May 21, 1939; May 23, 1939.

69. Kaplan diary, November 29, December 1, 1938.

70. Kaplan letters, November 19, 1938, and January 9, 1938.

71. Kaplan diary, January 6, 1935; Kaplan letters, December 3, 1937; December 18, 1938; January 6, 1939.

72. Lena correspondence, June 13, 1939.

73. Kaplan diary, August 1, 1905; December 29, 1918.

74. Kaplan diary, November 24, 1929; November 20, 1929; November 22, 1929.

75. Kaplan diary, November 26, 1929. See also, "Speculating on the Balfour Declaration. Differing Points of View in Different Quarters," *AH*, November 15, 1918.

76. Kaplan diary, August 24, 1939; November 19, November 22, 1938. See also August 24, 1938. Eisenstein's description can be found in a letter from Ira Eisenstein to Mordecai Kaplan, January 24, 1938, Ira Eisenstein correspondence, RG1_RS01, box 7, RRC Archives.

77. Kaplan diary, November 19, 1938.

78. Kaplan diary, November 19, 1938.

79. Mordecai M. Kaplan, "The State of Israel and the Status of the Jew," *The Reconstructionist* 15, no. 10 (June 24, 1949): 10; Lena correspondence, June 13, 1939; Kaplan letters, March 31, 1938.

80. *The New Haggadah for the Pesah Seder*, edited by Mordecai M. Kaplan, Eugene Kohn, and Ira Eisenstein for the Jewish Reconstructionist Foundation (New York, 1941), pp. 3, vi. See also, Mordecai M. Kaplan, "The New Haggadah," *The Reconstructionist* 7, no. 5 (April 18, 1941): 17–18.

81. Kaplan diary, April 29, 1941.

82. Kaplan diary, September 15, 1939; Lena correspondence, September 4, 1938. See also Mordecai M. Kaplan to Maurice Linder, October 3, 1944, box marked "M. Kaplan: Photographs, Sermons, Essays and Correspondence," SAJ Archives.

83. Mordecai Kaplan to Ira Eisenstein, September 2, 1938, Ira Eisenstein correspondence, box 7, RRC Archives; Kaplan diary, July 28, 1939; December 11, 1939.

84. "Postscript to Pesah," *The Reconstructionist* 7, no. 7 (May 16, 1941): 5–6; Kaplan diary, July 27, 1955.

85. Kaplan diary, April 21, March 24, 1941.

86. Kaplan diary, April 29, 1941. The text of the April 30, 1941, faculty letter can be found in full in Jack Wertheimer, "Kaplan vs. 'The Great Do-Nothings': The Inconclusive Battle over *The New Haggadah*," *Conservative Judaism* 45, no. 4 (Summer 1993): 24–28.

87. Kaplan diary, June 24, 1941; Eisenstein, *Reconstructing Judaism*, p. 165; Kaplan diary, June 6, June 24, 1941.

88. Kaplan's response of May 1, 1941, can be found in Wertheimer, "Kaplan vs. 'The Great Do-Nothings,' " pp. 29–30; Eisenstein, *Reconstructing Judaism*, p. 165.

89. Kaplan diary, May 19, 1941. On chosen-ness, see Kaplan diary, May 1–May 16, 1941, especially May 16, 11, 8, 1, 9, 1, 8. Writing several years later, Kaplan reaffirmed his commitment, noting, "I consider the omission of references to Israel as the Chosen People in *The New Haggadah* and in the forthcoming *Sabbath Prayer Book* to be one of the outstanding achievements of Reconstructionism." See Mordecai M. Kaplan, "Shall We Retain the Doctrine of Israel as the Chosen People?," *The Reconstructionist* 11, no. 1 (February 23, 1945): 20.

90. "Postscript to Pesah."

91. Kaplan diary, April 10, 1955.

92. Kaplan diary, October 6, 1938; September 11, 1933; August 27, 1955.

93. Kaplan diary, May 21, 1933; September 17, 1955.

94. Kaplan diary, August 27, 1955; April 10, 1939; October 2, October 30, 1942.

95. Kaplan diary, October 2, October 4, 1942.

96. Kaplan diary, March 19, 1943; Mordecai M. Kaplan, "God Is the Power that Makes for Salvation," in *The Meaning of God in Modern Jewish Religion* (New York: Behrman's Jewish Book House, 1937), pp. 40–103; Kaplan diary, January 1, January 7, 1943; Mortimer J. Cohen, "Mordecai M. Kaplan, Interpreter of Judaism: An Appreciation," *Jewish Exponent*, May 14, 1937, p. 9; Kaplan diary, April 6, 1955; August 5, 1934.

97. Mordecai M. Kaplan, "What Is Judaism?," *Menorah Journal* 1, no. 5 (December 1915): 311; Judy to My Darlings, September 12, 1938, Judith K. Eisenstein correspondence, RG1_RS01, box 27, subfolder 8, RRC Archives.

98. Kaplan diary, April 23, 1942; Louis Lubetkin to SAJ Board of Trustees, September 28, 1938, "Miscellaneous Box," SAJ Archives.

99. Kaplan diary, October 15, 1928; October 27, 1935; October 15, 1928; May 6, 1935.

100. Kaplan diary, April 30, 1932.

101. Kaplan diary, January 28, 1943; October 2, 1942.

102. Kaplan diary, November 30, 1942; Reuben I. Isaacson to SAJ Congregation, November 2, 1942, "Miscellaneous Box," SAJ Archives; Kaplan diary, April 23, 1942; July 30, 1932; April 23, 1942.

103. Kaplan diary, September 9, 1928; May 31, 1940; April 23, 1942.

104. Kaplan diary, October 23, 1942; Ira Eisenstein, "Rejoinder to Dr. Gaster," *Commentary*, March 1946, p. 87; Kaplan diary, January 23, 1945.

105. "Introduction," *Sabbath Prayer Book, with a Supplement Containing Prayers, Readings and Hymns and with a New Translation* (New York: Jewish Reconstructionist Foundation, 1945), pp. xvii, xviii, xx, 240–241, xxviii.

106. Eisenstein journal, January 9, 1943, RG 2, subfolder 4, RRC Archives; Kaplan diary, October 30, 1942; February 10, 1943; October 30, 1942; Eisenstein journal, January 9, 1943, RG 2, subfolder 4, RRC Archives.

107. Kaplan diary, December 19, 1942; Eisenstein journal, January 9, 1943, RG 2, subfolder 4, RRC Archives.

108. Kaplan diary, May 16, 1945.

109. Kaplan diary, May 5, 1945. Anticipating V-E Day, "people were very much in the mood for the celebration which we held today," Kaplan noted at day's close.

110. *"Asefas HaHerem," HaPardes* 19, no. 4 (July 1945): 2–4.

111. Much ink has been spilled over whether the book burning was a spontaneous gesture conceived in the heat of the moment or a planned, intentional one, the work of an individual or that of the rabbinical body. What matters most, I should think, is that no one took steps to put out the fire and the audience, including the officers of the Agudah, stood by as a sacred text went up in flames.

112. "Orthodox Rabbis 'Excommunicate' the Author of Prayer Book Though He Isn't a Member," *NYT,* June 15, 1945, p. 11; Kaplan diary, June 23, 1945. The condemnatory comments are drawn from Joshua Trachtenberg, "Religious Activities," *American Jewish Year Book, 1945–46,* vol. 47, p. 217; "Professor Mordecai M. Kaplan 'Excommunicated' by Orthodox Rabbis, His Prayer Book Banned," JTA (Jewish Telegraphic Agency), June 14, 1945; "Resolutions," *A Challenge to Freedom of Worship* (New York: Jewish Reconstructionist Foundation, 1945), pp. 12–15; and "Professor Mordecai M. Kaplan Excommunicated by Orthodox Rabbis," *Jewish Exponent,* January 25, 1945, p. 1. On Lieberman's behavior, see Kaplan diary, June 30, 1945. I'd like to thank Professor Marc Shapiro for sharing *A Challenge to Freedom of Worship* with me.

113. Sidney Morgenbesser, "Is Orthodoxy Consistent with Democracy?," *The Reconstructionist* 11, no. 10 (October 5, 1945): 22; "Resolution Adopted by the Executive Board of the Central Conference of American Rabbis, Meeting at Atlantic City, N.J., on June 8, 1945," in *Challenge to Freedom of Worship,* p. 14.

114. "Rabbinical Assembly Protests 'Excommunication' of Professor Mordecai Kaplan by Orthodox Rabbis," JTA, June 20, 1945; "Resolution Adopted by the Executive Council of the Rabbinical Assembly of America of New York and Approved by Convention," June 27, 1945, in *Challenge to Freedom of Worship,* pp. 13–14. A copy of Einstein's telegram can be found in Mel Scult, *Communings of the Spirit: The Journals of Mordecai M. Kaplan, 1942–1951* (Detroit: Wayne State University Press, 2020), vol. 3, p. 276.

115. Milton Steinberg to Mordecai Kaplan, June 13, 1945, Milton Steinberg Papers, box 3, folder 9, American Jewish Historical Society, Center for Jewish History, New York.

116. Meeting of the Board of Trustees, June 19, 1945, p. 2, SAJ Archives; "Order Now!," an advertisement for the prayer book that appeared in *Di Tsukunft*, September 1945, a copy of which Barbara Ann Schmutzler brought to my attention; Kaplan diary, June 23, 1945; "Mordecai Kaplan Responds to His 'Excommunication,' " *Jewish Advocate*, June 28, 1945, p. 1.

117. "Mordecai Kaplan Responds"; Kaplan diary, June 16, 1945; "Mordecai Kaplan Responds."

118. Mordecai M. Kaplan, "The Implications of the Herem," in *Challenge to Freedom of Worship*, pp. 7, 9, 10, 11.

119. Kaplan diary, June 23, 1945.

120. "Mordecai Kaplan Responds"; Kaplan diary, November 24, 1945.

121. "Dr. Mordecai Kaplan Taken to Task by Three Seminary Scholars," *Jewish Exponent*, December 7, 1945, p. 6. See also, "A Declaration about Dr. Kaplan's Siddur," *Jewish Forum* 29, no. 1 (January 1946): 7–8, 16.

122. Theodor Gaster, "Sabbath Prayer Book, with a Supplement Containing Prayers, Readings and Hymns with a New Translation," *Commentary*, February 1946, pp. 2, 4, 6. See also Theodor Gaster, "Modernizing the Jewish Prayerbook: Revisions That Sacrifice the Spirit," *Commentary*, April 1954. Both accessed at www.comentary.org.

123. "He Made a Little List," from "Tale of the Reconstructed Woman," ca. 1950, p. 5, box marked "Sheet Music," folder labeled "Texts for Performances at SAJ," SAJ Archives.

Chapter 5. Reconstruction

1. Kaplan diary, April 28, 1948; December 8, 1951.

2. Kaplan diary, June 9, 1951. A selection of "Random Thoughts" later appeared in the form of *Not So Random Thoughts*, a 1966 publication of the Reconstructionist Press, where the sto-

ried quote appeared twice, first within the introduction, where it's cited as the "past should have a vote, but not a veto," and on page 263, where it reads as "the ancient Israelites are entitled to a vote—but not a veto." I'm grateful yet again to Professor Mel Scult for chapter and verse. See also "Know How to Answer," *The Reconstructionist* 16, no. 16 (December 15, 1950): 29–31; 21, no. 6 (April 20, 1955): 31; Kaplan diary, October 24, 1946.

3. Kaplan diary, April 11, 1956; Mordecai M. Kaplan, *The Future of the American Jew* (New York: Macmillan, 1948), p. 527; Kaplan diary, December 31, 1951; December 8, 1951; Mordecai Kaplan to Harold Schulweis, May 1, 1956, Mordecai Kaplan Correspondence, SC-6102, AJA.

4. See, for example, "Good and Welfare," Minutes of the Board of Trustees, August 10, 1944; "Communication from Dr. Kaplan," Minutes of the Board of Trustees, October 5, 1944; "Copy of letter from Mordecai Kaplan to Maurice Linder, October 3, 1944," appended to the October 5, 1944, board minutes; "Resolution," January 16, 1945, Minutes of the Board of Trustees, all in SAJ Archives. Kaplan diary, June 1, 1946.

5. Kaplan diary, September 20, 1951; January 24, 1951; February 15, 1954; May 22, 1954.

6. Kaplan diary, November 23, 1944; May 14, 1948. Kaplan's journal for 1948 is a bit disjointed chronologically. While in Los Angeles, he made coterminous entries in a looseleaf notebook, the contents of which he "transcribed" and augmented several months later in his journal. I draw here on the second iteration of the May 14 entry.

7. Kaplan diary, December 3, 20, 1944; May 16, 1945; Moshe Davis, "Mordecai M. Kaplan: An Interpretation," *The Reconstructionist* 22, no. 12 (October 19, 1956): 17; Kaplan diary, May 9, 1948; July 1, 1951.

8. Kaplan diary, April 15, 1947; January 24, 1946.

9. Mordecai M. Kaplan, *A University of Judaism—A Compelling Need* (United Synagogue of America, 1946), pp. 6, 10, 8, 11, 17ff.

10. Kaplan, *Future of the American Jew*, p. 63.

11. Kaplan diary, May 16, 1945, December 20, 1946. See also, Deborah Dash Moore, "Another Glowing Chapter: The University of Judaism," in *Tradition Renewed: A History of the Jewish Theological Seminary*, ed. Jack Wertheimer (New York, 1997), vol. 1, pp. 793–819.

12. Kaplan diary, April 7, 1947; Mordecai Kaplan to Lena Kaplan, March 11, 14, 1947, Mordecai M. Kaplan Correspondence, RG1_RS01, box 14, subfolder marked "Lena R. Kaplan," RRC Archives.

13. Mordecai M. Kaplan to Lena Kaplan, March 18, 1947.

14. Kaplan diary, April 7, 1947; Mordecai M. Kaplan to Lena Kaplan, March 3, 4, 6, 1947.

15. Mordecai M. Kaplan to Lena Kaplan, March 11, 1947; Kaplan diary, August 15, 1947.

16. "Jewish Theologians Dedicate Coast Unit," *NYT*, December 29, 1948; "Western Unit Set Up by Jewish Seminary," *NYT*, February 13, 1948.

17. Kaplan diary, May 21, 1951; June 19, 1947; September 20, 1951; November 15, 1946; February 29, 1948; Milton Steinberg, "The Test of Time," *The Reconstructionist* 16, no. 1 (February 24, 1950): 20–25.

18. Kaplan diary, September 3, 1947; July 13, 1951; September 3, 1947; August 17, 1943.

19. Kaplan diary, April 11, 1949.

20. Kaplan diary, February 18, 1926; "Toward A Guide for Jewish Ritual Usage, Part I—Current Attitude," *The Reconstructionist* 17, no. 13 (October 31, 1941): 6.

21. *Toward A Guide for Jewish Ritual Usage* (New York, 1942). *The Reconstructionist* announced its availability—for free—in pamphlet form in January 1942. See "Ready for Distribution—'Toward A Guide for Jewish Ritual Usage,' " *The Reconstructionist* 7, no. 19 (January 23, 1942): 2. Its text initially appeared in *The Reconstructionist* in four parts, beginning in October 31, 1941, and running through January 9, 1942. Appearing under the same title, "Toward a Guide for Jewish Ritual Usage," it was credited to A. Elihu Michelson, a 1935 JTS graduate whose "summary report"

of a 1941 conference sponsored by the editorial board of *The Reconstructionist* formed its basis. For a detailed analysis, see Deborah Waxman, "Ethnicity and Faith in American Judaism: Reconstructionism as Ideology and Institution" (Ph.D. diss., Temple University, 2010), pp. 127–147. The sources for the sequential quotes are as follows: "Toward A Guide for Jewish Ritual Usage, Part III—Home Devotion and Synagogue Worship," *The Reconstructionist* 17, no. 15 (November 28, 1941): 10; "Toward A Guide for Jewish Ritual Usage, Part I—Current Attitude," 17, no. 13 (October 31, 1941): 6; "Toward A Guide for Jewish Ritual Usage, Part II—Principles of Evaluation," 17, no. 14 (November 14, 1941): 8; "Toward A Guide for Jewish Ritual Usage, Part I—Current Attitude," 17, no. 13 (October 31, 1941): 9, 10.

22. Kaplan diary, February 26, 1914; October 15, 1955; July 12, 1929; "Toward A Guide for Jewish Ritual Usage, Part IV—The Sabbath and Dietary Usages," *The Reconstructionist* 7, no. 16 (December 12, 1941): 16; Mordecai M. Kaplan, "Toward A Guide for Jewish Ritual Change," chapter 21 in *Future of the American Jew*, especially pp. 418, 20.

23. These quotes are culled from Kaplan, *Future of the American Jew*, pp. 413–428. See also "Toward A Guide for Jewish Ritual Usage, Part I," p. 7.

24. "Preface," *A Guide to Jewish Ritual* (New York: Reconstructionist Press, 1962), p. 3. See also pp. 6, 14, 16, 19–21, 44–46.

25. Kaplan diary, August 19, 1951; May 22, 1942; July 23, 1942; Mordecai Kaplan to Harold Schulweis, May 18, 1955, Mordecai M. Kaplan Correspondence, SC-6102, AJA.

26. Kaplan diary, February 4, 1917; October 7, 1948; September 3, 1947.

27. Kaplan diary, August 9, 1951; July 23, 1947; July 26, 1951. Kaplan's faith was put further to the test when two of his grandchildren, Deborah Jaffe and Andy (Ann) Eisenstein, told him of their plans to intermarry, leaving him "shocked and unnerved." After consulting with Judith and Ira, Hadassah and Sidney, Kaplan softened the content and tone of the letters he had intended to send the two prospective brides. Though opposition

to intermarriage, he wrote Andy, was one of the "basic principles" of Reconstructionism, "so far as I personally am concerned, whatever you do will in no way affect my love for you and my heartfelt prayer for your happiness with Evan Johnson. Your grandpa, Mordecai." See Kaplan diary, March 19, April 17, 1975; Mordecai Kaplan to Andy Eisenstein, March 16, 1975, Correspondence of Andy (Ann) Eisenstein with Mordecai M. Kaplan, RG1_RS01, box 26, subfolder 4, RRC Archives. On Deborah Jaffe's nuptials, see Mordecai Kaplan to Judith Eisenstein, July 5, 1968, and Judith Eisenstein to Mordecai Kaplan, July 17, 1968, Judith K. Eisenstein correspondence, RG1_RS01, box 26, subfolder 2, RRC Archives. On Andy's wedding plans, see Mordecai Kaplan to Andy Eisenstein, March 16, 1975, and Andy Eisenstein to Mordecai Kaplan, June 6, 1975, Correspondence of Andy (Ann) Eisenstein with Mordecai M. Kaplan, RG1_RS01, box 26, subfolder 4, RRC Archives; Ira Eisenstein to Mordecai Kaplan, March 27, 1975, Mordecai Kaplan to Ira Eisenstein, April 1, 1975, and Ira Eisenstein to Mordecai Kaplan, April 14, 1975, Ira Eisenstein correspondence, RG1_RS01, box 7B, RRC Archives.

28. Kaplan diary, June 13, 1951; Ira Eisenstein to Mordecai Kaplan, March 11, 1956, Ira Eisenstein correspondence, box 7, RRC Archives.

29. Kaplan diary, July 1, 1948; December 6, 1958; December 8, 1963; March 4, 1943; May 17, June 18, 1947; September 25, 1951; June 29, 1951; January 12, 1954.

30. For Heschel's most recent biography, see Julian E. Zelizer, *Abraham Joshua Heschel: A Life of Radical Amazement* (New Haven: Yale University Press, 2023), especially chapter 4, "New York City."

31. Kaplan diary, June 6, 1951; November 9, 1945; November 18, 1951; December 29, 1955; January 25, 1950.

32. Kaplan's journals, especially during the postwar era, are replete with withering comments about his students. A representative sample can be found on May 1, 1951; June 30, 1954; December 6, 1955; November 23, 1955; March 5, 1954; October 25, January 23, 1955; January 12, 1954.

33. Kaplan diary, February 6, 1951; January 25, 1950; January 12, 1954.

34. Kaplan diary, September 16, 1955; October 26, 1954; January 25, 1950; September 16, 1955; November 23, 1949. Lest Kaplan think otherwise, Heschel made a point of telling him of his admiration, writing on June 6, 1958, to "Professor Kaplan" as follows: "You know, I am sure, that even when I do not find myself in agreement with all your thoughts, I remain sensitive to your great intellectual passion and to your spiritual concern in our people and its teachings. In affection and esteem. Cordially, Abraham J. Heschel." Mordecai M. Kaplan Correspondence with Abraham J. Heschel, RG1, box 13, RRC Archives.

35. Kaplan diary, December 15, December 31, 1968; "Religion: Can Modern Man Pray?," *Newsweek* 72, no. 27 (December 30, 1968): 38–39; Kaplan diary, April 6, 1967.

36. Kaplan diary, August 28, 19, 1954.

37. Kaplan diary, January 11, May 1, 1958.

38. Kaplan diary, October 2, June 3, May 25, June 3, 1958; Mordecai Kaplan to Judith Eisenstein, February 12, 1959, Judith K. Eisenstein correspondence, RG1_RS01, box 26, subfolder 2.

39. Kaplan diary, June 3, 1958; Mordecai Kaplan to Judith Eisenstein, February 12, 1959.

40. Kaplan diary, June 2, 1958. I'd also like to thank Dan Rottenberg for sharing reminiscences of his grandfather, including the story of his overture to Kaplan, in his blog post, "Vol. 33: The Great Rabbi's (inadvertent legacy)," September 24, 2023, https://danrottenberg.substack.com/p/vol-33-the-great-rabbis-inadvertent.

41. Kaplan diary, May 3, 1959; see also transcript of interview with Rivkah Rieger Kaplan by Navah de Shalit, 1971–72, Jerusalem, Israel. I'd like to thank Ms. de Shalit, Rivkah's granddaughter, for sharing this document with me.

42. Kaplan diary, May 3, 8, 1959.

43. Kaplan diary, May 10, 1959.

44. Kaplan diary, June 23, 27, 1959; Mordecai Kaplan to Judith and Ira Eisenstein, July 10, 1959, Ira Eisenstein correspondence,

box 7, RRC Archives. A small cache of Rivkah's letters to Kaplan are housed at the RRC Archives. See, for instance, Rivkah R. Kaplan to Mordecai M. Kaplan, July 6, 1965; July 10, 1968, Rivkah R. Kaplan Correspondence with Mordecai M. Kaplan, RG1_RS01, box 14, subfolder marked "Rivkah R. Kaplan," RRC Archives; Mordecai Kaplan to Judith and Ira Eisenstein, September 7, 1962; Mordecai Kaplan to Ira Eisenstein, September 20, 1960, Ira Eisenstein correspondence, box 7, RRC Archives.

45. Kaplan diary, November 5, August 27, 1960; Mordecai Kaplan to Judith and Ira Eisenstein, September 20, October 12, 1960, Ira Eisenstein correspondence, box 7, RRC Archives; Kaplan diary, November 5, 1960.

46. Kaplan diary, November 11, 1960.

47. Kaplan diary, December 14, 1958; Mordecai M. Kaplan, "Foreword," *A New Zionism*, 2nd enlarged ed. (New York: Herzl Press, 1959). See also pp. 173, 26, 42; Kaplan diary, August 16, 1959; March 15, 1955.

48. Kaplan diary, July 6, 1959; Kaplan, *New Zionism*, p. 12.

49. Kaplan, *New Zionism*, p. 180.

50. Kaplan, *New Zionism*, pp. 28, 184; Mordecai M. Kaplan, "The Covenant Proposal Reviewed," *The Reconstructionist* 23, no. 3 (March 22, 1957): 16; Kaplan diary, February 5, 1960.

51. Kaplan diary, March 25, April 7, 1954; see also March 10, April 8, 21, 1954; Mordecai Kaplan to Judith and Ira Eisenstein, February 28, 1955, Ira Eisenstein correspondence, box 7, RRC Archives; Kaplan diary, December 15, 23, 1958. It was Zalman Shazar, at the time the head of the Jewish Agency's Department of Education and Culture in the Diaspora, who, while visiting with Kaplan at his home in the spring of 1954, put into his head the conceit that Reconstructionism should be represented at the World Zionist Congress. The April 7, 1954, entry in Kaplan's diary recounts this exchange.

52. Kaplan diary, May 22, 26,1954; Ira Eisenstein to Mordecai Kaplan, March 3,1955, Ira Eisenstein correspondence, box 7, RRC Archives; Kaplan diary, May 31, 1954.

53. Mordecai Kaplan to Judith Eisenstein, February 12, 1959, Judith K. Eisenstein correspondence, RG1_RS01, box 26,

subfolder 2, RRC Archives; Kaplan diary, May 15, 1960, July 6, 1959; Mordecai Kaplan to Ira Eisenstein, April 7, 1965, and July 28, July 29, and August 3, 1965, Ira Eisenstein correspondence, box 7, RRC Archives.

54. Kaplan diary, May 14, 1954; Eisenstein cited in Deborah Ann Musher, "Reconstructionist Judaism in the Mind of Mordecai Kaplan: The Transformation from a Philosophy into a Religious Denomination," *American Jewish History* 86, no. 4 (December 1998): 397–417, especially pp. 400, 400n9; Kaplan diary, June 21, 1955.

55. Kaplan diary, May 12, 1963; February 5, 1960. Kaplan's animadversions against the Seminary are strewn throughout his journal. What follows are among those he made as he edged toward retirement; they're just the tip of the iceberg. See, for example, October 5, 1949; July 8, 1951; April 14, 1958. See also Mordecai Kaplan to Harold Schulweis, July 5, 1963, Mordecai M. Kaplan Correspondence, SC-6102, AJA; Kaplan diary, July 6, 1963.

56. Kaplan diary, May 16, July 17, 1963; Mordecai Kaplan to Judy and Ira Eisenstein, July 11, July 18, 1963, Ira Eisenstein correspondence, box 7, RRC Archives.

57. Kaplan diary, May 10, 1960; May 12, 1965.

58. Kaplan diary, January 17, 1968; May 3, 1967.

59. Mordecai Kaplan to Ira Eisenstein, March 24, 1965, Ira Eisenstein correspondence, box 7, RRC Archives.

60. Mordecai Kaplan to Judy and Ira Eisenstein, July 4, 1961, Ira Eisenstein correspondence, box 7, RRC Archives; Mordecai Kaplan to Judy and Ira Eisenstein, March 14, 1974, Judith K. Eisenstein correspondence, RG1_RS01, box 26, folder 2, RRC Archives; Rivkah Rieger Kaplan's comments appeared in a brief note that she had appended to her husband's March 14, 1974, letter.

61. Author's Zoom interview with Hanan Shlonsky, Holon, Israel, February 28, 2023. Unceasing in her efforts to improve her husband's mental well-being, Rivkah encouraged another grandson, Ur Shlonsky, to make a point of engaging Kaplan in discussion and of encouraging his friends to swing by for a chat. Author's Zoom interview with Ur Shlonsky, Geneva, Switzerland, July 11, 2024.

62. Mordecai Kaplan to Ira Eisenstein, September 7, 1954; Ira Eisenstein to Mordecai Kaplan, September 10, 1954, Ira Eisenstein correspondence, box 7, RRC Archives. More than twenty years later, in the wake of the UN's 1975 declaration of Zionism as racism, Kaplan once again trumpeted the idea of Israel becoming the fifty-first state. "When, if not now, is the time to hold a Jewish Reconstitutional Convention" at which to propose that Israel join the Union, he suggested to Philip Klutznick, president of the World Jewish Congress. The "idea isn't as bizarre as it seems," he went on to say, explaining that not only would the measure safeguard Israel's security, it would also "enhance the American celebration of the 200th anniversary of its own founding." Kaplan diary, November 15, 16, 17, 1975. Ira Eisenstein to Mordecai Kaplan, January 14, 1970; Ira Eisenstein to Mordecai Kaplan, March 10, 1965, Ira Eisenstein correspondence, box 7, RRC Archives.

63. All of the following letters are in Ira Eisenstein correspondence, RRC Archives. Ira Eisenstein to Mordecai Kaplan, July 25, 1961, box 7; Ira Eisenstein to Mordecai Kaplan, February 26, 1965, box 7; Ira Eisenstein to Mordecai Kaplan, April 23, 1972, box 7B; Ira Eisenstein to Mordecai Kaplan, June 29, 1972, box 7B; Ira Eisenstein to Mordecai Kaplan, July 12, 1972, box 7; Ira Eisenstein to Mordecai Kaplan, February 9, 1972, box 7B; Ira Eisenstein to Mordecai Kaplan, June 29, 1972, box 7B.

64. Eisenstein journal, June 26, 1972, RG 2, subfolder 2, RRC Archives; Ira Eisenstein to Mordecai Kaplan, July 10, 1972, and June 29, 1972, Ira Eisenstein correspondence, box 7B, RRC Archives.

65. Mordecai Kaplan to Ira Eisenstein, June 28, 1972, Ira Eisenstein correspondence, box 7B, RRC Archives; Kaplan diary, July 11, 1972; Mordecai Kaplan to Ira Eisenstein, June 28, July 12, 1972, Ira Eisenstein correspondence, box 7B, RRC Archives.

66. Kaplan diary, September 25, 1972; November 1, 1972; October 22, 1972; November 1, 1972; Mordecai Kaplan to Judith Eisenstein, March 14, 1974, Judith K. Eisenstein correspondence, RG1_RS01, box 26, folder 2, RRC Archives.

67. Kaplan diary, April 13, 1973.

68. Mordecai Kaplan to Ira Eisenstein, March 10, 1971, Ira Eisenstein correspondence, box 7B, RRC Archives; Mordecai Kaplan to Judith Eisenstein, March 14, 1974, Judith K. Eisenstein correspondence, RG1_RS01, box 26, folder 2, RRC Archives.

69. Kaplan diary, April 25, 1979; December 16, 1979; March 6, 1980; November 27, 1978; April 25, 1979.

70. Ira Eisenstein to Mordecai Kaplan, January 20, 1980, Ira Eisenstein correspondence, box 7B, RRC Archives; Kaplan diary, August 1, 1976. Kaplan wrote out his speech in full in that day's journal entry.

71. Rivkah Rieger Kaplan to Navah Haber-Schaim, July 3, 1981, May 28, 1982, courtesy Navah de Shalit, Jerusalem, Israel; "Kaplan, Reconstructionist Founder, Hailed on 100th Year," JTA (Jewish Telegraphic Agency), June 19, 1981.

72. Mordecai Kaplan to Ira Eisenstein, April 1, 1966, Ira Eisenstein correspondence, box 7, RRC Archives; Kaplan diary, May 25, 1942; Mordecai M. Kaplan, "A Heart of Wisdom," *The Reconstructionist* 17, no. 6 (May 4, 1951): 12.

Chapter 6. Portrait Gallery

1. Rivkah Rieger also made and had reproduced a lithographic line drawing of Kaplan, ca. 1966, copies of which are in private hands.

2. Kaplan diary, December 8, 1951; May 16, 1951; April 2, 1968; May 14, June 1, 1927.

3. On another occasion, the 1932 dedication of a bronze plaque bearing his likeness, Kaplan commented that the piece, which was to be hung in the Teachers Institute library, was "probably good from an artistic point of view, but it is certainly not calculated to make me fall in love with myself." Kaplan diary, April 3, 1932. See also, Kaplan diary, November 3, 1930; Ira Eisenstein to Mordecai Kaplan, April 7, 1966, Ira Eisenstein correspondence, box 7B, RRC Archives; Kaplan diary, May 27, 1929; March 22,

1926; February 20, 1954; December 6, 1955; September 29, 1930; March 1, 1954.

4. Kaplan diary, March 5, 1934; January 2, 1930.

5. Mordecai Kaplan to Harold Schulweis, May 21, 1970, Kaplan Correspondence, SC-6102, AJA; Kaplan diary, April 15, 1934.

6. Kaplan diary, December 8, 1963; Sidney Morgenbesser, "Mordecai Kaplan Some Thirty Years Ago," *Sh'ma*, October 14, 1974, p. 148, http://shma.com; Kaplan diary, July 3, 1948.

7. Meeting Minutes, Meeting-House of Mr. Sylvan Robison, April 3, 1917, "Early Kaplan," box 1, folder 13, RRC Archives; Kaplan diary, November 20, 1972.

8. Kaplan diary, May 7, 1942; December 18, 1944; September 7, 1934; April 17, 1955.

9. Kaplan diary, February 15, 1955; Theodor Gaster, "Sabbath Prayer Book, Published by the Jewish Reconstructionist Foundation," *Commentary*, February 1946, pp. 3, 4. www.commentary.org.

10. Kaplan diary, June 8, 1940; Eisenstein journal, September 7, 1941, RG 2, subfolder 4, RRC Archives; Ira Eisenstein to Mordecai Kaplan, April 9, 1971, Ira Eisenstein correspondence, box 7B, RRC Archives.

11. Kaplan diary, April 17, 1955; June 8, 1940; see also, Kaplan diary, February 8, 1948.

12. Kaplan diary, December 12, 1906, RRC Archives; Kaplan diary, March 2, 1926; January 1, 1929; February 2, 1935; December 8, 1928; November 3, 1929; Eisenstein journal, September 7, 1941, RG 2, subfolder 4, RRC Archives.

13. Milton Steinberg, "The Test of Time," *The Reconstructionist* 16, no. 1 (February 24, 1950): 25.

14. "Religion: The Reconstructionist," *Time*, June 13, 1961, https://time.com; Emil L. Fackenheim, "Mordecai Kaplan, A Critic's Tribute," *Sh'ma*, October 18, 1974, p. 145, http://shma.com; Mordecai Kaplan to Ira Eisenstein, September 2, 1938, Ira Eisenstein correspondence, box 7, RRC Archives.

Reconstructing a Life

1. Kaplan diary, March 10, 1955.

2. Kaplan diary, April 11, 1949.

3. Kaplan diary, November 23, 1963. The cartoon can be found on the page opposite the August 14, 1932, entry.

4. Kaplan diary, April 13, 1958; November 21, 1928; June 25, 1929; Charles Liebman, "Reconstructionism in American Jewish Life," *American Jewish Year Book*, vol. 71, 1970, p. 27.

5. Kaplan diary, February 8, 1950; July 3, 1929; July 1, 1951; November 21, 1928; January 9, 1960.

6. Kaplan diary, July 14–15, 1932.

7. Kaplan diary, November 9, 1973.

ACKNOWLEDGMENTS

TAKING THE MEASURE OF Mordecai M. Kaplan was a daunting task, but I was assisted, enlightened, set straight, and buoyed by a battery of people, whose ranks included members of his family, former students and congregants, as well as archivists, librarians, and colleagues.

To Kaplan's dedicated grandchildren, keepers of the flame, go my warmest thanks for sharing their memories, insights, and photographs over numerous cups of tea, bowls of soup, and Zoom. Ann Eisenstein in Brooklyn, Miriam Eisenstein in Washington, D.C., Dr. Daniel and Karol Musher in Houston, and Dr. David and Ruth Musher in Manhattan couldn't have been more forthcoming or more patient with my barrage of questions about this, that, and the other thing.

Rivkah Rieger Kaplan's grandchildren were also extremely generous with their time and memories. Navah de Shalit in Jerusalem, Hanan Shlonsky in Tel Aviv, Or Shlonsky in Geneva, and Ron Rieger Kopito in Palo Alto furnished me with sharply detailed, lively accounts of Kaplan's life in Jerusalem alongside their indomitable grandmother, Rivkah, and with some arresting visual images, to boot.

Closer to home, in the Big Apple, Professor Mel Scult was unflagging in his enthusiasm for my efforts and unstinting when it came to the exchange of information. Having devoted his life to Kaplan, it could not have been easy for him to entertain my Johnny-come-lately questions or cotton to the perspective I brought to bear, but, throughout, he was graciousness itself, a model of collegiality. Eric Caplan, vice president and academic advisor of the Kaplan Center, and Jane Susswein, its president, were unfailingly helpful, fielding pesky inquiries, pointing me in the right direction, and sharing tranches of information. Tamar Chipkin Orvell, whose beloved father, Israel, was one of Kaplan's most steadfast of friends and champions, made available their extant correspondence.

The process of research brought me into touch with the architectural historians Andrew Dolkart and Anthony Robins, who helped me to understand what rendered the Upper West Side apartment house a distinctive phenomenon, and Kenneth Cobb, assistant commissioner, New York City Department of Records and Information Services, faithful steward of New York City's history, and dear friend since forever (or at least since graduate school days), showered me with materials—maps, photographs, tax records—that enabled me to piece together and visualize the neighborhood's coming of age.

When it came to the American Jewish experience, Joe Weber, managing archivist, and Jae Heisler, project archivist, of the Jacob Rader Marcus Center of the American Jewish Archives in Cincinnati, Ohio, responded to my numerous requests with enthusiasm and efficiency. On my behalf, they even opened up and shared the contents of a relevant collection that had long been unprocessed, enabling me to enliven my account. Erin Hess, archivist of the Mordecai Kaplan Archives/Reconstructionist Archives at the Rabbinical Reconstructionist College outside of Philadelphia, also went far beyond the call of duty, making sure I left no box unexamined and cheerfully enduring my outbursts when I happened upon one felicitous discovery after another. Susan Berman, senior director of collaborative governance, facilitated my access to and use of this material, as did Deborah Waxman, president of Reconstructing Judaism and a most wonderful interlocuter on all things Kaplan. My colleague and friend David Kraemer, librarian of the Jewish Theological Seminary; Havva Zellner, digital librarian; and former archivist Mary Silverstein were extremely obliging at every turn, as was Sharon Liberman Mintz, the Seminary's curator of Jewish art, whose support was invaluable and unstinting.

A few blocks away, at the Society for the Advancement of Judaism, Barbara Ann Schmutzler tended to the congregation's papers with her characteristic verve and sensitivity, protecting them as best she could from the ravages of time and the boiler room. Debbie Rudt, SAJ's executive director, literally opened doors for me. Further downtown, the Dorot Jewish Division of the New York Public Library was, as always, a wellspring of primary source materials about American Jewish life.

When I wasn't entombed in an old microfilm machine, stuck in a book, or swimming in a sea of papers, I held forth on my latest find, taking advantage of my colleagues' goodwill. Some even managed to get a word in edgewise, sharing anecdotes, interpreting a passage that had me stumped, or suggesting another approach. Sadly, two among them are no more: David Ellenson, the historian's historian, and Peter Schweitzer, the great collector of American Judaica and a close friend for more than thirty years, passed away within a few months of one another, leaving me, and many others, bereft of their warmth and smarts.

At one point or another along the way, Carole Balin; Shelly Buring; Jon Butler; Barry Chazan; Maurice Corson; Jeremy Dauber; Hasia Diner; Arnie Eisen, chancellor emeritus of the Jewish Theological Seminary and an ardent Kaplan fan; Zev Eleff; Ayala Feder; Sam Freedman; Naomi Gamoran; Melila Hellner-Eshed; Ben Jacobs; Barbara Kirshenblatt-Gimblett; Laura Arnold Leibman; Derek Penslar; Carl Perkins; Chana Pollack; Dan Rottenberg; Daniel B. Schwartz; Jeffrey Shandler; Marc Shapiro; Abe Socher; Eliyahu Stern; Michael Strassfeld; Magda Teter; Erika Vogel; Elliot Zashin; Froma Zeitlin; Jerry

Zelizer; Julian Zelizer; and Daniel Zemel deepened and sharpened my thinking, for which I'm most grateful.

Steve Zipperstein did even more. A wise counsel, a most excellent sounding board, a nimble editor, he became in the course of this enterprise a friend as well.

The myriad complexities of book making fell to the resolute Heather Gold and her resourceful assistant Chelsea Connelly; copyeditor extraordinaire Eliza Childs; the indefatigable Erica Hanson, production editor; and indexer Kay Banning, all of whom acquitted themselves with abundant good spirit, expertise, and sensitivity. Lori and Steve Ross, stalwart, generous supporters of my work within and without the George Washington University, made sure I had what I needed to pull out all the stops.

My beloved husband, Joz, couldn't have been more accommodating, attentive, good-humored, and gung ho, even when I spent more time with Mordecai Kaplan than with him. Whether putting me through the paces of our nightly debrief or reading for the umpteenth time a particularly recalcitrant formulation, he prodded and poked at all the right places, wielded a fierce editorial pen, and lifted me up when I wobbled. For this, and, most of all, for our wonderful life together, I dedicate this book to him.

INDEX

Note: Italic page numbers refer to illustrations.

Jewish Lives is a prizewinning series of interpretative biography designed to explore the many facets of Jewish identity. Individual volumes illuminate the imprint of Jewish figures upon literature, religion, philosophy, politics, cultural and economic life, and the arts and sciences. Subjects are paired with authors to elicit lively, deeply informed books that explore the range and depth of the Jewish experience from antiquity to the present.

Jewish Lives is a partnership of Yale University Press and the Leon D. Black Foundation. Ileene Smith is editorial director. Anita Shapira and Steven J. Zipperstein are series editors.

PUBLISHED TITLES INCLUDE:

Abraham: The First Jew, by Anthony Julius
Rabbi Akiva: Sage of the Talmud, by Barry W. Holtz
Ben-Gurion: Father of Modern Israel, by Anita Shapira
Judah Benjamin: Counselor to the Confederacy, by James Traub
Walter Benjamin: The Pearl Diver, by Peter E. Gordon
Bernard Berenson: A Life in the Picture Trade, by Rachel Cohen
Irving Berlin: New York Genius, by James Kaplan
Sarah: The Life of Sarah Bernhardt, by Robert Gottlieb
Leonard Bernstein: An American Musician, by Allen Shawn
Hayim Nahman Bialik: Poet of Hebrew, by Avner Holtzman
Léon Blum: Prime Minister, Socialist, Zionist, by Pierre Birnbaum
Franz Boas: In Praise of Open Minds, by Noga Arikha
Louis D. Brandeis: American Prophet, by Jeffrey Rosen
Mel Brooks: Disobedient Jew, by Jeremy Dauber
Martin Buber: A Life of Faith and Dissent, by Paul Mendes-Flohr
David: The Divided Heart, by David Wolpe
Moshe Dayan: Israel's Controversial Hero, by Mordechai Bar-On
Disraeli: The Novel Politician, by David Cesarani
Alfred Dreyfus: The Man at the Center of the Affair, by Maurice Samuels
Einstein: His Space and Times, by Steven Gimbel
Becoming Elijah: Prophet of Transformation, by Daniel Matt
The Many Lives of Anne Frank, by Ruth Franklin
Becoming Freud: The Making of a Psychoanalyst, by Adam Phillips

Betty Friedan: Magnificent Disrupter, by Rachel Shteir
Emma Goldman: Revolution as a Way of Life, by Vivian Gornick
Hank Greenberg: The Hero Who Didn't Want to Be One, by Mark Kurlansky
Peggy Guggenheim: The Shock of the Modern, by Francine Prose
Ben Hecht: Fighting Words, Moving Pictures, by Adina Hoffman
Heinrich Heine: Writing the Revolution, by George Prochnik
Lillian Hellman: An Imperious Life, by Dorothy Gallagher
Herod the Great: Jewish King in a Roman World, by Martin Goodman
Theodor Herzl: The Charismatic Leader, by Derek Penslar
Abraham Joshua Heschel: A Life of Radical Amazement, by Julian Zelizer
Houdini: The Elusive American, by Adam Begley
Jabotinsky: A Life, by Hillel Halkin
Jacob: Unexpected Patriarch, by Yair Zakovitch
Franz Kafka: The Poet of Shame and Guilt, by Saul Friedländer
Mordecai M. Kaplan: Restless Soul, by Jenna Weissman Joselit
Carole King: She Made the Earth Move, by Jane Eisner
Rav Kook: Mystic in a Time of Revolution, by Yehudah Mirsky
Stanley Kubrick: American Filmmaker, by David Mikics
Stan Lee: A Life in Comics, by Liel Leibovitz
Primo Levi: The Matter of a Life, by Berel Lang
Maimonides: Faith in Reason, by Alberto Manguel
Groucho Marx: The Comedy of Existence, by Lee Siegel
Karl Marx: Philosophy and Revolution, by Shlomo Avineri
Louis B. Mayer and Irving Thalberg: The Whole Equation, by Kenneth Turan
Golda Meir: Israel's Matriarch, by Deborah E. Lipstadt
Menasseh ben Israel: Rabbi of Amsterdam, by Steven Nadler
Moses Mendelssohn: Sage of Modernity, by Shmuel Feiner
Harvey Milk: His Lives and Death, by Lillian Faderman

Arthur Miller: American Witness, by John Lahr
Moses: A Human Life, by Avivah Gottlieb Zornberg
Amos Oz: Writer, Activist, Icon, by Robert Alter
Proust: The Search, by Benjamin Taylor
Yitzhak Rabin: Soldier, Leader, Statesman, by Itamar Rabinovich
Ayn Rand: Writing a Gospel of Success, by Alexandra Popoff
Walther Rathenau: Weimar's Fallen Statesman, by Shulamit Volkov
Man Ray: The Artist and His Shadows, by Arthur Lubow
Sidney Reilly: Master Spy, by Benny Morris
Admiral Hyman Rickover: Engineer of Power, by Marc Wortman
Jerome Robbins: A Life in Dance, by Wendy Lesser
Julius Rosenwald: Repairing the World, by Hasia R. Diner
Philip Roth: Stung by Life, by Steven J. Zipperstein
Mark Rothko: Toward the Light in the Chapel, by Annie Cohen-Solal
Ruth: A Migrant's Tale, by Ilana Pardes
Menachem Mendel Schneerson: Becoming the Messiah, by Ezra Glinter
Gershom Scholem: Master of the Kabbalah, by David Biale
Bugsy Siegel: The Dark Side of the American Dream, by Michael Shnayerson
Solomon: The Lure of Wisdom, by Steven Weitzman
Stephen Sondheim: Art Isn't Easy, by Daniel Okrent
Steven Spielberg: A Life in Films, by Molly Haskell
Spinoza: Freedom's Messiah, by Ian Buruma
Alfred Stieglitz: Taking Pictures, Making Painters, by Phyllis Rose
Barbra Streisand: Redefining Beauty, Femininity, and Power, by Neal Gabler
Henrietta Szold: Hadassah and the Zionist Dream, by Francine Klagsbrun
Leon Trotsky: A Revolutionary's Life, by Joshua Rubenstein

Warner Bros: The Making of an American Movie Studio, by David Thomson
Elie Wiesel: Confronting the Silence, by Joseph Berger
Ludwig Wittgenstein: Philosophy in the Age of Airplanes, by Anthony Gottlieb

FORTHCOMING TITLES INCLUDE:

Hannah Arendt, by Masha Gessen
The Ba'al Shem Tov, by Ariel Mayse
Bob Dylan, by Sasha Frere-Jones
George Gershwin, by Gary Giddins
Ruth Bader Ginsburg, by Jeffrey Rosen
Jesus, by Jack Miles
Louis Kahn, by Gini Alhadeff
Henry Kissinger, by Dennis Ross
Fiorello La Guardia, by Brenda Wineapple
Mahler, by Leon Botstein
Norman Mailer, by David Bromwich
Robert Oppenheimer, by David Rieff
Rebecca, by Judith Shulevitz
Edmond de Rothschild, by James McAuley
Jonas Salk, by David Margolick
Susan Sontag, by Benjamin Taylor
Gertrude Stein, by Lauren Elkin
Sabbatai Tsevi, by Pawel Maciejko
Billy Wilder, by Noah Isenberg